Corporate Takeover Law and Management Discipline

This book examines the effectiveness of corporate takeovers. Particularly, it identifies the extent to which the interests of shareholders and employees can be complementarily protected when a takeover is made. The dominant ideologies of corporate takeovers include synergistic gains and managerial disciplinary role. *The UK Takeover Code* is a regulatory response to the role of managers of target companies only. Also, the regulatory framework for takeovers in the United States is largely focused on target companies. Identifying the limitations of these regulatory framework, the book demonstrates that managements can influence the role of takeovers, thereby undermining its synergistic and disciplinary values.

The relevance of institutional control over the important role of managements is identified.

Addressing the challenges of managerial influence over takeover functions is argued to be capable of promoting a complementary benefit to shareholder and employee interests, thereby challenging the shareholder and stakeholder primacy debate in corporate law, particularly in relation to takeovers.

This book will be essential reading for scholars and students interested in the market for corporate control, corporate law and company law.

Dr Francis Okanigbuan Jnr is a Lecturer in the School of Law, Liverpool John Moores University. He was a Research Fellow on the Arts and Humanities Research Council funded project 'Business Judgment and the Courts' in the Centre for Business Law and Practice, School of Law, University of Leeds. He was a Teaching Assistant at the University of Manchester and Associate Lecturer, at the Manchester Metropolitan University. He is a graduate-member of the Institute of Chartered Secretaries and Administrators. His research interests include takeovers (the market for corporate control), corporate law, corporate governance, law and economics of regulation and comparative law.

Routledge Research in Corporate Law

Available titles in this series include:

Regulation and the Credit Rating Agencies
Restraining Ancillary Services
Daniel Cash

Law and Responsible Supply Chain Management
Contract and Tort Interplay and Overlap
Edited by Vibe Ulfbeck, Alexandra Andhov and Kateřina Mitkidis

Shareholder Primacy and Global Business
Re-clothing the EU Corporate Law
Lela Mélon

Corporate Law, Codes of Conduct and Workers' Rights
Vanisha Sukdeo

Insolvency Law and Multinational Groups Theories, Solutions and Recommendations for Business Failure
Daoning Zhang

Employee Rights in Corporate Insolvency
A UK and US Perspective
Hamiisi Junior Nsubuga

Shareholder Protection Reconsidered
Derivative Action in the UK, Germany and Greece
Georgios Zouridakis

Corporate Takeover Law and Management Discipline
Francis Okanigbuan Jnr

For more information about this series, please visit: www.routledge.com/Routledge-Research-in-Corporate-Law/book-series/CORPORATELAW

Corporate Takeover Law and Management Discipline

Francis Okanigbuan Jnr

Routledge
Taylor & Francis Group
LONDON AND NEW YORK

First published 2020
by Routledge
2 Park Square, Milton Park, Abingdon, Oxon OX14 4RN

and by Routledge
605 Third Avenue, New York, NY 10017

Routledge is an imprint of the Taylor & Francis Group, an informa business

First issued in paperback 2021

British Library Cataloguing-in-Publication Data
A catalogue record for this book is available from the British Library

Library of Congress Cataloging-in-Publication Data
A catalog record for this book has been requested

ISBN 13: 978-1-138-60002-7 (hbk)
ISBN 13: 978-1-03-223825-8 (pbk)
ISBN 13: 978-0-429-47112-4 (ebk)

Typeset in Galliard
by Apex CoVantage, LLC

Contents

Preface

Several interests are affected by the economic success or failure of a corporation as a going concern. This does not only include the major corporate constituents: management board (executive management and supervisory directors), shareholders, creditors and employees. The list extends to communities, customers, suppliers, the government and so on. When a corporate acquisition is made, the list can be extended to 'prospective investors'. This list comprises financial and non-financial stakeholders of corporations whose interests are affected directly or indirectly by corporate acquisitions. We have seen the effects of takeovers on the interests of these stakeholders and we are also witnesses to the development of the regulatory framework of takeovers to address the situation. I think it is a good development that the challenges of takeovers are getting recognised. However, as the propensity for economic gains increases when a takeover is imminent, so does the scope for loss to the financial and non-financial stakeholders.

It was never contemplated that the book would provide holistic analyses of the challenges of takeovers with solutions; that is inconceivable. It only attempted a critical exposition of the weakness of takeovers as a mechanism of the market for corporate control. Through Chapters 2, 3, 4, 5, 6 and 7, the comparative approach of the book provides insight into shareholder and employee interests. This was considered particularly relevant because of the palpable fear of loss of employment when acquisition is imminent and the costs of acquisitions that undermine acquiring shareholder interests. We can see that so much attention is given to employment matters when a takeover is imminent despite the fact that employees are non-financial stakeholders. Of course, the role of the management board is central to takeovers, and that is the reason that Chapter 2 focuses on institutional support to strengthen takeover markets where managers operate, in anticipation of the analysis about managerial dominance of corporate governance and the MCC in Chapter 6.

I am grateful to Nathalie Taylor for her timely contribution to the case search at the Aldham Robarts Library, Liverpool John Moores University. I also thank the anonymous reviewers of the sample draft when this book was being conceived.

Francis Okanigbuan Jnr
Liverpool, September 2019

Table of cases

United Kingdom

New Zealand

United States

Table of statutes

Part I

1 General introduction

1.1 Introduction

A company is a complex whole, so are its challenges. Among the several challenges facing a modern corporation are conflict of interests[1] and issues of accountability. The existence of these challenges and the threats that they pose to corporate values led to the development of internal systems of corporate control, led by the board of directors of companies.[2] As an internal disciplinary mechanism, the board is expected to limit the incidence of conflict of interests through its effective monitoring and supervisory roles. However, despite the existence of boards of directors, these challenges have not been effectively addressed. Conflict of interests remains a serious problem, and it can be responsible for the poor performance of firms. For example, it may lead to the undervaluation of the assets of companies, exposing such companies to risks and external pressure from the market for corporate control.[3] Corporate acquisition is one of the ways that the market for corporate control is exhibited. It has become a recurrent feature in exerting external pressure on companies, directly or indirectly.[4] Even though a company is not a subject of a takeover bid, an indirect pressure may be signalled as soon as a competitor of similar economic strength becomes the target of a takeover bid.[5]

Traditional finance theory suggests that corporate entities that are 'poorly managed' are likely to become takeover targets, because external investors believe that at optimal management level, the value of the firm can be enhanced beyond its current level.[6] This can be achieved through the synergistic objective

1 Corporate managers as agents can be influenced by personal interests in making investment decisions. See generally Ralph A. Walkling and Michael S. Long, 'Agency Theory, Managerial Welfare and Takeover Bid Resistance' (1984) 15 *The Rand Journal of Economics* 54.
2 Pieter W. Moerland, 'Alternative Disciplinary Mechanisms in Different Corporate Systems' (1995) 26 *Journal of Economic Behaviour & Organisation* 17, 25.
3 Henry G. Manne, 'Mergers and the Market for Corporate Control' (1965) 73 *Journal of Political Economy* 110, 112.
4 Note 2, 23. See generally, Henry G. Manne, note 3.
5 Barry M. Mitnick, *The Political Economy of Regulation: Creating, Designing and Removing Regulatory Forms* (New York, Columbia University Press, 1980) 328.
6 Michael C. Jensen, 'The Takeover Controversy: Analysis and Evidence' in John C. Coffee, Louis Lowenstein, and Susan Rose-Ackerman (eds.), *Knights, Raiders and Targets: The Impact*

of acquisitions, whereby the value of the combined entity is greater than the sum of the separate entities values.[7] However, in light of the litany of challenges that occurs post-acquisition, namely, loss of value to acquiring companies and shareholders,[8] and challenges to stakeholders, such as employee dismissal,[9] the synergistic role of takeovers is being undermined.

Several studies have examined the role of acquisitions as it affects the interests of shareholders of target[10] and acquiring[11] companies. Others have examined the

---

of the Hostile Takeover (New York, Oxford University Press, 1988) 318; David Hirshleifer and Anjan V. Thakor, 'Corporate Control through Board Dismissals and Takeovers' (1998) 7 *Journal of Economics & Management Strategy* 489, 511.

7 Lynn Hodgkinson and Graham H. Partington, 'The Motivation for Takeovers in the UK' (2008) 35 *Journal of Business Finance & Accounting* 102. Even though takeovers appear to discipline 'non-performing managers', the quest for synergy remains the driving force for takeovers. See Michael Jensen, 'Takeovers: Folklore and Science' in Peter J. Buckley and Pervez N. Ghauri (eds.), *International Mergers and Acquisition: A Reader* (London, Thompson, 2002) 71; Peter Dodd and Richard Ruback, 'Tender Offers and Stockholder Returns: An Empirical Analysis' (1977) 5 *Journal of Financial Economics* 351; Michael Bradley, 'Interfirm Tender Offers and the Market for Corporate Control' (1980) 53 *Journal of Business* 345; Michael Bradley, Anand Desai, and Han E. Kim, 'The Rationale Behind Interfirm Tender Offers: Information or Synergy?' (1983) 11 *Journal of Financial Economics* 183.

8 Sara B. Moeller, Frederik P. Schlingemann, and René M. Stulz, 'Do Shareholders of Acquiring Firms Gain from Acquisitions?' (2003) *National Bureau of Economic Research* Working Paper Series, 9523 www.nber.org/papers/w9523 accessed 8 May 2018; Mahendra Raj and Michael Forsyth, 'Hubris among UK Bidders and Losses to Shareholders' (2003) 8 *International Journal of Business* 1, 8–15; Elazar Berkovitch and M. P. Narayanan, 'Motives for Takeovers: An Empirical Investigation' (1993) 28 *Journal of Finance and Quantitative Analysis* 347, 351; Robert F. Bruner, 'Does M & A Pay? A Survey of Evidence for the Decision Maker' (2002) *Journal of Applied Finance* 48, 64–65; Michael Firth, 'Corporate Takeovers, Stockholder Returns and Executive Rewards' (1991) 12 *Managerial and Decision Economics* 421, 425–427.

9 Myeong-Gu Seo and N. Sharon Hill, 'Understanding the Human Side of Merger and Acquisition: An Integrative Framework' (2005) 41 *The Journal of Applied Behavioral Science* 422.

10 James F. Cotter, Anil Shivdasani, and Marc Zenner, 'Do Independent Directors Enhance Target Shareholder Wealth during Tender Offers?' (1997) 43 *Journal of Financial Economics* 195, 196; Blanaid Clarke, 'The Takeover Directive: Is a Little Regulation Better Than No Regulation?' (2009) 15 *European Law Journal* 174, 188; Peter Holl and Dimitis Kyriazis, 'The Determinants of Outcome in UK Takeover Bids' (1996) *International Journal of Economics and Business* 165; Darren Henry, 'Directors' Recommendations in Takeovers: An Agency and Governance Analysis' (2005) 32 *Journal of Business Finance & Accounting* 129; Noel O'Sullivan and Pauline Wong, 'Board Composition, Ownership Structure and Hostile Takeovers: Some UK Evidence' (1999) 29 *Accounting and Business Research* 139; Gregg A. Jarrell, James A. Brickley, and Jeffry M. Netter, 'The Market for Corporate Control: The Empirical Evidence Since 1980' (1988) 2 *The Journal of Economic Perspectives* 49, 58.

11 Paul Mason et al., 'Does Shareholder Voting Matter? Evidence from the Takeover Market' (2018) 53 *Wake Forest Law Review* 157; Donald C. Langevoort, 'The Behavioural Economics of Mergers and Acquisitions' (2011) 12 *Tennessee Journal of Business Law* 65; Afra Afsharipour, 'Reevaluating Shareholder Voting Rights in M&A Transactions' (2017) 70 *Oklahoma Law Review* 127; Marco Becht, Andrea Polo, and Stefano Rossi, 'Does Mandatory Shareholder Voting Prevent Bad Acquisition?' (2016) 29 *Review of Financial Studies* 3035.

extent to which the interests of other stakeholders, such as employees, can be protected.[12] These studies address the challenges of takeovers from the separate viewpoints of shareholder value and stakeholder value. These approaches have largely been influenced by the dominant argument in the corporate law literature, that is, whether the corporation, as a going concern, should be run for the interests of shareholders or stakeholders. The restricted scope of these theories has failed to provide a comprehensive approach to the challenges of corporate acquisitions.

This book adopts a different approach. It provides important analysis on the complementary protection of shareholder value and stakeholder interests in the administration of corporate acquisitions. The book addresses the challenges of inefficient outcomes in corporate acquisitions. It identifies the extent to which the interests of shareholders and stakeholders such as employees can be complementarily protected.

The effects of acquisitions and the interests that are affected are similar across jurisdictions. For example, shareholder value, employee interests and corporate value are similarly affected in different jurisdictions. Hence, further to the objective of this book, the regulatory control over the role of corporate managements in acquisitions in the United Kingdom and the United States – Delaware General Corporations Law – are examined. Companies in the United States and the United Kingdom concluded the most expensive acquisition deals globally.[13] Thus, it is justifiable to ascertain the extent to which managements can influence acquisition activities in these jurisdictions, relative to the role of the regulatory framework for acquisitions.

The remainder of the chapter is structured as follows. First, the persistent challenges of acquisitions are identified. Next, the theoretical perspectives of corporate acquisitions are briefly illustrated. Then, the aim and scope of the book are outlined. Finally, an outline of the chapters with the relevant scope is presented.

1.2 The persistent challenges of corporate acquisition

The key participants in a corporate entity are: shareholders, creditors, employees, directors and managers.[14] Viewed from the lens of the contractual theory, the nature of a corporation as a going concern constitutes a nexus of contracts[15] amongst these corporate actors. These contracts are embodied in the relationships which exist among the key participants. Among these participants, the interests of managements and creditors may be protected without specific reference to takeover regulations. Company directors and managers are directly involved

12 See Chapter 4, section 4.4, Chapter 5, section 5.5.

13 See the analyses in Chapter 8, section 8.2.

14 See Brian R. Cheffins, *Company Law: Theory, Structure and Operation* (New York, Oxford University Press, 2000) 47.

15 Michael C. Jensen and William H. Meckling, 'Theory of the Firm: Managerial Behaviour, Agency Cost and Ownership Structure' (1976) 3 *Journal of Financial Economics* 305, 310–311.

in the negotiation process during takeovers. They have the capacity to negotiate their compensation packages. Also, creditors can be protected by secured credit. The combination of the assets of firms through takeovers can enhance the security of the credit facilities that unsecured creditors provide to companies. Shareholders and employees may not have the capacity to protect their interests, except by reference to specific regulations. For example, shareholders of target companies are mainly protected by the regulatory framework of takeovers in the United Kingdom and in European Union countries. Corporate managements are required not to act in the manner that would interfere with a takeover bid without the authority of the shareholders of target companies.[16] Also, all shareholders of the same class in a target company must be given equivalent treatment when a bid is made.[17] In the United States, particularly under the *Delaware General Corporation Law*, managements have discretionary powers, and they can exercise managerial business judgment.[18] Their obligation to their shareholders when a takeover bid is made is governed by their fiduciary duties. This includes the obligation to act with care and speak with candour when advising their shareholders whether they should accept an offer. Meanwhile, the interests of shareholders of acquiring companies are only protected in limited circumstances in the UK, where shareholders are required to vote to approve the acquisition objectives of managements in certain transactions.[19] This voting mechanism does not apply in the United States, despite the empirical evidence which suggest that acquiring shareholders record losses or insignificant gains from acquisitions,[20] and the desire of acquiring shareholders to be actively involved in takeover decisions.[21] Apart from shareholders, employees cannot successfully protect their interests when a corporate acquisition is made. This is evident in the continuous large-scale employee dismissal when takeovers are concluded. Employee dismissal has become a recurrent feature of takeovers. This was demonstrated in the botched

16 The board neutrality rule or non-frustration rule – *Directive 2004/25/EC of The European Parliament and of the Council of 21 April 2004 on Takeover Bids (EU Takeover Directive)* art. 9(2) and The UK City Code on Takeovers and Mergers 2016 B1 General Principles 3.

17 The equal opportunity rule – *The UK City Code on Takeovers and Mergers 2016*, General Principles 1. See also, the mandatory bid rule, which is triggered when the acquirer alone or acting in concert with others acquire more than 30% of the shares of the company, or not more than 50% of the shares when acting in concert with others. See *The UK City Code on Takeovers and Mergers 2016*, r 9; *EU Takeover Directive* art 5.

18 *Delaware General Corporation Law*, § 141. *In Aronson v Lewis*, 473 A.2d 805 (Del. 1984), 812, business judgment rule was described as the 'rebuttable presumption that in making a business decision the directors of a corporation acted on an informed basis, in good faith and in the honest belief that the action taken was in the best interests of the company'.

19 *UK Listing Rules* 10.2 (3), R 10 (annex 1.1) (1G). See the analysis in Chapter 4, section 4.3.2.

20 Chapter 4, section 4.3.2 (ii).

21 Warren Buffet who owned 9.4% stakes in Kraft indicated that he would block the deal if he could. Graeme Wearden, 'Warren Buffett Blasts Kraft's Takeover of Cadbury' *The Guardian* Wednesday 20 January 2010 www.theguardian.com/business/2010/jan/20/warren-buffett-blasts-kraft-cadbury accessed 13 June 2018.

takeover of AstraZeneca by Pfizer. During negotiations for the takeovers, concerns were raised about the interests of the employees of AstraZeneca. The Chief Executive of Pfizer stated, while appearing before the House of Commons Business, Innovation and Skills Committee, that Pfizer cannot guarantee that the jobs in AstraZeneca would be 'safe'.[22] As noted, the regulatory framework for takeovers appears to preserve the traditional role of company managements in making investment decisions in relation to takeovers.[23] Shareholder approval is only required in limited circumstances when takeover bids are made. Consequently, company shareholders, especially acquiring shareholders, may not be expected to play significant roles during takeovers, despite the losses that are recorded by acquiring shareholders.

Lack of investor confidence and unemployment crises can affect national economic growth and stability. For example, in October 2007, a consortium of the Royal Bank of Scotland Group (UK) RBS, Fortis (Belgian) and Banco Santander (Spanish), known as RFS Holdings B.V. in a deal considered to be the largest acquisition in the banking sector, acquired the Dutch bank ABN AMRO Bank N.V. for about €71 billion. One year after the acquisition, the UK government bailed RBS from an impending collapse, largely as a result of capital strain from the acquisition.[24] The Dutch Government nationalised ABN AMRO Bank in 2009 and took control of the Fortis operation of the bank in the Netherlands as part of the bailout plans after the bank struggled financially as a result of the acquisition by the consortium.[25] Similarly, the Belgian government in collaboration with the

22 Rupert Neate and Jennifer Rankin, 'Pfizer Admits Takeover of AstraZeneca Would Lead to Cuts in UK Jobs and R&D' *The Guardian* Tuesday 13 May 2014 www.theguardian.com/business/2014/may/13/pfizer-astrazeneca-uk-job-cuts-mps-hostile accessed 19 June 2018.

23 Arguably, takeovers may not be considered to be a usual investment decision of managements that should not require managerial supervision and regulatory control. They are affected by their sporadic nature, dissimilarity from managements' regular experiences, opportunistic nature, limited access to information, risks, among other factors. See Philippe C. Haspeslagh and David B. Jemison, *Managing Acquisitions: Creating Value through Corporate Renewal* (New York, Free Press, 1991) 52–55.

24 FSA Board Report, 'The Failure of the Royal Bank of Scotland' *Financial Services Authority* 2011, 407 www.fca.org.uk/publication/corporate/fsa-rbs.pdf accessed 31 May 2018; Harry Wilson, Philip Aldrick, and Kamal Ahmed, 'The Royal Bank of Scotland Investigation: The Full Story of How the Biggest Bank in the World Went Burst' *The Telegraph* 5 March 2011 www.telegraph.co.uk/finance/newsbysector/banksandfinance/8363417/Royal-Bank-of-Scotland-investigation-the-full-story-of-how-the-worlds-biggest-bank-went-bust.html accessed 31 May 2018.

25 'Nationalisation of ABN AMRO' www.government.nl/topics/state-owned-enterprises/nationalisation-of-financial-institutions-abn-amro-asr-and-sns-reaal/nationalisation-of-abn-amro accessed 31 May 2018; ABN AMRO Bank Press Release, 'Completion of ABN AMRO Bank and Fortis Bank Nederland Legal Merger' 30 June 2010 www.abnamro.com/en/newsroom/press-releases/2010/completion_of_legal_merger.html accessed 31 May 2018; Yvette Essen, 'Financial Crisis: Fortis' Dutch Assets are Nationalised' *The Telegraph* 3 October 2008 www.telegraph.co.uk/finance/financialcrisis/3131247/Financial-Crisis-Fortis-Dutch-assets-are-nationalised.html accessed 31 May 2018.

Netherlands and Luxembourg announced a bailout plan for Fortis.[26] The over-ambitious attempt by the acquiring managers of the affected banks almost led to the collapse of these banks. This would have consequently led to severe economic crisis in the affected countries, including challenges to the interests of investing shareholders and employees. Thus, it is important to identify the scope of the challenges of takeovers as it affects shareholder and employee interests. While acquisition can be considered to be an investment decision, the non-value-creation impact of acquisition remains a challenge to its value-creation objections.

1.3 Theoretical perspectives of takeovers

Takeovers can be used to create value, by replacing low productive management personnel with a different set of management that can enhance the economic value of the firm.[27] This is the value-creation hypothesis of takeovers.[28] This hypothesis also emphasises that the value of firms can be enhanced by fusing the operations and assets of different companies into a single entity. A combination of the operations of two companies can save costs through economies of scale, whereby a combined firm can produce more resources in less time, using a more formidable input. This hypothesis is based on the synergistic gains and disciplinary role of takeovers.

Takeovers can also be used as a tool towards redirecting and redistributing resources of the firm from one corporate constituent to another, without necessarily adding value. This is the value redistribution hypothesis of takeovers.[29] When investors purchase shares at a premium and they gain control of corporate powers, they can renegotiate the existing contracts with the management and employees. The management of the acquired company may be dismissed; a large number of employees may also be disengaged. The underlying thesis of this hypothesis is that, through takeovers, the interests of some corporate constituents may be 'traded'.[30] For example, the interests of employees are often traded

26 Tina Wang, 'Fortis Pulled Back from the Brink' *Forbes* www.forbes.com/topstories/2008/09/28/fortis-bailout-pingan-markets-equity-cx_tw_0928markets01.html accessed 31 May 2018; Ian Traynor Brussels, 'Fortis: Belgium Acts to Prevent Financial Group's Collapse' *The Guardian* 29 September 2008 www.theguardian.com/money/2008/sep/29/insurance.europeanbanks accessed 31 May 2018.

27 David J. Denis and Diane K. Denis, 'Performance Changes Following Top Management Dismissals' (1995) 50 *The Journal of Finance* 1029, 1054.

28 See generally note 3 (Manne); Richard P. Rumelt, 'Diversification Strategy and Profitability' (1982) 3 *Strategic Management Journal* 359–369.

29 Andrei Shleifer and Lawrence H. Summers, 'Breach of Trust in Hostile Takeovers' in Alan J. Auerbach (ed.), *Corporate Takeovers: Causes and Consequences* (Chicago, University of Chicago Press, 1988) 33–68. See also Michael C. Jenson, 'Takeovers: Folklore and Science' (1984) 62 *Harvard Business Review* 109, 114.

30 Premiums paid to shareholders of target companies may represent losses to shareholders of acquiring companies. These losses can be mitigated by a reduction of employees post-takeover.

to mitigate the general expenditure of a corporation after engaging in a costly acquisition. This does not add wealth to corporate entities or acquiring shareholders, it merely reduces further corporate expenditure.

1.4 Aim and scope

This book aims at ascertaining the extent to which the interests of company shareholders and employees can be complementarily protected during takeovers. In furtherance of this objective, the regulatory framework of takeovers in the United Kingdom and the United States – *Delaware General Corporation Law* – are examined. This comparison is necessary in view of the worldwide dominant acquisition traffic in the United States and the United Kingdom.

Takeovers have a relative universal application; it is not limited to any particular jurisdiction. Also, takeovers affect virtually the same set of interests in a company in virtually all jurisdictions – shareholders, employees managements, directors, creditors and other stakeholders – including the United Kingdom and the United States. A comparative analysis would provide a focal point for understanding the challenges of takeovers and the ways that these challenges affect the interests of the categories of corporate constituents that are most likely to be undermined when acquisitions are made, namely, shareholders and employees, having regard to the role of management.

The role of company management in acquisitions is central to the ways that the interests of the various corporate constituents can be determined. Particularly, there are different scopes of protection available to shareholders of target companies and those of acquiring companies in the United Sates and the United Kingdom. The role of managements relative to the regulatory framework for corporate acquisitions in these jurisdictions determines the extent to which the interests of the shareholders and employees are protected. This book provides an expository analysis on how managements dominate acquisitions and how they can determine the extent to which shareholder and employee interests can be enhanced or undermined when acquisitions are made. A constructive analysis is provided to show how shareholder and employee interests can be complimentarily protected, without necessarily undermining the general role of managements, when acquisitions are made.

1.5 Outline

The book is divided into three Parts, I, II and III. It comprises nine chapters.

Part I contains the general introduction and background to the challenges of corporate acquisition in relating to shareholder and employee interests. An analysis of the regulatory framework of institutions relative to takeovers is also presented. Finally, the theoretical framework for a takeover is examined. It illustrates how the identified challenges arise, and how they can manifest from the role of managements. These are presented in Chapters 1, 2 and 3.

Chapter 1: General introduction

Chapter 1 introduces the book. It identifies the background to the problem and the objective of the book. Also, it briefly highlights how the challenges of takeovers in relation to shareholder and employee interests are determined by reference to the scope of managerial functions when takeover decisions are made. The chapter illustrates the importance of the comparative approach of the book, especially in relation to takeover regulation in the UK and the *Delaware General Corporation Law*. It also contains an outline of the chapters.

Chapter 2: The regulatory framework of institutions

Chapter 2 examines the theoretical framework of the new institutional economics (NIE) in relation to the objective of the book. It identifies the role of institutions as a mechanism for regulating human behaviour and relationships from an economic perspective. It briefly illustrates the critical factors in earlier models of economic theories that led to the development of the NIE: these include a critique of the neo-classical economics and the old institutional economics. The different levels from which institutions emerge are also illustrated in relation to how the regulatory functions of institutions can be developed in a particular society. Further, the chapter examines the main themes of the NIE: namely, property rights ownership, transaction costs and agency relationship. They are examined in relation to how their application determines the objectives of the NIE and how they can be applied to corporate acquisition challenges. The property rights and agency relationship concepts are examined in relation to company shares and ownership rights of shareholders and the relationship between company management and shareholders as agents and principals.

As the 'owners'[31] of the property rights in shares, it is illustrated that the need to provide an effective mechanism to protect shareholder interests during takeovers is justified. Also, mitigating transaction costs is one of the major objectives of the NIE. The chapter illustrates how employee disengagements during takeover may indirectly encourage managements to incur higher transaction costs during takeovers.

Chapter 3: The theoretical framework of corporate takeovers

In Chapter 3, the theoretical framework for corporate takeovers is examined. The examination of the framework for takeovers is important because it identifies how takeovers affect the different interests in a corporate entity. The chapter includes an illustration of the nature and characteristics of the different modes through which takeovers can be activated. Also, it examines the different hypotheses of takeovers. It reviews some of the existing research on the factors that can

31 'Owners' in this regard does not refer to shareholders as owners of the companies in which they invest. They are merely the owners of the property rights in the shares that they own.

influence takeovers. These include synergy, the disciplinary role of takeovers and the hubris hypothesis. The role of corporate managements is central to takeovers. They can largely determine the extent to which the interests of one or more of the corporate constituents can be enhanced. It includes a review of some of the relevant studies on the role of management.
It identifies the extent that synergy, the disciplinary role of takeovers and managerial hubris can be promoted or restricted. This includes the devices that can be used to 'frustrate' a takeover. Further, agency problems and employee issues are identified and briefly examined as part of the major problems of takeovers. In relation to the challenges of takeovers as they affect shareholders and employees, the contractual theory and entity theory of the firm are briefly examined in this chapter.

Part II examines the regulatory framework of takeovers. It is illustrated and examined in relation to shareholder and employee interests in the United Kingdom and the United States. This includes an examination of the limitations of corporate governance and the market for corporate control in both restricting and strengthening management functions in corporate acquisitions.

These are examined in Chapters 4, 5 and 6.

Chapter 4: Takeover regulation in the United Kingdom

Chapter 4 examines the regulatory framework for takeovers in the United Kingdom. Particularly, it identifies the extent to which the interests of shareholders and employees can be protected during takeovers in the United Kingdom. Pursuant to this objective, it identifies how the current regulatory framework for takeovers was established and the historical development of the regulation. It identifies the role of managements as an important factor that led to the development of takeover regulation in the United Kingdom. Managerial interference in takeover bids was indicated to have led to successive conflicts of interest between shareholders and managements. Thus, the development of the takeover regulations was meant to essentially ensure that a free and competitive market operates in the United Kingdom. The chapter highlights the need for the role of managements to be restricted during takeovers to ensure that this objective is achieved. *The City Code on Takeovers and Mergers 2016* and the *European Council Directive on Takeovers and Mergers 2004* are examined in the chapter.

The effect of takeovers on employment remains an issue in the United Kingdom despite the existence of employment protection regulation: the *Transfer of Undertakings (Protection of Employment) Regulations 2006* (TUPE). It was established pursuant to the *European Commission Acquired Rights Directive 1977 amended in 2001*. The chapter examines TUPE to ascertain the extent to which employee interests can actually be protected. While the *EU Takeover Directive* recognises the need to protect employees during takeovers, substantial provisions relating to employment protection can actually be found in TUPE.

Chapter 5: The regulatory framework for takeovers in the United States (Delaware)

This chapter examines the framework for takeover regulation in the state of Delaware. The examination is done in relation to the interests of shareholders of target and acquiring companies. Also, the extent to which the interests of employees are protected during takeovers is examined. At the core of these examinations is the scope of the statutory role of corporate management during takeovers and the effect of the business judgment rule on shareholder and employee interests.

Chapter 6: Management board: corporate governance and the market for corporate control MCC

Chapter 6 examines the role of managements in relation to corporate governance and the market for corporate control. It identifies the limit of corporate governance and the role of the market for corporate control in management discipline. It illustrates how the scope of management functions in takeovers can undermine the managerial disciplinary role of the market for corporate control. Ultimately, it shows that the inherent challenges that restrict the role of corporate governance in managerial discipline can also be present in the market for corporate control.

Part III contains Chapters 7, 8 and 9. It includes detailed analyses of the extent to which employee interests can provide a complimentary protection for shareholders. It is examined by reference to the role of managements in acquisitions. Also, the scope for judicial review of takeovers – United Kingdom and the United States, Delaware – in relation to the interests of shareholders is examined before the concluding chapter.

Chapter 7: Complementary interests of shareholders and employees

Much focus has been directed towards promoting shareholder value during takeovers without realising that the interests of other constituents such as employees' can indirectly be linked with the interests of shareholders, especially shareholders of acquiring companies. This chapter examines the link between the role of managements, shareholder interests and employee interests in takeovers. It illustrates how the role of managements can be restricted towards ensuring that employee dismissal during takeovers is avoided or clearly justified to ultimately promote shareholder interests and corporate value.

Chapter 8: Judicial intervention in corporate acquisitions

The scope for judicial intervention in takeovers is examined in Chapter 8 in relation to shareholder interests. This is examined by reference to the regulatory framework for takeovers in the UK and the Delaware General Corporation Law. In light of the shareholder value approach of corporation law and corporate governance rules in the UK and US, there is insignificant scope for judicial

intervention in takeovers in relation to employee interests. Hence, judicial intervention in relation to employees will not be examined.

Chapter 9: A new paradigm for takeover administration

Chapter 9 concludes with forward-looking analyses. It illustrates the irrelevance of shareholder and stakeholder dichotomy and explains the extent to which it creates an impediment to corporate growth and value especially in relation to takeovers. Too much focus has been directed at the shareholder and stakeholder value approaches that the role of managements has been given limited attention. This chapter concludes by emphasising the development of creative ways to challenge management functions so that they can be positioned and given the needed support towards enhancing corporate value rather than merely engaging in value redistribution. The restricted objective of the book limits the analysis. There is scope for future research in exploring other relevant areas, such as the link between the capital structure of the payments made for acquisitions, the role of management and other external factors.

References

Afsharipour, A., 'Reevaluating Shareholder Voting Rights in M&A Transactions' (2017) 70 *Oklahoma Law Review* 127.

Becht, M., Andrea Polo, and Stefano Rossi, 'Does Mandatory Shareholder Voting Prevent Bad Acquisition?' (2016) 29 *Review of Financial Studies* 3035.

Berkovitch, E. and M. P. Narayanan, 'Motives for Takeovers: An Empirical Investigation' (1993) 28 *Journal of Finance and Quantitative Analysis* 347.

Bradley, M., 'Interfirm Tender Offers and the Market for Corporate Control' (1980) 53 *Journal of Business* 345.

Bradley, M., A. Desai, and Han E. Kim, 'The Rationale Behind Interfirm Tender Offers: Information or Synergy?' (1983) 11 *Journal of Financial Economics* 183.

Bruner, R. F., 'Does M & A Pay? A Survey of Evidence for the Decision Maker' (2002) *Journal of Applied Finance* 48.

Cheffins, B. R., *Company Law: Theory, Structure and Operation* (New York, Oxford University Press, 2000).

Clarke, B., 'The Takeover Directive: Is a Little Regulation Better Than No Regulation?' (2009) 15 *European Law Journal* 174.

Cotter, J. F., Anil Shivdasani, and Marc Zenner, 'Do Independent Directors Enhance Target Shareholder Wealth during Tender Offers?' (1997) 43 *Journal of Financial Economics* 195.

Denis, D. and Diane K. Denis, 'Performance Changes Following Top Management Dismissals' (1995) 50 *The Journal of Finance* 1029, 1054.

Dodd, P. and R. Ruback, 'Tender Offers and Stockholder Returns: An Empirical Analysis' (1977) 5 *Journal of Financial Economics* 351.

Firth, M., 'Corporate Takeovers, Stockholder Returns and Executive Rewards' (1991) 12 *Managerial and Decision Economics* 421.

Haspeslagh, P. C. and David B. Jemison, *Managing Acquisitions: Creating Value through Corporate Renewal* (New York, Free Press, 1991).

Henry, D., 'Directors' Recommendations in Takeovers: An Agency and Governance Analysis' (2005) 32 *Journal of Business Finance & Accounting* 129.

Hirshleifer, D. and A. V. Thakor, 'Corporate Control through Board Dismissals and Takeovers' (1998) 7 *Journal of Economics & Management Strategy* 489.

Hodgkinson, L. and G. H. Partington, 'The Motivation for Takeovers in the UK' (2008) 35 *Journal of Business Finance & Accounting* 102.

Holl, P. and Dimitis Kyriazis, 'The Determinants of Outcome in UK Takeover Bids' (1996) *International Journal of Economics and Business* 165.

Jarrell, G. A., James A. Brickley, and Jeffry M. Netter, 'The Market for Corporate Control: The Empirical Evidence Since 1980' (1988) 2 *The Journal of Economic Perspectives* 49, 58.

Jensen, M. C. 'The Takeover Controversy: Analysis and Evidence' in John C. Coffee, Louis Lowenstein, and Susan Rose-Ackerman (eds.), *Knights, Raiders and Targets: The Impact of the Hostile Takeover* (New York, Oxford University Press, 1988).

Jensen, M. C., 'Takeovers: Folklore and Science' in Peter J. Buckley and Pervez N. Ghauri (eds.), *International Mergers and Acquisition: A Reader* (London, Thompson, 2002).

Jensen, M. C. and W. H. Meckling, 'Theory of the Firm: Managerial Behaviour, Agency Cost and Ownership Structure' (1976) 3 *Journal of Financial Economics* 305, 310–311.

Langevoort, D. C., 'The Behavioural Economics of Mergers and Acquisitions' (2011) 12 *Tennessee Journal of Business Law* 65.

Manne Henry, G., 'Mergers and the Market for Corporate Control' (1965) 73 *Journal of Political Economy* 110.

Mason, P., et al., 'Does Shareholder Voting Matter? Evidence from the Takeover Market' (2018) 53 *Wake Forest Law Review* 157.

Mitnick, B. M., *The Political Economy of Regulation: Creating, Designing and Removing Regulatory Forms* (New York, Columbia University Press, 1980).

Moeller, S. B., Frederik P. Schlingemann, and René M. Stulz, 'Do Shareholders of Acquiring Firms Gain from Acquisitions?' (2003) *National Bureau of Economic Research Working Paper Series*, 9523 www.nber.org/papers/w9523 accessed 8 May 2018.

Moerland, P. W., 'Alternative Disciplinary Mechanisms in Different Corporate Systems' (1995) 26 *Journal of Economic Behaviour & Organisation* 17.

Myeong-Gu, Seo and N. Sharon Hill, 'Understanding the Human Side of Merger and Acquisition: An Integrative Framework' (2005) 41 *The Journal of Applied Behavioral Science* 422.

O'sullivan, N. and Pauline Wong, 'Board Composition, Ownership Structure and Hostile Takeovers: Some UK Evidence' (1999) 29 *Accounting and Business Research* 139.

Raj, M. and Michael Forsyth, 'Hubris among UK Bidders and Losses to Shareholders' (2003) 8 *International Journal of Business* 1.

Rumelt, R. P., 'Diversification Strategy and Profitability' (1982) 3 *Strategic Management Journal* 359.

Shleifer, A. and L. H. Summers, 'Breach of Trust in Hostile Takeovers' in Alan J. Auerbach (ed.), *Corporate Takeovers: Causes and Consequences* (Chicago, University of Chicargo Press, 1988).

Walkling, R. A. and M. S. Long, 'Agency Theory, Managerial Welfare and Takeover Bid Resistance' (1984) 15 *The Rand Journal of Economics* 54.

Other online sources

Essen, Y., 'Financial Crisis: Fortis' Dutch Assets are Nationalised' *The Telegraph* 3 October 2008 www.telegraph.co.uk/finance/financialcrisis/3131247/Financial-Crisis-Fortis-Dutch-assets-are-nationalised.html accessed 31 May 2018.

Neate, R. and Jennifer Rankin, 'Pfizer Admits Takeover of AstraZeneca Would Lead to Cuts in UK Jobs and R&D' *The Guardian* Tuesday 13 May 2014 www.theguardian.com/business/2014/may/13/pfizer-astrazeneca-uk-job-cuts-mps-hostile accessed 19 June 2018.

Wang, T., 'Fortis Pulled Back from the Brink' *Forbes* www.forbes.com/topstories/2008/09/28/fortis-bailout-pingan-markets-equity-cx_tw_0928markets01.html accessed 31 May 2018; Ian Traynor Brussels, 'Fortis: Belgium Acts to Prevent Financial Group's Collapse' *The Guardian* 29 September 2008 www.theguardian.com/money/2008/sep/29/insurance.europeanbanks accessed 31 May 2018.

Wearden, G., 'Warren Buffett Blasts Kraft's Takeover of Cadbury' *The Guardian* Wednesday 20 January 2010 www.theguardian.com/business/2010/jan/20/warren-buffett-blasts-kraft-cadbury accessed 13 June 2018.

Wilson, H., Philip Aldrick, and Kamal Ahmed, 'The Royal Bank of Scotland Investigation: The Full Story of How the Biggest Bank in the World Went Burst' *The Telegraph* 5 March 2011 Nationalisation of ABN AMRO' www.government.nl/topics/state-owned-enterprises/nationalisation-of-financial-institutions-abn-amro-asr-and-sns-reaal/nationalisation-of-abn-amro accessed 31 May 2018.

2 The regulatory framework of institutions

2.1 Introduction

This chapter examines the characteristics and functions of institutions as tools for regulating human behaviour and relationships from the perspective of the new institutional economics.

First, the chapter briefly examines the limitations of the neo-classical and the old institutional economics theories. This is important because it identifies the factors that influenced the development of the new institutional economics. Second, the framework of the new institutional economics (NIE) is illustrated. Next, the different levels of institutional establishment and the process of change of these institutions are illustrated. Then a brief evaluation of the main themes of the NIE is presented. It identifies the relevance of the new institutional economics to the regulation of corporate takeovers with reference to shareholder and employee interests. Finally, the influence of institutions over market behaviour is examined, before the conclusion.

2.2 The neo-classical economics and the old institutional economics theories

The new institutional economics is relatively new by reference to the development of economic theories. It emerged after the neo-classical economic theory and the 'old economics theory'; however, it is not essentially a recent development.[1] It is a concept which attempts to explain economic behaviour from an institutional perspective. Prior to the emergence of this theory, the 'old' economics theory was developed as a critique to the much earlier neo-classical economics theory.

Neo-classical economics[2] comprises certain assumptions about the human economic society. It assumes that humans have rational preferences among outcomes

1 Its title, 'new' institutional economics, is meant to differentiate its concept from the previous economics theory which is now regarded as 'old' economics theory.

2 'Neo-classical economics' is believed to have been first used in reference to the theoretical assumptions of its hypothesis in Thorstein Veblen, 'The Preconceptions of Economic Science' (1900) 14 *Quarterley Journal of Economics* 240, 261.

that can be identified and associated with a value and that individuals maximise utility, firms maximise profits and people act independently on the basis of full access to relevant information.[3] Hence, it suggests that institutions are unnecessary because economies are characterised by efficient markets, which depict a world of instrumental rationality where ideas do not matter. The neo-classical economics theory is also based on the assumption that humans have perfect understanding of their surrounding environments and that they have access to perfect information, hence transactions are regulated by a perfect market where such transactions are costless.[4] Also, neo-classical economics is forward-looking; it depicts a world of functional and optimal efficiency and an ideal world. However, its idealistic characteristic is its greatest shortcoming. It fails to take account of the characteristic form of human relationship which is represented in the present human society of scarcity of resources which leads to competition. In view of this, a different proposition which completely rejects the neo-classical economic theory emerged. This became known as the 'old' institutional economics.[5]

The old – classical – institutional economics is concerned with resource allocation and the level at which resources are utilised. It argues that economics should be socially determined through cultural change. The market is seen as an invisible hand which is used as an unproductive tactic by businesses to generate income for the privileged few, as opposed to the general welfare of the people.[6] This theory supports the idea that the market should be replaced with institutions which are capable of enforcing and achieving social control for the purpose of ensuring that production and profits originate for the purposes of social welfare.[7] The major limitation of the old institutional economics theory is its exclusion of markets. The functions of the market can hardly be wholly replaced by institutions. The market forms the platform through which transactions and exchange occur[8] and the old institutional economics fails to consider this important role of the market. Its overwhelming focus on the exclusive importance of the role of institutions in promoting economic welfare undermines the indispensable nature of human interaction and exchange. This severely limits the scope of its thesis.

3 E. Roy Weintraub, 'Neo-Classical Economics' in *The Concise Encyclopedia of Economics* (Library of Economics and Liberty, 1993) www.econlib.org/library/Enc1/NeoclassicalEconomics.html accessed 11 March 2018.

4 In the real world, transactions are costly. See general generally John Joseph Wallis and Douglas North, 'Measuring the Transaction Sector in the American Economy 1870–1970' in Stanley Engerman and Robert Gallman (eds.), *Long Term Factors in American Economic Growth* (Chicago, University of Chicago Press, 1986) 95–162.

5 It emerged from the works of *Thorstein Veblen* in Thorstein Veblen, *The Theory of the Leisure Class: An Economic Study of Institutions* (New York, Macmillan & Co. Ltd, 1915).

6 Malcolm Rutherford, 'Intitutional Economics: Then and Now' (2001) 15 *The Journal of Economic Perspectives* 173, 175.

7 Wesley C. Mitchell, 'Making Goods and Making Money' in Wesley C. Mitchell (ed.), *The Backward Art of Spending Money* (New York, Augustine M. Kelley, 1923) 137–148.

8 See the discussion in section 2.5.3.

While the neo-classical economics focused entirely on the view that the market is made up of an existing perfect framework which characterises economies, the old institutional economics assumes that markets are not perfectly characterised, and that institutions can determine economic factors. The extreme thematic approaches of these theories did not provide any satisfactory explanations of the present state of the economic society. The market as presently constituted is characterised with a lot of imperfections, but it remains relevant. Also, institutions – as humanly devised constraint – are important for purposes of regulating the economic players to achieve efficient outcomes.[9] In view of these, another economics theory which attempts to strike a desirable balance between these theories emerged, namely, the 'new' institutional economics. The new institutional economics recognises institutions as the ultimate driving force of economic change and development. It recognises that transactions are costly as a result of inadequate information and scarcity, leading to the existence of imperfect markets and competition, and individual choices can be influenced by the norms derived from cultural environments.[10] Without effective institutions, these norms which influence behaviour can promote market imperfections. The challenges caused by imperfect markets can be addressed by establishing effective institutions to regulate market functions, thereby promoting efficient markets.

2.3 The framework of the new institutional economics

The new institutional economics supports the view that choices made by individuals are derived from their cultural backgrounds and that these choices are based on norms and values which are peculiar to individuals or groups among ethnic lines.[11] As a result of the differences in culture and mental attitudes, there are differences in perception. Hence, people often have different understandings as to how things work around the world, irrespective of any formal education which they may have had. In such a world, choices of rational decision-makers become largely unpredictable, since these choices are made on the basis of different individual modes. Information can be difficult to access and this can lead to an imperfect market which is characterised by competition. As such, human behaviour becomes largely unpredictable.

The unpredictable nature of human behaviour makes it difficult to incorporate expectations to guide behaviour. One of the main challenges of policy development process is to determine how human behaviour is expected to respond to new policies. This challenge can be largely addressed by reference to the

9 Douglas C. North, 'Economic Performance through Time' (1994) 84 *The American Economic Review* 359, 360–361.

10 Douglas C. North, 'Institutions and Economic Theory' (1992) 36 *The American Economist* 3–6, 4–5.

11 See the analysis in Ronald A. Heiner, 'The Origin of Predictable Behaviour' (1983) 73 *The American Economic Review* 560, 573, 580.

developmental framework of the new institutional economics. Particularly, it is possible to predict the behaviour of people from a certain geographical location, who have common customary practices. The incorporation of the cultural values and customs from the informal institutional environment into the mainstream of the institutional framework can create a high level of valid expectations. The behaviours that are sought to be constrained by such an institutional framework that has been developed pursuant to the relevant informal institutions can be expected to follow a certain pattern.[12]

In recognition of these, the new institutional economics is essentially concerned with the possibility of limiting these uncertainties through established institutions.[13] The use of institutions to administer and regulate human interactions and relationships is a form of state intervention. It is a response to the uncertainties and inadequacies of contracts and the inability of human relationships and interactions to predict future events and make anticipatory provisions for these occurrences. The need for state intervention is a major theme of the entity theory of the corporation.[14] The new institutional economics is a form of state intervention; it essentially implements the objectives of the entity theory.

In view of the uncertain nature of human behaviour in a world where choices are based on cultural factors, the institutional framework which is made of rules is used to control behaviour and structure human interactions and relationships.[15] These institutions are important because of the ultimate role which they play in governance. Since information is in fact uncertain and not easily accessible, transactions become costly. Costs are often determined by the legal system, political system, social system, educational system and other related factors of a country. In light of these, the performance of a given economy is largely determined by existing institutions.[16] Consequently, the new institutional economics is not only

12 See Geoffrey M. Hodgson, 'The Approach of Institutional Economics' (1998) 36 *Journal of Economic Literature* 166, 179. For example, the 'comply or explain' approach to the *UK Corporate Governance Code* differs from the approach to regulating corporate governance in the United States. The UK approach was developed in view of the expectation that companies in the UK (that the code applies to) would abide by the approach without the need for strict regulations that apply in the United States. The Financial Reporting Council is responsible for developing the codes, it is made up of different personalities from the financial and governance sectors in the UK. This ensures that a wide consultation is made before the code is developed. Thus, it creates an expectation that the codes would be obeyed and the approach that has been adopted would be respected by the 'corporate players'.

13 While the 'old' institutional economics identifies institutions as settled habits of thought common to the generality of men (a way of thought, of action embedded in the habits of a group), the 'new' institutional economics excludes the notion of habit. It regards institutions as humanly devised constraints that shape human interaction.

14 The contractual theory and entity theory of the corporation are briefly reviewed and examined in relation to takeovers in Chapter 3, sections 3.6.3 and 3.6.4.

15 Note 10, 4.

16 Ronald Coase, 'The New Institutional Economics' (1998) 88 *The American Economic Review* 72, 73.

concerned with the existence of institutions,[17] it is also concerned with how the institutions are created and how they function. In response to this, four levels of institutional framework were developed.[18] These levels of institution are illustrated in the following section.

2.4 Institutions: levels of development and change

The new institutional economics is different from previous economic theories because it accepts the market as a platform for economic interactions, strengthened by institutions to ensure efficiency of the market functions. More importantly, it is further concerned with how the institutions are created and developed.[19] One of the hypotheses of the theory is that a study of the developmental processes of institutions will create an understanding of how institutions emerge and how they can be changed or transformed.[20] Since institutions are relevant because they can be used to regulate the market towards efficiency, institutions can be relevant only to the extent that they are actually capable of enhancing the market functions. As such, institutions must be tailored towards the needs of the markets.

The needed foundation of the structure for efficient markets can be determined by reference to cultural values and choices which govern human behaviour and relationships.[21] Cultural values and choices emerge from the practices of particular local customs and they influence the ways in which an entire institutional framework are created. The process of developing institutions has its foundation in informal institutions. These informal institutions comprise cultural value, culturally derived choices and other local practices. Since they influence the formation and development of formal institutions and the entire institutional framework, they can largely determine how institutional functions can effectively respond to the challenges that they were created to address. Thus, institutions may effectively relate to the markets where reference is made to local practices which are based on human relationships. In view of this, institutions emerge through cultural evolution, trade practices and the constant value of human relationships.[22] In recognition of these, four levels of institutional development and change have emerged. These levels illustrate how institutions emerge, how they can be changed or transformed and more importantly, how they affect economics. They include: informal institutions, formal institutions, level of governance and the level of resource allocation – the market.

17 Rules that regulate individuals and organisations.

18 See Oliver E. Williamson, 'The New Institutional Economics: Taking Stocks, Looking Ahead' (2000) 38 *Journal of Economic Literature* 595, 596–600.

19 Douglas C. North, 'The New Institutional Economics' (1986) 142 *Journal of Institutional and Theoretical Economics* 230, 230.

20 Ibid. 234–235.

21 Note 11, 573.

22 Cultural evolution depicts norms and values and trade practices connect people of different cultural backgrounds through human relations.

The first level consists of informal institutions, they include: customs, traditions, values, religion and culture. At this level of institution, changes are very slow, because social institutions are largely embedded[23] and they form part of the unique way of the peoples' understanding of the environment around them. They are embedded because they are transmitted from generation to generation. At the second level is the formal institution. They consist of formal rules such as constitutions and property rights.[24] They often change from time to time and they are basically derived from the informal rules of level one. The function of institutions at this level is to provide a mechanism for the unification of the different close-knitted society within a larger macrocosm.[25] Institutions at this level are not closely embedded; hence changes may occur more frequently when compared with informal institutions. But the changes are not often cumulative; they are triggered by a sharp break from established principles which may be caused by political, civil or financial turmoil.[26]

The third level is the level of governance; it is the level where the formal rules which have been developed from the informal rules are applied. This is the level where human behaviour which is exhibited through established organisations is controlled and co-ordinated through the formal rules. At this level, conflicts are mitigated since organisations interact with the larger society. Ordinarily, in a perfect world, the rules which have been established at level two should govern human interaction to the exclusion of government intervention. But because of uncertainties and costs of transactions, the mere creation of rules is not sufficient in itself. Governance becomes necessary to enforce contractual relations for the purpose of mitigating conflicts to realise mutual gains.[27] This has been described as a unit of transaction which encompasses conflict, mutuality and order.[28] The fourth level is the level of the market. It is the level of production which is carried out by a firm. It is the level of output which is engineered by the productive capacity of the firm after the rules which emerged from level two have been applied to level three.

23 Human interactions designed by cultures have been described as the most enduring of human association. Such interactions are believed to confer benefit on close-knit groups where individual actions are for the collective good, rather than for individual purposes. See Samuel P. Huntington, *The Clash of Civilizations and the Remaking of the World Order* (London, Simon & Schuster, 1996) 43–44; Victor Nee, 'Sources of New Institutionalism' in Mary C. Brinton and Victor Nee (eds.), *New Institutionalismin Sociology* (New York, Russell Sage Foundation, 1998) 8–10.

24 Douglas C. North, 'Institutions' (1991) 5 *Journal of Economic Perspectives* 97.

25 Constitutions and property rights are often used as *grundnums*. They serve as a common restraint to the behavioural patterns of the people that make up the nation state. It is impracticable to practice diverse cultural behaviour at the same time or to decide which culture should be adopted as supreme among different cultures.

26 Note 18, 598.

27 Ibid. 599.

28 John R. Commons, 'The Problem of Correlating Law, Economics and Ethics' (1932–1933) 8 *Wisconsin Law Review* 1, 3–4.

These levels of institutional framework function effectively through continuous interrelations.[29] This is indicative of the major concepts of the new institutional economics; namely, the formation of institutions, the way they emerge and the way they influence economics.

The framework of the new institutional economics is mainly concerned with the ways in which the institutions that are the determinants of economics are formed. Since organisations[30] are expected to engage in transactions according to existing institutional framework – rules – the extent to which institutions can function effectively may be largely determined by the relevance which the organisations attach to the institutions. As such, institutions may function effectively only to the extent that they can be suitably applicable to the challenges and problems which exist within a given society. In view of this, it was rightly observed that the institutional framework which has been developed as a response to the challenges of an economic problem may not be successfully applied to a different economy. They may only be successfully applied to the extent that they can be adaptable.[31]

It can be observed that the new institutional economic theory is functional at *levels two* and *three*, while *levels one* and *four* represent institutions of existing norms and markets. Since the market factors are dependent on the institutional factors, the *fourth level* may be included as a functional part of the theory. In view of this, the interactions among *levels two, three, and four* distinguish the new institutional economics theory from the neo-classical and old economic theories. These levels which have been described as the mainstreams[32] of the new institutional economics theory: property rights theory, transaction cost economics and agency theory – contractual relations – are briefly examined next.

2.5 Main streams in economics of institutions

The new institutional economics consists of two basic foundations. First, that its theoretical framework should have the capacity to cause an interrelation of neo-classical economic theory with an analysis of the way institutions modify the choices which have been made available to humans. Second, that this framework must build upon the basic determinants of institutions so that the set choices

29 The preceding levels impose constraints on the subsequent levels. But the levels are nevertheless interconnected through the response which originates from the lower levels back to the higher levels by way of feedback.

30 Organisations are the actors. They consist of people or group of people who are connected by the same beliefs and views, such as political parties, religious organisations, trade unions and professional bodies.

31 See Douglas C. North, *The New Institutional Economics and Development* (Washington, Washington University, 1993) 8 www.deu.edu.tr/userweb/sedef.akgungor/Current%20topics%20in%20Turkish%20Economy/north.pdf accessed 7 February 2018.

32 Rudolf Richter, 'The New Institutional Economics: Its Start, Its Meaning, Its Prospects' (2005) 6 *European Business Organization Law Review* 161, 173; Claude Menard, 'Methodological Issues in New Institutional Economics' (2001) 8 *Journal of Economic Methodology* 85, 86–87; See generally Eric G. Furubotn and Rudolf Richter, 'The New Institutional Economics: A Different Approach to Economic Analysis' (2008) 28 *Economic Affairs* 15.

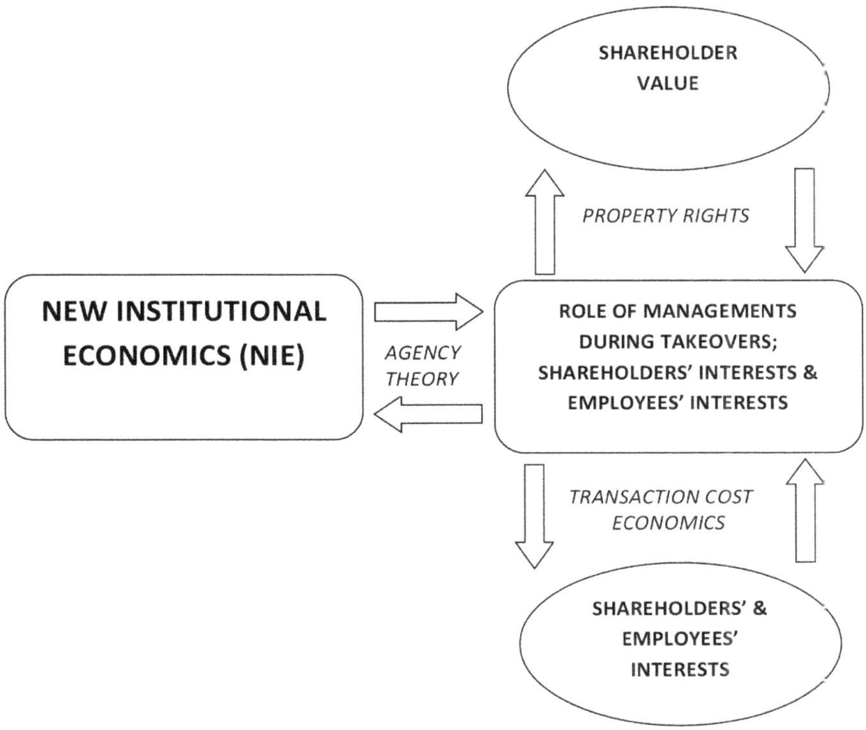

Figure 2.1 The NIE Framework for Takeover Regulation

Source: Author

cannot only be defined, but also have the capacity to analyse the way in which institutions change and therefore alter the available choice which may be set.[33] On their own, these theoretical foundations do not provide any tangible framework for achieving the collective objective of institutional economic functions. Rather, the central objective of these foundations has given rise to the needed tangible frameworks of property rights, transactions cost economics and agency theory – contractual relationship.

Figure 2.1 depicts the NIE framework for takeover regulations. It identifies the role of managements as central in the determination of the extent to which the interests of shareholders, employees and the company can be enhanced.

2.5.1 Property rights of shareholders

The importance which is attached to the value of properties both tangible and intangible is largely a function of the level of control which may be exerted

33 Note 19, 230.

over such properties. The level of control can be expressed as the rights to use, control[34] and the combination of both. The new institutional economics is concerned with the level of control to which property rights can be put. Company Managements can determine the level of control, as shown in Figure 2.1. Since scarcity leads to competition, allocation of resources should be determined by reference to established standard.[35] As observed: 'When it is too costly for one party to specify a long list of the particular rights it desires over another party's assets, it may be optimal for that party to purchase all the rights except those specifically mentioned in the contract'.[36] Thus, property rights theory as a framework of the new institutional economics determines the standard which governs the relationship amongst people for the exchange of ownership rights. The role of property right is to determine the use of resources.[37] This role is important because it forms the basis of exchange of the scarce resources. It determines whether resources are to be put to permanent or temporary use.[38] Also, it creates a platform for the use of scarce resources by demarcating the rights to use the resources where an exclusive right over the resources cannot be granted.[39] Property rights determine the value of resources. When resources are exclusively held by a person or group of persons, there is a greater incentive to improve on the value of the asset by investment.[40] Also, it is illustrated that the property right of sale can improve allocation of resources in the following ways. First, allowing sale signals scarcity which invariably enhances the value of goods. Second, the existence of markets allows those who value the assets the most to have the ability to purchase the assets.[41] More importantly, the role of property right is largely dependent on the role of the state pursuance to

34 These include the rights to change and transfer (a totality of right over property or the residual rights of control). Oliver Hart and John Moore, 'Property Rights and the Nature of the Firm' (1990) 98 *The Journal of Political Economy* 1119, 1121.

35 Armen A. Alchian, 'Pricing and Society' (The Institute of Economic Affairs *Occasional Paper* (17; Westminster, 1967) cited in Eirik G. Furubotn and Svetozar Pejovich, 'Property Rights and Economic Theory: A Survey of Recent Literature' (1972) 10 *Journal of Economic Literature* 1137, 1139.

36 Sanford J. Grossman and Oliver D. Hart, 'The Costs and Benefits of Ownership: A Theory of Vertical and Lateral Integration' (1986) 94 *Journal of Political Economy* 691, 692.

37 Lee J. Alston and Bernardo Mueller, 'Property Rights and the State' in Clause Menard and Mary M. Shirley (eds.), *Handbook of New Institutional Economics* (Dordrecht, Netherlands Springer, 2008) 573–590.

38 It determines whether a property can be used as collateral to secure a loan. Also, the decision whether to turn a piece of land into a farm land or to build estate on such land is determined by reference to property rights.

39 Jongwook Kim and Joseph T. Mahoney, 'Property Rights Theory, Transaction Costs Theory and Agency Theory: An Organizational Economics Approach to Strategic Management' (2005) 26 *Managerial and Decision Economics* 223, 226.

40 Alston and Mueller note 37, 574. See also Harold Demsetz, 'Information and Efficiency: Another Viewpoint' (1969) 12 *Journal of Law and Economics* 1, 12–13.

41 Ibid. (H Demsetz).

its functions. Where property rights are created, they must be clearly defined, enforced and protected by the apparatus of the state.[42]

In corporate acquisitions, the interests of shareholders are directly related to the value of their investments in the company in the form of shares. Shareholders have property rights in the shares that are the main subject of transfer. The rights that are attached to shares, which include the right to vote, right to receive dividends, right to participate in capital distribution,[43] are important only to the extent that shareholders can actually enforce their rights, subject to company law and other regulations. These rights, which emanate from the property rights doctrine, can only be meaningful if takeovers are included in the circumstances where the rights can be applied, enforced and enjoyed without hindrance. As indicated in Figure 2.1 the role of managements is central in the determination of whether the property rights of shareholders can actually be freely exercised. The ability of the state to establish effective institutions that can regulate takeovers by challenging managerial behaviour towards enforcing property rights can determine the extent of the aforementioned functions. Also, Figure 2.1 shows that the extent to which the interests of shareholders can be protected during takeovers depends on two main factors amongst other considerations. First, whether company managements can genuinely promote shareholder interests when they make takeover decisions where takeovers are considered to be a usual investment decision for which managements are responsible to act as agents of shareholders. Second, alternatively, whether there are effective institutional mechanisms that can effectively regulate takeovers to ensure that managements promote the property rights of shareholders.

Managements can engage in acquisitions for the genuine reasons of seeking to promote corporate value and shareholder interests. However, in view of the fact that conflict of interests characterises the agency relationship of shareholders and managements,[44] this may not always be guaranteed. Agency conflict which can be demonstrated in costly and overambitious acquisitions can lead to negligible or zero gains to acquiring shareholders.[45] Hence it is imperative that effective institutional mechanisms are established to regulate and administer takeovers to ensure that property rights of shareholders can be protected from managerial hubris.

Property right does not function independently of other institutional frameworks of transaction costs and agency costs; rather, it provides the platform on which they function. This means that the transaction cost economics and agency

42 Note 37 Alston and Mueller, 573. See also Ugo Mattei, L. Antoniolli Deflorian, and A. Rossato, 'Comparative Law and Economics' in Boudewijn Bouckaert and Gerrit De Geest (eds.), *Encyclopedia of Law and Economics* (Vol. 1, Cheltenham, UK, Edward Elgar, 2000) 515.

43 The rights attached to shares are enjoyed by the beneficial owners of the shares. Andrew McGee, *Shares and Share Capital under the Companies Act 2006* (Bristol, Jordan Publishing Ltd, 2009) 71–107; see also Harold Demsetz, 'Toward a Theory of Property Rights' (1967) 57 *The American Economic Review* 347, 358–359.

44 See section 2.5.3.

45 See the discussions in Chapter 3, section 3.4.3, Chapter 5, section 5.4.

theory – contracts – functions of the institutional economic theory are dependent on the scope of the property rights functions. Thus, property right influences incentives and behaviour.[46]

2.5.2 Transaction cost economics (costs of takeovers)

Transaction cost economics is a basic feature of the new institutional economics theory. It is concerned with the transactions that can lead to the exchange of property rights and their attendant costs. The existence of property rights invariably leads to transactions of which property rights are exchanged for value. These transactions are often influenced by both human[47] – Figure 2.1 indicates that managements can determine how values are allocated – and environmental factors[48] which increase the costs of these transactions. In a perfect world where these factors are absent, transactions where exchanges occur would be costless. The new institutional economics recognises that human and environmental factors influence the costs of transactions. Hence it is concerned with the process of organising transactions towards minimising these costs to attain efficiency.[49] The existence of property rights is relevant to the new institutional economics theory to the extent that it provides an institutional framework for the clear definition of rules which govern human relations. The property rights will not be functional by its mere existence, rather a system of governance through which these rights can be positively organised towards its enforcement makes the transaction cost economics theory an indispensable unit of the framework of the new institutional economics theory.[50] The protection of property rights becomes as important as its creation. As observed, 'the TCE – transaction cost economics – tries to explain how trading partners choose, from the set of feasible institutional alternatives, the arrangement that offers protection for their relationship-specific investments at the lowest total cost(s)', to reduce transaction costs.[51] This implies that the transaction cost economics theory builds on the property rights theory because it indicates the existence of an institutional framework which defines the rights it sets out to implement and the intensity of relationships. The

46 Note 35 Furubotn and Pejovich, 1139. They influence incentives at the level of governance (transaction cost economics) and behaviour at the level of the market (agency theory).

47 These are endogenous factors within a firm such as bounded rationality and opportunism.

48 They are exogenous factors which affect a firm's productivity and transactions, such as uncertainties and complexities.

49 Robert J. David and Shin-kap Han, 'A Systematic Assessment of the Empirical Support for Transaction Cost Economics' (2004) 25 *Strategic Management Journal* 39, 40.

50 Douglas W. Allen, 'Transaction Costs' in Steven G. Medema, Boudewijn Bouckaert, and Gerrit De Geest (eds.), *Encyclopedia of Law and Economics* (Aldershot, Edward Elgar, 1999) 898–899.

51 Howard A. Shelanski and Peter G. Klein, 'Empirical Research in Transaction Cost Economics, a Review and Assessment' in Glenn R. Carroll and David J. Teece (eds.), *Firms, Markets and Hierarchies: The Transaction Cost Economics Perspective* (New York, Oxford University Press Inc., 1999) 91; Robert H. Sitkoff, 'The Economic Structure of Fiduciary Law' (2011) 91 *Boston University Law Review* 1039, 1044.

function of the transaction cost economics within the main stream of the new institutional economics is to eliminate or reduce the incompleteness which characterises contractual relations and transactions because of future uncertainties.

One of the greatest challenges of takeovers is the level of uncertainty that characterises employment issues. Even though all takeovers do not lead to employment reduction, as soon as negotiations for a takeover become apparent, there are often concerns for employment security. While shareholders may not experience gains that correspond with the size of the company post-takeover, managements may decide to disengage some employees to mitigate the effects of the costs of the takeovers.[52] In some cases, negotiating parties make promises to protect employment, only to renege on such promises post-takeover. This uncertainty which characterises takeovers in relation to employment is often caused by lack of appropriate institutional structure that regulates takeovers and incorporates employment issues into the takeover framework in specific corporate jurisdictions. This means that the incompleteness which characterises employment contracts can indirectly increase transaction costs during takeovers. Where appropriate regulatory mechanisms are established to ensure that employees are not easily disengaged by managements to reduce the costs of takeovers, company managements would make more prudent acquisitions. Also, they would focus on value-yielding takeovers that would not necessarily require reduction of employment post-takeovers. The objective of the regulation that is contemplated here is to ensure that the role of managements is clearly defined towards promoting corporate value during takeover. A regulatory framework that can effectively restrain managements from engaging in overambitious acquisitions can lead to lower takeover transaction costs. This would likely mitigate losses to acquiring shareholders.[53]

As indicated in Figure 2.1, the role of managements can largely determine the extent to which transaction costs can be high or low in relation to takeovers. Hence, it may be argued that as long as managements can freely engage in large-scale employment reduction post-takeovers, they are likely to engage in costly acquisitions irrespective of whether or not such acquisitions would enhance shareholder wealth and corporate value. It is impossible for parties to draw up a complete contract that will clearly define their rights with regards to any possible future eventuality,[54] because it is too costly to do so.[55] Thus, transaction cost economics plays a governance role, to protect parties from the hazards which may occur by virtue of the uncertainties during exchange.[56]

52 Azimjon Kuvandikov, Andrew Pendleton, and David Higgins, 'Causes of Employment Reductions after Corporate Takeovers' 2012, 1–34 http://ilera2012.wharton.upenn.edu/RefereedPapers/PendletonAndrew%20AzimjonKuvandikov%20David%20Higgins.pdf accessed 21 March 2018.

53 See analysis in Chapter 7.

54 Oliver E. Williamson, *Markets and Hierarchies: Analysis and Antitrust Implications* (New York, Macmillan Publishing Co, Inc., 1975) 23.

55 John C. Coffee, Jr., 'The Uncertain Case for Takeover Reform: An Essay on Stockholders, Stakeholders and Bust-Ups' (1988) *Wisconsin Law Review* 435, 448.

56 Peter G. Klein, 'New Institutional Economics' in Boudewijn Bouckaert and Gerrit De Geest (eds.), *Encyclopedia of Law and Economics* (Cheltenham, Edward Elgar Publishing Ltd, 1998) 466.

Transaction cost which plays a governance role[57] serves as an important link between institutions and the market.[58] It governs relationships by applying established institutional guidelines to the level of the market. This can mitigate the extra costs of transactions which are caused by uncertainties arising from factors that are both internal and external to organisations. These internal and external factors which influence individual behaviour can be controlled at the level of governance through effective institutions.

During negotiations for a takeover, while institutional frameworks can protect the property rights of shareholders, the interests of other corporate constituents such as employees are also affected, and their interests can be related to shareholder interests. Takeovers are expensive, and when a takeover becomes more costly, the effects of the costs can be shared by shareholders – especially those of the acquiring companies – and the company employees. The institutional framework can influence the level of governance and this can have a direct impact on transaction costs. Employment reduction can be influenced by costly takeover transactions; to mitigate corporate cash outflow and the loss to the shareholders of the acquiring company. In the absence of an effective institutional framework that can mitigate the costs of takeovers, the interests of employees would remain uncertain. Thus, an appropriate institutional framework which can regulate takeovers towards promoting shareholder value while defining and preserving employee interests is desirable.

2.5.3 Agency relationship between managements and shareholders

The new institutional economics theory is generally concerned with the promotion of an efficient market through established institutions and governance mechanisms. While institutions define property rights, the governance functions ensure that the costs of transactions are minimised or eliminated. These important aspects of the new institutional economics have been briefly examined in the preceding sections of this chapter. The platform where transactions occur, namely the market, is also important. It is the level where individuals interact through contractual relationships to achieve mutual objectives. Usually, at the level of the market where contracts are concluded, there is often the problem with delegation of authority as a result of certain intervening factors. Since investors often rely on agents to manage their capital towards productive use, their interests can be undermined by some intervening factors. These often prevent agents who have been appointed to manage the investments from achieving the objective of the investors. These include information asymmetry[59] and opportunism. These can

57 See the 'Three-Level Schema' in Oliver E. Williamson, 'Transaction Cost Economics and Organization Theory' in Neil J. Smelser and Richard Swedberg (eds.), *The Handbook of Economic Sociology* (New York, Princton University Press, 1994) 80.

58 The institutions here refer to the established property rights and the market is the level where humans actually interact (agency and contractual relationships).

59 When information is asymmetric, only managements know the true position of the company. They can use this for their own advantage. See for example, Sam Mensah, 'The Impact of

cause agents to have conflicting objectives with their principals; hence, agents can pursue personal objectives to maximise their own value at the expense of the principal-investor. Agency problems[60] interfere with the market functions by increasing the costs of transactions. This is depicted in Figure 2.1. The role of managements can determine how agency relationship is expressed, especially in relation to conflict of interests and shareholder value. When institutions are established at the level of property rights, and adequate governance mechanisms towards the enforcement of these rights are functional and agency costs can be reduced or eliminated, market efficiency will likely be achieved.

The agency theory which originated from the concept of 'separation of ownership and control'[61] uses a modern corporation as an analogy where ownership and control of investment capital resides in principals and agents respectively. As a result of the intervening factors, the objective of the firm becomes divided between the principal's and the agent's. In view of this, it is important to ensure that the agents act for the best interests of the principal. To encourage the agent to act in the best interest of the principal, the principal must engage certain mechanisms to ensure that the interests of the agents align with those of the principal. This may be achieved through improved information systems and incentive programmes.[62] Incentive contracts often include the specification of residual rights of control, to determine who can make decisions on unforeseen matters relating to the contract between the principal and agent in the productive function of the firm.[63] In achieving this objective, certain costs arise, these include: monitoring costs, bonding cost and residual loss.[64] The monitoring costs represent the expenditure incurred by the principal in monitoring the business activities of the agent through mechanisms such as auditing, while bonding costs are those expenditures which accrue from the agency contract itself, including commitments from the agent and incentives offered to the agent to enhance performance output. The residual loss is different from those incurred from monitoring and bonding. They include loss which should have been counted as gains of trade

---

Asymetric Information on Proxy Outcomes: An Empirical Test' (1998) 33 *The Financial Review* 69, 73–74.

60 See generally Michael C. Jensen and William H. Meckling, 'Theory of the Firm: Managerial Behaviour, Agency Cost and Ownership Structure' (1976) 3 *Journal of Financial Economics* 305, 310–311; Eugene F. Fama and Michael C. Jenson, 'Separation of Ownership and Control' (1983) 26 *Journal of Law and Economics* 301.

61 See generally Adolfe A. Berle and Gardiner C. Means, *The Modern Corporation and Private Property* (New York, Macmillan, 1932).

62 Joana G. Geraldi, 'New Institutional Economics' (Management Internationaler Projekte, 2007) 2, 8 www.studocu.com/en/document/universitaet-hamburg/international-economics/other/new-institutional-economics-summary/388514/view accessed March 2018.

63 David E. M. Sappington, 'Incentives in Principal: Agent Relationships' (1991) 5 *The Journal of Economics Perspectives* 45, 62.

64 See Charles W. L. Hill and Thomas M. Jones, 'Stakeholder-Agency Theory' (1992) 29 *Journal of Management Studies* 131, 138–140. See also note 60, Michael C. Jensen and William H. Meckling, 308.

but because of the inability to supervise all the actions of the agents, these losses occur anyway.[65]

The function of institutions at the level of the agency theory with respect to takeovers is to properly define the role of management during takeovers. The definition of the role of managements can be done with an appropriate institutional framework with reference to property rights and transaction cost economics. It can help to provide a regulatory control over transaction costs by ensuring that the role of managements during takeovers aligns as best as possible with the interests of shareholders, managements and the company.

New institutional economics is particularly concerned with the principal-agent relationship because, first, it is the level of the market in the institutional framework where resources are allocated. Also, it is concerned with promoting efficiency in contractual relationships by attempting to reduce the general costs of transacting – which is caused by opportunism – through incentive alignments which determine how risks are allocated between principal and agent.[66] In view of the fact that one of the main objectives of the new institutional economics is to promote efficiency in the allocation of resources, it is also concerned with the elimination or reduction of the marginal deficiencies of contractual relationships. This means that the challenges of conflict of interests can hinder the effectiveness of management functions when a takeover is made. Effective takeover regulations can be used to re-define the scope of managerial discretion and their role generally. This can ensure that agency conflicts are mitigated and the decisions of managements can be made to reflect their positions as agents of their shareholders when a takeover is made, to enhance corporate value, shareholder and other stakeholder interests.

2.6 How institutions can influence market discipline

While the new institutional economics is generally concerned with how institutions emerge and how they can be changed over time, it is also particularly concerned with how institutions can be used to achieve a higher level of corporate productivity and market efficiency.

Two levels of institutional functions can be deduced here. First is the emergence and definition of institutions, which exist at the level of institutional environment. It is the set of fundamental political, social and legal ground rules that establishes the basis for production, exchange and distribution. It includes the rules governing property rights.[67] At this level, institutions are seen as sets of ordered relationships among people: they define rights, exposure to the rights

65 Some of these aspects of losses are not caused by the agents, they occur because of circumstances beyond the control of the agent.

66 See generally Bengt Holmstrom and Paul Milgrom, 'Multitask Principal-Agent Analyses: Incentive Contracts, Asset Ownership and Job Design' (1991) 7 *Journal of Law, Economics & Organisation* 24.

67 Lance E. Davis and Douglas C. North, *Institutional Change and American Economic Growth* (Cambridge, Cambridge University Press, 1971) 6.

of others, privileges and responsibilities.[68] Institutions function at this level as a constraint and act on a composite level.

At the second level of institutional function are institutions of governance. Here institutions operate at the level of individual transactions.[69] It is the level where the first level of institution is applicable to human interpersonal relationships. This level determines whether established institutional frameworks can achieve the desired objective of market efficiency.

The market is characterised by uncertainties in view of the principal-agency problems and market expropriation. The extent to which established institutional frameworks can reduce or eliminate these challenges depends on how they function at the level of the market.

The problems of principal-agent relationship occur as a result of lack of a definite contractual relationship between a principal and an agent. Where it is possible to define all the terms of a contract which determine the relationship between a principal and an agent, it would be unlikely for parties to be involved in any dispute when they enter into contractual relationships. Opportunism is another factor which undermines principal-agent relationship. As long as there is the expectation that individual advantage will be realised, the self-disbelieved promises will characterise individual transactions.[70] Although, institutional frameworks may not create contracts between agents and principals, they can reduce the elements of uncertainty and complexity, as well as opportunistic behaviour which characterise such contracts. Also, since a party cannot determine the level of satisfaction which is sought by another party as well as all contingent matters which may originate during the pendency of the contract, institutions can thus determine the extent to which compensation can be appropriated.[71]

Market expropriation[72] can occur where there is a relationship which confers economic benefit during exchange. Expropriation occurs because of imbalance in contractual relationships. Parties with higher bargaining powers often consider their ability to expropriate as an added gain in the exchange which is different from the gains which they have earned from the contractual relationship. Employer-employee relationship is an example of an imbalanced contractual relationship where the employer occupies the position of advantage. It has

68 A. Allan Schmid, 'Analytical Institutional Economics: Challenging Problems in the Economics of Resources for a New Environment' (1972) 54 *American Journal of Agricultural Economics* 893, 893.

69 Oliver E. Williamson, *The Mechanism of Governance* (New York, Oxford University Press, 1996) 5.

70 Erving Goffman, *Strategic Interaction* (Philadelphia, University of Pennsylvania Press, 1969) 105.

71 The problems of principal-agent relationship (as it relates to shareholders of offeree companies during takeovers) was one of the factors which influenced the emergence of *The City Code on Takeovers* and Mergers in the United Kingdom. See *The City Code on Takeovers and Mergers* section 2(a).

72 Market expropriation is a wide concept. It includes expropriation by suppliers and rivals. For the purpose of this this analysis, expropriation of employees by employers will only be considered here.

been observed that one of the functions of institutions is to co-ordinate the relationship between a legal superior and a legal inferior; this includes managerial transactions which have been described as characterising the relationship between employers and employees.[73] The relationship between employer and employee creates deficiencies in bargaining powers. As a result of human asset specificity,[74] economic conditions and psychological state of mind, it is often impracticable for employees to protect themselves from expropriation. Established institutional frameworks can be used to regulate this relationship, to limit the extent of expropriation by setting appropriate standards for compensation as 'deemed' protection for employees.

The principal-agent relationship and employer–employee relationship are clearly based on contractual relationships. The extent to which value is allocated in these contracts depends largely on how the contracting parties can effectively enforce their respective contractual rights. In view of the uncertainties and other external factors already considered, the enjoyment of these rights invariably becomes a matter of the extent to which these rights not only exist, but their enforcement is guaranteed. Guarantees which characterise enforcement of contracts as binding obligations and protection of contractual parties in the event of contingencies introduce the framework of institutions into the market functions to attain efficiency. Thus, the new institutional economics seeks to regulate the role of the market actors, using effective institutions, rather than merely replacing the market with institutions.

While the market function is given as a constant value[75] in the framework of the new institutional economics – being a platform for human interaction and exchange – institutions are important to the extent that they can actually influence the market function towards efficiency. This means that market efficiency depends on the following: first, the effectiveness of established institutional frameworks, and second, the degree to which these institutional frameworks are responsive to the challenges posed by the market function.[76] Institutions are necessary to promote market efficiency. To promote and preserve this efficiency, institutional frameworks must be regularly changed so that they can effectively respond to recent and recurrent challenges.

Corporate takeovers are an important aspect of the market for corporate control. In view of the plethora of interests which characterise takeovers, regulatory

73 John Groenewegen, Antoon Spithoven, and Annette Van Den Berg, *Institutional Economics, an Introduction* (New York, Palgrave Macmillan, 2010) 13–14.

74 This includes Firm's specific knowledge that employees may accumulate overtime that would make them essentially valuable only within one company. Ibid. 121.

75 The market function is regarded as constant because as a platform for exchange, interactions are always directed towards economic value. People interact and exchange property rights only to the extent that it would enhance their economic interests. Also, general contractual relationships can be created at the level of the market.

76 Robert C. O. Matthews, 'The Economics of Institutions and the Sources of Growth' (1986) 96 *The Economic Journal* 903, 908–911.

control over takeovers have been considered to be necessary.[77] Since takeover markets are regulated by established institutional frameworks, institutions must be continuously reviewed to suit current trends in takeover markets.

Although it may be a challenge to make changes and restructure institutions, the challenges which may occur from failure to restructure current institutions could be enormous. As such, it was rightly observed that failures to carry out institutional changes are obstacles to development.[78]

The conceptual framework of the new institutional economics supports the theoretical arguments for shareholder and employee interests in takeovers. Its main stream of property rights, transaction costs and agency theory are used to examine the problems as it affects shareholders and employees. The next section concludes the chapter.

2.7 Conclusion

Interactions at the level of the market characterise the high point of human relationship leading to exchange. The market is an important platform for exchange and its functions can be further strengthened to eliminate or reduce the effects of uncertainties. The new institutional economics is concerned with the creation of institutions to protect the market functions towards a more efficient system of human exchange. Institutions matter and without the appropriate institutions, no market economy of any significance would be possible.[79]

This chapter examined the institutional framework which supports market efficiency. The new institutional economics was examined. It was revealed that the new institutional economics was established to build on the main concepts of the neo-classical economics. It accepts the market functions and identifies institution as a mechanism that can be used to strengthen the important function of the market. Also, it emerged that the new institutional economics is not merely concerned with the introduction of institutions; it is actually concerned with the ways that institutions are created. This explains the importance of the informal institutions as forming a part of the levels of institutional development.

The chapter also showed that aspects of the institutional framework are especially concerned with how established institutions can be defined, protected and enforced. This was examined by reference to the main streams of the new institutional economics of property rights, transaction costs and the principal-agent theory. In light of the aim of the book, the problems which characterise principal-agent

77 In the United Kingdom, corporate takeovers are regulated by the European Parliament, *Directive 2004/25/EC of the European Parliament and of the Council on Takeover Bids* 2004 the *UK Code on Takeovers And Mergers 2016*.

78 See Douglas C. North, 'Institutions and Performance of Economies over Time' in Claude Menard and Mary M. Shirley (eds.), *Handbook of Institutional Economics* (Heidelberg, Netherlands, Springer, 2005) 29.

79 Ronald H. Coase, 'The Institutional Structure of Production' (1992) 82 *The American Economic Review* 713, 714.

relationships and market expropriation during takeovers were shown to persist as a result of the lack of a functional institutional framework that can effectively regulate takeovers. This problem affects the interests of company shareholders and employees at the level of the market. It was shown that providing a platform for the creation of functional institutions or the strengthening of existing institutions can ensure that takeovers are effectively regulated and administered.

Chapter 3 concludes Part I. It examines the theoretical framework of takeovers. The chapter illustrates the problems that arise during takeovers and it shows the need for the establishment of the effective institutions that have been examined in this chapter.

References

Alchian, A. A., 'Pricing and Society' The Institute of Economic Affairs *Occasional Paper* (17; Westminster, 1967).

Allen, D. W., 'Transaction Costs' in Steven G. Medema, Boudewijn Bouckaert, and Gerrit De Geest (eds.), *Encyclopedia of Law and Economics* (Aldershot, Edward Elgar, 1999).

Alston, L. J. and Bernardo Mueller, 'Property Rights and the State' in Clause Menard and Mary M Shirley (eds.), *Handbook of New Institutional Economics* (Dordrecht, Netherlands, Springer, 2008).

Berle, A. A. and Gardiner C. Means, *The Modern Corporation and Private Property* (New York, Macmillan, 1932).

Coase, R. H., 'The Institutional Structure of Production' (1992) 82 *The American Economic Review* 713.

Coase, R. H., 'The New Institutional Economics' (1998) 88 *The American Economic Review* 72.

Coffee, J. C., Jr., 'The Uncertain Case for Takeover Reform: An Essay on Stockholders, Stakeholders and Bust-Ups' (1988) *Wisconsin Law Review* 435.

Commons, J. R., 'The Problem of Correlating Law, Economics and Ethics' (1932–1933) 8 *Wisconsin Law Review* 1.

David, R. J. and Shin-K. Han, 'A systematic Assessment of the Empirical Support for Transaction Cost Economics' (2004) 25 *Strategic Management Journal* 39.

Davis, L. E. and Douglas C. North, *Institutional Change and American Economic Growth* (Cambridge, Cambridge University Press, 1971).

Demsetz, H., 'Information and Efficiency: Another Viewpoint' (1969) 12 *Journal of Law and Economics* 1.

Demsetz, H., 'Toward a Theory of Property Rights' (1967) 57 *The American Economic Review* 347.

Fama, E. F. and Michael C. Jenson, 'Separation of Ownership and Control' (1983) 26 *Journal of Law and Economics* 301.

Furubotn, E. G. and Svetozar Pejovich, 'Property Rights and Economic Theory: A Survey of Recent Literature' (1972) 10 *Journal of Economic Literature* 1137.

Furubotn, E. G. and Rudolf Richter, 'The New Institutional Economics: A Different Approach to Economic Analysis' (2008) 28 *Economic Affairs* 15.

Geraldi, J. G., 'New Institutional Economics' (Management Internationaler Projekte, 2007) 2, 8 www.studocu.com/en/document/universitaet-hamburg/international-economics/other/new-institutional-economics-summary/388514/view accessed March 2018.

Goffman, E., *Strategic Interaction* (Philadelphia, University of Pennsylvania Press, 1969).

Groenewegen, J., Antoon Spithoven, and Annette Van Den Berg, *Institutional Economics, an Introduction* (New York, Palgrave Macmillan, 2010).

Grossman, S. J. and Oliver D. Hart, 'The Costs and Benefits of Ownership: A Theory of Vertical and Lateral Integration' (1986) 94 *Journal of Political Economy* 691.

Hart, O. and John Moore, 'Property Rights and the Nature of the Firm' (1990) 98 *The Journal of Political Economy* 1119.

Heiner, R. A., 'The Origin of Predictable Behaviour' (1983) 73 *The American Economic Review* 560.

Hill, C. W. L. and Thomas M. Jones, 'Stakeholder-Agency Theory' (1992) 29 *Journal of Management Studies* 131, 138–140. See also note 60: Michael C. Jensen and William H. Meckling, 308.

Hodgson, G. M., 'The Approach of Institutional Economics' (1998) 36 *Journal of Economic Literature* 166.

Holmstrom, B. and Paul Milgrom, 'Multitask Principal-Agent Analyses: Incentive Contracts, Asset Ownership and Job Design' (1991) 7 *Journal of Law, Economics & Organisation* 24.

Huntington, S. P., *The Clash of Civilizations and the Remaking of the World Order* (London, Simon & Schuster, 1996).

Jensen, M. C. and William H. Meckling, 'Theory of the Firm: Managerial Behaviour, Agency Cost and Ownership Structure' (1976) 3 *Journal of Financial Economics* 305.

Kim, J. and Joseph T. Mahoney, 'Property Rights Theory, Transaction Costs Theory and Agency Theory: An Organizational Economics Approach to Strategic Management' (2005) 26 *Managerial and Decision Economics* 223.

Klein, P. G., 'New Institutional Economics' in Boudewijn Bouckaert and Gerrit De Geest (eds.), *Encyclopedia of Law and Economics* (Cheltenham, Edward Elgar Publishing Ltd, 1998).

Kuvandikov, A., Andrew Pendleton, and David Higgins, 'Causes of Employment Reductions after Corporate Takeovers' 2012 http://ilera2012.wharton.upenn.edu/RefereedPapers/PendletonAndrew%20AzimjonKuvandikov%20David%20Higgins.pdf accessed 21 March 2018.

Mattei, U. L., Antoniolli Deflorian, and A. Rossato, 'Comparative Law and Economics' in Boudewijn Bouckaert and Gerrit De Geest (eds.), *Encyclopedia of Law and Economics* (Vol. 1, Cheltenham, UK, Edward Elgar, 2000).

Matthews, R. C. O., 'The Economics of Institutions and the Sources of Growth' (1986) 96 *The Economic Journal* 903.

Mcgee, A., *Shares and Share Capital under the Companies Act 2006* (Bristol, Jordan Publishing Ltd, 2009) 71.

Menard, C., 'Methodological Issues in New Institutional Economics' (2001) 8 *Journal of Economic Methodology* 85.

Mensah, S., 'The Impact of Asymetric Information on Proxy Outcomes: An Empirical Test' (1998) 33 *The Financial Review* 69.

Mitchell, W. C., 'Making Goods and Making Money' in Wesley C. Mitchell (ed.), *The Backward Art of Spending Money* (New York, Augustine M. Kelley, 1923).

Nee, V., 'Sources of New Institutionalism' in Mary C. Brinton and Victor Nee (eds.), *New Institutionalismin Sociology* (New York, Russell Sage Foundation, 1998).

North, D. C., 'Economic Performance through Time' (1994) 84 *The American Economic Review* 359.

North, D. C., 'Institutions' (1991) 5 *Journal of Economic Perspectives* 97.
North, D. C., 'Institutions and Economic Theory' (1992) 36 *The American Economist* 3.
North, D. C., 'Institutions and Performance of Economies over Time' in Claude Menard and Mary M. Shirley (eds.), *Handbook of Institutional Economics* (Heidelberg, Netherlands, Springer, 2005).
North, D. C., 'The New Institutional Economics' (1986) 142 *Journal of Institutional and Theoretical Economics* 230.
North, D. C., *The New Institutional Economics and Development* (Washington, Washington University, 1993) 8 www.deu.edu.tr/userweb/sedef.akgungor/Current%20topics%20in%20Turkish%20Economy/north.pdf accessed 7 February 2018.
Richter, R., 'The New Institutional Economics: Its Start, Its Meaning, Its Prospects' (2005) 6 *European Business Organization Law Review* 161.
Rutherford, M., 'Intitutional Economics: Then and Now' (2001) 15 *The Journal of Economic Perspectives* 173.
Sappington, D. E. M., 'Incentives in Principal: Agent Relationships' (1991) 5 *The Journal of Economics Perspectives* 45.
Schmid, A. A., 'Analytical Institutional Economics: Challenging Problems in the Economics of Resources for a New Environment' (1972) 54 *American Journal of Agricultural Economics* 893.
Shelanski, H. A. and Peter G. Klein, 'Empirical Research in Transaction Cost Economics, a Review and Assessment' in Glenn R. Carroll and David J. Teece (eds.), *Firms, Markets and Hierarchies: The Transaction Cost Economics Perspective* (New York, Oxford University Press Inc., 1999).
Sitkoff, R. H., 'The Economic Structure of Fiduciary Law' (2011) 91 *Boston University Law Review* 1039.
Veblen, T., 'The Preconceptions of Economic Science' (1900) 14 *Quarterley Journal of Economics* 240.
Veblen, T. and Thorstein Veblen, *The Theory of the Leisure Class: An Economic Study of Institutions* (New York, Macmillan & Co. Ltd., 1915).
Wallis, J. J. and Douglas North, 'Measuring the Transaction Sector in the American Economy 1870–1970' in Stanley Engerman and Robert Gallman (eds.), *Long Term Factors in American Economic Growth* (Chicago, University of Chicago Press, 1986).
Weintraub, E. R., 'Neo-Classical Economics' in *The Concise Encyclopedia of Economics* (Library of Economics and Liberty, 1993) www.econlib.org/library/Encl/NeoclassicalEconomics.html accessed 11 March 2018.
Williamson, O. E., *Markets and Hierarchies: Analysis and Antitrust Implications* (New York, Macmillan Publishing Co, Inc., 1975).
Williamson, O. E., *The Mechanism of Governance* (New York, Oxford University Press, 1996).
Williamson, O. E., 'The New Institutional Economics: Taking Stocks, Looking Ahead' (2000) 38 *Journal of Economic Literature* 595.
Williamson, O. E., 'Transaction Cost Economics and Organization Theory' in Neil J. Smelser and Richard Swedberg (eds.), *The Handbook of Economic Sociology* (New York, Princton University Press, 1994).

3 The theoretical framework of corporate takeovers

3.1 Introduction

This chapter identifies the underlying effects of takeovers. It includes an examination of the challenges of conflict of interests and agency problems in takeovers.

Traditional finance theory recognises different mechanisms for corporate regulation, namely, the internal and external mechanisms. While the internal mechanism is based on managerial compensation, structure of the board of directors and control by large shareholders, the external control mechanisms consist of the activities of the market as a means of controlling corporate powers.[1] In the United States, internal corporate control is regulated with statutes,[2] whereas in the United Kingdom,[3] the internal mechanism of corporate control is mainly administered through corporate governance codes. This leaves enforcement powers with shareholders who have limited monitoring capacities by reasons of coordination problems, monitoring costs and different incentives.[4] A failure of internal control may lead to the intervention of external control measures of takeovers as a function of the market for corporate control.

A corporate takeover is an important aspect of the market for corporate control. It functions as an external mechanism[5] for corporate accountability.[6] The

1 Alvaro Cuervo, 'Corporate Governance Mechanisms: A Plea for Less Code of Good Governance and More Market Control' (2002) 10 *Blackwell Publishers* 84, 84.

2 The United States, partly regulates corporate governance with legislative provisions such as the *Sarbanes-Oxley Act 2002.*

3 The first corporate governance code was the Cadbury Report, 1992. The most recent code is the *UK Corporate Governance Code 2018.*

4 Sridhar Arcot, Valentina Bruno, and Antoine Faure-Grimaud, 'Corporate Governance in the UK: Is the Comply or Explain Approach Working'? (2010) 30 *International Review of Law and Economics* 193, 193; see also David Seidl, Paul Sanderson, and John Roberts, *Applying 'Comply or Explain': Conformance with Codes of Corporate Governance in the UK and Germany* (Cambridge, Centre for Business Research, University of Cambridge, 2009) 2 www.cbr.cam.ac.uk/fileadmin/user_upload/centre-for-business-research/downloads/working-papers/wp389.pdf accessed 12 March 2018.

5 The internal mechanisms involve the use of codes of governance and/or mandatory rules to direct and control the internal affairs of companies.

6 Charlie Weir, David Laing, and Phillip J. Mcknight, 'Internal and External Governance Mechanisms: Their Impact on the Performance of Large UK Public Companies' (2002) 29 *Journal*

market for corporate control refers to the entire processes leading to the transfer of control and ownership of companies[7] from one set of investors and managers to another,[8] through different mechanisms. In a broad sense, it connotes the rights to determine the management of corporate resources, which include the rights to hire, fire and set the compensation of top-level managers.[9] When a company with publicly traded shares is *poorly* managed, this may effectively reduce the share prices, and the holders of the shares may respond to such mismanagement by selling their shares. Corporate raiders or outside investors may take the opportunity to buy as many shares as possible to enable them to gain control.[10]

The market for corporate control can also be largely controlled by corporate managements. Figure 2.1[11] in Chapter 2 depicts the central role of managements in takeover administration. It indicates that managements can largely determine the extent to which value can be distributed in the firm amongst the various corporate constituents. The agency relationship objective of the new institutional economics identifies the potential for conflict of interests. Institutional control over management functions is not aimed at undermining managers, rather it is meant to challenge management functions towards effectiveness in ensuring that investment decisions add value to the corporation and its constituents, rather than merely enlarging the size of the corporation. When the role of managements is successfully challenged, property rights can be protected and transaction costs can be mitigated in the absence of needlessly costly acquisitions, and market efficiency can be promoted. Thus, market activities[12] which may be aimed at taking over the control of a company, either directly or indirectly, can thrive in an efficient manner. Further to this, synergistic gains and the disciplinary effects of takeovers can be promoted as the bedrock of the market for corporate control as an alternative mechanism to corporate governance.

First, the chapter identifies the nature and characteristics of the different types of corporate takeovers. Second, the various devices that can be used to initiate takeover process are examined. Next, the chapter evaluates the different takeover hypotheses: this is done by reference to the extent to which takeovers can

---

of Business, Finance & Accounting 579; see also Pieter W. Moerland, 'Alternative Disciplinary Mechanisms in Different Corporate Systems' (1995) 26 *Journal of Economic Begbaviour and Organisation* 17, 23; James P. Walsh and James K. Seward, 'On the Efficiency of Internal and External Corporate Control Mechanisms' (1990) 15 *Academy of Management Review* 421, 423; Randal Morck, Andrei Shleifer, and Robert Vishny, 'Alternative Mechanisms for Corporate Control' (1989) 79 *The American Economic Review* 842.

7 In this book, companies and corporations are used synonymously, also, target companies and offeree companies are used interchangeably.

8 See the Organisation for Economic Co-operation and Development (OECD), 'Glossary of Statistical Terms' 2008, 1–605 at 323.

9 Michael C. Jenson and Richard S. Ruback, 'The Market for Corporate Control: The Scientific Evidence' (1983) 11 *Journal of Financial Economics* 5.

10 Henry G. Manne, 'Cash Tender Offers for Shares: A Reply to Chairman Cohen' (1967) *Duke Law Journal* 231, 236.

11 See Chapter 2, section 2.5.

12 Particularly, the purchase of shares.

actually enhance the value of a corporate entity. Then, some of the mechanisms that are used by company management to 'frustrate' takeovers are examined. Finally, conflict of interests – agency problems – and employment issues in relation to takeovers are identified briefly. This includes an analysis of the contractual relationship among managements, shareholders and employees. It identifies the limitations of the contractual theory and it briefly illustrates the role of the entity theory before the conclusion.

3.2 Types of corporate takeovers: nature and characteristics

Investors seeking to gain corporate control may achieve their objective through friendly takeover, hostile takeover, reverse takeover[13] or a backflip takeover. Friendly takeover may also be referred to as 'a negotiated takeover'. It involves series of negotiations between the acquiring investors(s) and the target board. The shareholders of the target company receive cash and/or shares in the acquiring company as part of the process leading to the successful completion of the takeover. This type of takeover is not controversial: as its name suggests, its entire process aims at creating synergies between the acquirer and the target company.[14] Hostile takeovers are attempts by acquiring companies towards gaining control of corporate powers through different methods. These include direct negotiations with shareholders in the target company and the purchase of shares in the target company discreetly. A hostile takeover may also commence as a result of failed negotiations of a friendly takeover attempt. In view of the nature of this type of takeover, it has been suggested that hostile takeovers are the most effective ways of getting rid of non-performing managers without bribing them.[15]

In light of the direct negotiations between the shareholders and the outside investors, a hostile takeover has the characteristics of promoting private benefit to the negotiating parties, rather than conferring any form of social value. As indicated, hostile takeovers can be privately beneficial even though they are not socially desirable.[16] They can lead to a renegotiation of contracts of labour and employee dismissal,[17] contrary to the theory of a corporation as a nexus

13 See the LegalMatch online library www.legalmatch.com/law-library/article/business-takeover-lawyers.html accessed 29 December 2018.

14 Randall Morck, Andrei Shleifer, and Robert W. Vishny, 'Characteristics of Targets of Hostile and Friendly Takeovers' in Alan J. Auerbach (ed.), *Corporate Takeovers: Causes and Consequences* (Chicago, IL, University of Chicago Press, 1988) 102.

15 Andrei Shleifer and Robert W. Vishny, 'Value Maximization and the Acquisition Process' (1988) 2 *Journal of Economic Perspectives* 7, 11.

16 Andrei Shleifer and Lawrence H. Summers, 'Breach of Trust in Hostile Takeovers' in Alan J. Auerbach (ed.), *Corporate Takeovers: Causes and Consequences* (Chicago, IL, University of Chicago Press, 1988) 34–35.

17 Ibid. A. Shleifer and L. H. Summers. While it is contended that hostile acquisitions are largely associated with job losses post-acquisition, it has also been suggested that friendly acquisitions can also lead to intial decrease in job demand. See Martin J. Conyon et al.,

of contracts.[18] While the outside investor(s) negotiate with the shareholders of the target company on terms suitable to both parties, managers could also seek to remain relevant with a view towards protecting their interests by attempting to convince shareholders that they are performing efficiently through increased reported earnings to avoid losing their jobs.[19] They are also more likely to engage in acts that could make them entrenched and remain in control of corporate powers.[20] While friendly takeovers are mainly non-controversial, hostile takeovers represent a control contest amongst the incumbent managers, shareholders and the outside investors. In light of this, the nature of this type of takeover suggests that it is mostly activated through the mechanisms of the direct purchase of shares, particularly tender offers and proxy contests.

A reverse takeover is the type of corporate takeover where the shareholder(s) of a private firm purchase a large majority of the stock of a public company for the purpose of gaining control over the latter.[21] It is a medium of gaining public company status without the usual process of re-registration. Finally, backflip takeover occurs where an acquiring company becomes the subsidiary of the acquired company. This type of takeover occurs where the acquired company has well-known market brands, but it became a takeover target because of its challenging financial status. The next section examines the different methods through which the control of the corporate powers of a company may be sought and obtained.

3.3 The takeover devices

A takeover may occur through any of the following.

3.3.1 Direct purchase of shares (tender offer or open market bid)

Direct purchase of shares represents the most obvious and direct method through which the controlling powers of a company may be acquired by outside investors. This method, which enables investors to directly acquire the controlling powers

---

'Do Hostile Mergers Destroy Jobs?' (2001) 45 *Journal of Economic Behaviour & Organization* 427.

18 Eugene F. Fama, 'Agency Problems and the Theory of the Firm' (1980) 88 *Journal of Political Economy* 288.

19 Cintia M. Easterwood, 'Takeovers and Incentives for Earnings Management: An Empirical Analysis' (1998) 14 *Journal of Applied Business Research* 29.

20 Andrew Christie and Jerold L. Zimmerman, 'Efficiency and Opportunistic Choices of Accounting Procedures: Corporate Control Contests' (1994) 69 *The Accounting Review* 539, 541–543.

21 Kimberly C. Gleason, Leonard Rosenthal, and Roy A. Wiggins, III, 'Backing into Being Public: An Explanatory Analysis of Reverse Take-Overs' (2005) 12 *Journal of Corporate Finance* 54, 56. See also Philip Brown, Andrew Ferguson, and Peter Lam, 'What's in a Shell? Analysing the Gain to Shareholders from Reverse Takeovers' (2010) *Social Science Research Network* 1, 5 file:///C:/Users/user/Downloads/SSRN-id1896004.pdf accessed 20 April 2018.

of the company, may be attempted through one or more of the following ways, namely:

a) The direct purchase of shares from an individual or individuals who have a controlling block of shares.
b) The gradual acquisition of a controlling number of shares through anonymous open market transactions.
c) A tender offer to purchase shares at a specific price above the usual market price.
d) An offer of marketable securities in exchange for the required number of shares.

The last method (d) is often used by corporate investors instead of a cash tender offer which is commonly used by individuals or group of investors.[22] a) and b) are mainly used when the majority shares are held by a single or few individuals.

A tender offer occurs when a prospective buyer offers or invites the shareholders of a target company to offer for sale or tender their shares at a stated price, usually above the market price.[23] As indicated, tender offers may either be a 'cash tender offer' or 'a public exchange offer'. A cash tender offer involves the use of cash by outside investors to purchase a certain number of shares directly from the shareholders of the target company through the bidding process, usually at a premium. Where a tender offer is made by exchange, the outside investors usually offer company securities to the shareholders of the target company in exchange for certain number of shares. It may include a combination of cash and shares.[24] A tender offer may include an agreement to keep an offer for sale open within a specific period of time.[25] The nature of the offer may also contain the condition that a certain percentage of the total shares should be offered for sale. The conditions may also include the right of the investor to withdraw the offer.[26]

The major challenge to successful tender offers is the opposition from the board of the target companies. A board that is composed of mainly executive directors may oppose a tender offer to prevent the successful completion of a takeover.[27] These managers who may also have a certain percentage of shareholding in the company may not be concerned about their personal loss from

22 See generally note 10, 239.

23 See generally Frank H. Easterbrook and Daniel R. Fischel, *The Economic Structure of Corporate Law* (Cambridge, MA, Harvard University Press, 1991).

24 Robert W. Hamilton, 'Some Reflections on Cash Tender Offer Legislation' (1969) 15 *New York Law Forum* 269, 270.

25 Ibid. 271–272, citing Samuel L. Hayes and Russell A. Taussi, 'Tactics of Cash Takeover Bids' (1967) 45 *Harvard Business Review* 135, 140.

26 Daniel R. Fischel, 'Efficient Capital Market Theory, the Market for Corporate Control and the Regulation of Cash Tender Offers' (1978) 57 *Texas Law Review* 1, 6.

27 James F. Cotter, Ani Shivdasani, and Marc Zenner, 'Do Independent Directors Enhance Target Shareholder Wealth during Tender Offers?' (1997) 43 *Journal of Financial Economics* 195, 196. See also Greg A. Jarrell, James A. Brickley, and Jeffry M. Netter, 'The Market for

such resistance. As suggested, they may be prepared to suffer a decline in the value of their shareholding in their bid towards maintaining control and enjoying the pecuniary and non-pecuniary benefits arising from the power of control.[28] On the contrary, a board which is mainly composed of independent directors may oppose the bid for the purpose of ensuring the enhancement of the wealth of the shareholders of the company,[29] or to generally enhance corporate value. Opposition to a takeover bid is capable of leading to a renegotiation between the investors and the target company. This could lead to an upward review of the bid price. In certain circumstances, managerial resistance to a takeover bid may have a negative impact on shareholder wealth. Resistance to a tender offer may not always lead to an upward review of the offer. It could discourage the bidder to continue with the bid. The outside investors may be compelled to withdraw their bid, leading to a loss of shareholder wealth,[30] especially where there are no suitable competing bids.

Where dispersed target shareholders are faced with only one potential buyer, they would be in a much more disadvantageous position compared to a single shareholder with majority shareholding. It may be difficult for dispersed owners to organise themselves to form a major block of shareholders with the aim of threatening to frustrate the takeover, by insisting on receiving a higher price for their shares.[31] While the effect of competing bids may show positive results for the shareholders of target firms, it may nevertheless derail the success of the takeover. Where there are multiple bids from several outside investors, the chances of each of the investors succeeding in the purchase of the sought-after shares decreases, as each bid is a threat to the other. One or more bidder(s) will be unsuccessful in the bid to purchase shares from the target shareholders, since demand for shares among the bidders will exceed the available amount of the outstanding shares.[32] This has the effect of fragmentising the shareholding amongst the different bidders, with the possible implication of the absence of a clear-cut majority holder, thereby frustrating the purpose of the tender offer.

Another factor which may negate the objective of the tender offer process is the general nature of shareholding in the target firm. That is, the ratio of shareholding between the shareholders of the target firm and the managers and board of directors of the firm. The larger the fraction of shares held by the board members and managers of the target company, the greater the proportion of other

---

Corporate Control: The Empirical Evidence since 1980' (1988) 2 *The Journal of Economic Perspectives* 49, 58.

28 James F. Cotter and Marc Zenner, 'How Managerial Wealth Affects the Tender Offer Process' (1994) 35 *Journal of Financial Economics* 63, 87.

29 See note 27 (Cotter, Shivdasani and M. Zenner), 205.

30 Note 28, 86.

31 See generally Lucian A. Bebchuk, 'The Case for Facilitating Competing Tender Offers' (1982) 95 *Harvard Law Review* 1028, 1039.

32 Ralph A. Walkling, 'Predicting Tender Offer Success: A Logistic Analysis' (1985) 20 *Journal of Financial and Quantitative Analysis* 461, 464.

shares that must be tendered for the tender offer to succeed, hence the less likely that the tender offer will succeed.[33]

Competition among bidders makes tender offers more credible and prevents any abnormally low bids and – although driven by self-interested pursuit of the bargain – it ensures that target shareholders are fairly compensated.[34] However, it could be faced with many challenges. First, the problem of free-riding may be encountered. Free-riding by the shareholders of the target firm[35] and free-riding by the competitive bidders may characterise a takeover bid. While some shareholders may be willing to sell their shares at a premium to an outside investor, other shareholders may refuse to sell theirs. Some shareholders may refuse to sell their shares because of the general expectations that the outside investors, having gained control, would improve the value of the shares of the target company. Hence, they would refuse to sell their shares even at a premium, thereby free-riding on the efforts of other shareholders who are willing to sell their shares to make the transfer of control possible. This has the effect of defeating the tender offer exercise.

It has been suggested that the free-rider problem could be mitigated by reducing the value of the remainder of shares after the successful completion of the tender offer. The initial shareholders may agree by way of a corporate charter, allowing the raiders to dilute the share value of the non-tendering shareholders, after they take over the firm. This can be done by either allowing the raider to be paid an excess salary, issue new shares below the market value or sell the outputs or some of the assets of the firm to another firm owned by the raider.[36] This can effectively 'dilute' the value of the shares of the remainder of the shareholders that refused to sell their shares.

This view may not be justifiable to those categories of shareholders, who believe that the present managers are good enough to continue to run the firm. Shares may be considered to be the property rights of shareholders and they reserve the right to dispose or hold on to their shares. While tender offers appear to promote the interests of target shareholders and outside investors, the real motives of the outside investors may be difficult to identify.[37] Proxy contest is examined next.

3.3.2 Proxy contests

Proxy contests occur when there is active competition between two or more groups, usually the incumbent managers and a group of dissident shareholders.

33 Charles R. Knoeber, 'Golden Parachutes, Shark Repellents, and Hostile Tender Offers' (1986) 76 *The American Economic Review* 155, 162.

34 Steven C. Bradford, 'Stampeding Shareholders and Other Myths: Target Shareholders and Hostile Tender Offers' (1989–1990) 15 *Journal of Corporation Law* 417, 420.

35 Robert Marquez and Bilge Yilmaz, 'Information and Efficiency in Tender Offers' (2008) 76 *Journal of the Econometric Society* 1075, 1093.

36 Sanford J. Grossman and Oliver D. Hart, 'Takeover Bids, the Free-Rider Problem and the Theory of the Corporation' (1980) 11 *The Bell Journal of Economics* 42, 46.

37 Tim Jenkinson and Colin Mayer, 'The Assessment: Corporate Governance and Corporate Control' (1992) 8 *Oxford Review of Economic Policy* 1, 3.

The aim is to either solicit proxies to elect their candidates or to vote in favour of desired policies or against such policies.[38] Typically, proxy contests occur between the management of the company and some dissident shareholders whereby company shareholders either vote for the slate of directors proposed by management or for a rival slate proposed by the dissidents who seek to replace them.[39] Proxy contests may occur for the purpose of gaining control of the management of the company, by seeking a majority position of the board. It could alternatively occur for the purpose of proposal contests, in which dissidents seek to vote to defeat a management-sponsored proposal or to initiate their own proposal.[40] Where the dissident shareholders are successful with the election of new directors, a new management team is appointed, but where they fail to replace the directors, the management team retain their positions.

Shareholders may increase their support for outside investors in proxy contests, where they believe that the current managers are not sufficiently promoting their interests. Companies which have a low rate of dividend payment, relative to other companies in the same industry are more likely to become targets of a proxy contest.[41] This may pose a threat to the incumbent managers and they may devise alternative means of winning the support of the shareholders. The management may alter the capital structure of the company by sourcing funds outside the company to finance an increase in the level of dividend payment. They may try to boost short-term distribution to shareholders by raising additional debts for the purpose of financing special dividends.[42] This may have an adverse effect on the long-term objectives of a company, since long-term values are used to promote short-term objectives. Capital restructuring may also be used by management to succeed in the proxy contests. They may choose to issue debts in exchange for the equities of the passive investors who are not necessarily interested in control contest. This increases the equity of the incumbent and provides them with more leverage to be successful in the proxy contest. Since they must control at least 50% of the votes to be certain of victory, they could issue the amount of debt required to achieve this purpose.[43]

Also, poor earnings can instigate a change in management when the earning capacity of the company experiences a downward trend.[44] This suggests that a

38 G. D. Hancock, 'Battles for Control: An Overview of Proxy Contests' (1992) 18 *Managerial Finance* 59.

39 Linda E. Deangelo, 'Managerial Competition, Information Costs and Corporate Governance: The Use of Accounting Performance Measures in Proxy Contests' (1988) 10 *Journal of Accounting and Economics* 3, 5.

40 The analysis is concerned with *proxy contest* that is aimed towards gaining control of the management of a company which precedes a takeover.

41 G. D. Hancock and Mbodja Mougoue, 'The Impact of Financial Factors on Proxy Contest Outcomes' (1991) 18 *Journal of Business Finance & Accounting* 541, 544.

42 Lucian A. Bebchuk and Marcel Kahan, 'A Framework for Analyzing Legal Policy towards Proxy Contests' (1990) 78 *California Law Review* 1071, 1102–1103.

43 See generally Milton Harris and Artur Raviv, 'Corporate Control Contests and Capital Structure' (1986) 20 *Journal of Financial Economics* 55, 63, 69.

44 Note 39, 12.

firm with low earnings is more likely to be the subject of a proxy contest. The determinants of the earning powers of a company have been calculated with reference to earnings per share (EPS) and price earnings ratio (P/E).[45]

The threat of a proxy contest may lead to an improvement in the operating performance of the firm.[46] Managements can obtain shareholder support by dismantling unproductive empires and focusing on only those areas that can yield a high level of productivity.[47]

Although, these measures may lead to improved firm performance in the short term, as rightly observed, it has the effect of sacrificing the long-term goals of the company for short-term profits.[48] The implication of the short-term approach that can be used by managements to gain shareholder support during proxy contexts is an indication of the presence of agency conflict.[49] Agency conflict can influence managers to promote short-term objectives. For example, certain corporate investments with long-term value may be dismantled by managements through divestments to raise cash for dividend payments. In light of information asymmetry, shareholders may not be able to ascertain the true state of affairs and they would support managements in the proxy contests. This can undermine the disciplinary role of the market for corporate control, which the proxy contest is meant to achieve in this regard, since managements are able to influence and gain shareholder support. The new institutional economics seeks to address this challenge, to ensure that agency conflicts are mitigated. This can be achieved by ensuring that effective institutions are established to restrict and challenge the role of managements, to promote shareholder interests and the overall corporate value.

Where the divestments occur as a justified response to actual unproductive empires, it may be argued that such unproductive empires could have earlier been created by management. When the empires are dismantled, they provide only an apparent gain to shareholders, since the existence of the empires and the

45 (EPS) is calculated by dividing a company's net income (dividend payments are excluded from a company's earnings to determine the net income) by its outstanding shares. (P/E) is calculated by dividing a company's market value per share by its earnings per share. See generally note 41, 544.

46 Vyacheslav Fos, 'The Disciplinary Effects of Proxy Contests' (2011) 1 *Social Science Research Network* 17–19 http://ssrn.com/abstract=1705707, accessed 11 March 2018; Assem Safieddine and Sheridan Titman, 'Leverage and Corporate Performance: Evidence from Unsuccesful Takeovers' (1999) 54 *The Journal of Finance* 547, 557–559.

47 Michael C. Jensen, 'Agency Costs of Free Cash Flow, Corporate Finance, and Takeovers' (1986) 76 *The American Economic Review* 323, 328. The incumbent has the advantage of getting more votes in the proxy contest because they maintain shareholder lists, they are experienced in soliciting votes for annual meetings, as well as developing relationships with the shareholders, including the uninformed shareholders. See John Pound, 'Proxy Contests and the Efficiency of Shareholder Oversight' (1988) 20 *Journal of Financial Economics* 237–365, 240.

48 Jeremy C. Stein, 'Takeover Threats and Managerial Myopia' (1988) 96 *Journal of Political Economy* 62, 63, 71.

49 See section 3.6.1 and Chapter 2, section 2.5.3.

dismantling of the empires may both serve the interests of managements. Since shareholders are not often aware of the existence of unproductive empires, the dismantling of the empires at the time that managements are seeking the support of shareholders in a proxy contest show that there is indeed the need to establish appropriate and effective institutional control measures as indicated by the new institutional economics, to challenge the role of management. As long as managements can influence the decisions of shareholders in a proxy contest, the disciplinary role of proxy contest can be undermined.

Proxy contests are favourably viewed by the market as a medium through which poorly performing managers are removed from management responsibilities.[50] This implies that only those proxy contests which successfully lead to a takeover would likely enhance the wealth of the company, while companies which resist a takeover bid are suggested to experience a post-decline of value.[51] This further suggests that proxy contests which lead to change of management are most likely to enhance shareholder wealth, through an improvement in the value of the company.

Contrary to the suggestion that only proxy contests which lead to a successful takeover enhances shareholder wealth, shareholder value may be enhanced from the activities of the dissidents.[52] The contests are capable of providing incentives to management from their lacklustre performance, by 'waking them from their slumber'. In response to the claim of inefficiency, the managers may develop a strategy towards a change of policy in pursuit of short-term economic growth, which may become visible to shareholders during the period that the company is faced with threats of proxy contests. If the shareholders are convinced, the outside investors may become unsuccessful in their bid to gain control. Even if they do not succeed in gaining control, the pressure exerted on management may have helped to enhance the economic value of the firm. This can also occur where the dissidents gain a minority representation, where they fail to gain full corporate control. This suggests that proxy contests may be beneficial to shareholders irrespective of the result of the contests.[53]

While management positions may be secured through the means that they use to persuade shareholders, their position in the company may be short-lived. Even if they retain their positions during and immediately after the proxy contests, these managers may nevertheless lose their positions through resignations in the manner which may be attributed to the earlier contests[54] which have ended at the material time. The apparent efficiency which they managed to show to gain shareholders' support in the heat of the contest may begin to wane with the passage of time.

50 J. Harold Mulherin and Annette B. Poulsen, 'Proxy Contests and Corporate Change: Implications for Shareholder Wealth' (1998) 47 *Journal of Financial Economics* 279, 305.

51 Ibid. 303.

52 Erica Laudano, 'One Man's Junk Mail Is Another Man's Treasure: Proxy Contests and Corporate Governance' (2004) 3 *Connecticut Public Interest Law Journal* 430, 446.

53 Ibid. 445–447.

54 Ibid. 441. See also Harry Deangelo and Linda Deangelo, 'Proxy Contests and the Governance of Publicly Held Corporations' (1989) 23 *Journal of Financial Economics* 29, 49.

Proxy contests remain an important mechanism for gaining the power of corporate control as an alternative to the direct purchase of shares by tender offer or open market bid. Although it tends to save costs of purchasing shares at a premium, as in the case of tender offer, the costs of access to information and contacting shareholders may be a setback to the exercise.

As a result of the cost implication and free-rider problems, it was indicated that proxy contests are a rarely used method of gaining corporate control for the purpose of managerial discipline.[55] This may no longer represent the situation in recent times. The use of proxy contests has been on the increase. Proxy contests may be encouraged by the unavailability of capital for financing the financially motivated hostile takeovers.[56] The antitakeover barriers[57] adopted by several corporations could also encourage proxy contests, as well as the increase in state legislations which regulate takeovers through tender offers, amongst other reasons.[58]

Besides tender offers, open market bids and proxy contests, friendly mergers play an active role as a function of the market for corporate control. However, mergers are agreements between different firms to combine their operations for the purpose of forming a single entity, hence, mergers will not be examined in this chapter. A scheme of arrangement can also be used to take over the control of a company. It does not have the character of corporate acquisitions as a mechanism of the market for corporate control because it can include arrangements with creditors who did not intend to obtain control of the company.

Several factors influence takeovers. Companies are taken over as a result of the corporate strategy of the acquiring firm for reasons best known to them. Developments in the fields of corporate finance and economics may have led to the emergence of certain theories which may explain the reasons for corporate takeovers; these are referred to as the takeover hypotheses. They are briefly examined next.

3.4 The takeover hypotheses and justification for takeovers

The takeover hypotheses identify the role of takeovers and their effects on companies, shareholders and other stakeholders. They include the disciplinary role, synergistic gains and the hubris hypothesis.

3.4.1 The disciplinary hypothesis

Since takeovers often lead to the dismissal of managers of target companies, it has been suggested that takeovers lead to the elimination of inefficient managers,[59]

55 Note 23, 78.
56 Note 52, 430.
57 David Ikenberry and Josef Lakonishok, 'Corporate Governance through Proxy Contests: Evidence and Implications' (1993) 66 *The Journal of Business* 405.
58 Note 38, 59. Citing J. Queenan, 'The Proxy Wars: There Are More of Them and They Are Meaner' (1988) *Barrons* 88.
59 Richard A. Brealey, Stewart C. Myers, and Franklin Allen, *Principles of Corporate Finance* (New York, McGraw-Hill/Irwin, 2008) 887.

amongst other reasons. Often, when companies are taken over, the usual contract of continuous employment is apparently terminated. The disciplinary hypothesis of a takeover promotes the view that the value of the target company is likely to be enhanced where there is a threat of takeover by a raider who actually knows that the present economic value of the company can be improved if the company has a better management team than it presently has.[60] In support of this hypothesis, it was observed that managers who are slow to recognise that many old practices and strategies are no longer viable are finding that takeovers are doing the job for them.[61] In view of this, corporate managers may be constrained to constantly review their managerial strategies and policies to meet the needs of their companies in terms of growth and productivity, to reduce the incidence of slow growth or underperformance. In this subsection, the disciplinary effect of takeovers is examined in relation to whether a hostile takeover is caused by poor performance, the effects of company size on managerial competence and, last, the effectiveness of the disciplinary functions of takeovers.

Generally, it appears that managerial disciplinary hypothesis is a function of hostile takeover.[62] The disciplinary hypothesis has been linked with hostile takeover because of the absence of the usual negotiations leading to the takeover, especially negotiations leading to job security or compensation. Hence managers tend to oppose bids, to protect their positions amongst other reasons. They resist the takeover bid because they are most likely to be replaced as managers post-takeover since they are regarded as being inefficient managers.

It was suggested that their inefficient character often originates from incompetent management which makes the assets of the company underpriced,[63] as a result of managerial discretionary behaviour[64] and the agency cost of free cash flow.[65] While these views contend that the disciplinary hypothesis is related to hostile takeover, which is caused by poor performance, alternative arguments indicate otherwise. One of such alternative arguments did not identify poor performance as a significant factor which leads to hostile takeovers. It reports that the link between underperformance and hostile takeover bids is the result of a miss-specified empirical model. It also contends that good firms could be targets

60 See generally David Scharfstein, 'The Disciplinary Role of Takeovers' (1988) 55 *The Review of Economic Studies* 185, 192. Some managers may pursue acquisitions even where such acquisitions may not enhance shareholder value, provided that such pursuit of growth is consistent with the corporation's mission statement or it provides a utilitarian value in terms of the interests of the society at large. See generally John Dobson, 'Size Matters: Why Managers Should Pursue Corporate Growth, Even at the Expense of Shareholder Value' (2004) 23 *Business and Professional Ethics Journal* 45.

61 Michael C. Jensen, 'Takeovers: Their Causes and Consequences' (1988) 2 *The Journal of Economic Perspectives* 21, 24.

62 See generally, note 14.

63 Note 14, 120.

64 See generally Oliver E. Williamson, *The Economics of Discretionary Behaviour: Managerial Objective in a Theory of the Firm* (Chicago, IL Markham Publishing Company, 1964).

65 See note 47, Jensen, 328–329.

corporate control is not severe enough to deter this behaviour; more research is needed in this area.

Meanwhile, there are suggestions that takeovers have not been adequately proven to be an effective disciplinary mechanism. The inability to clearly show that takeovers effectively discipline managers may be caused by the use of conflicting takeover motives presented in the studies. The methods used in measuring the performance of management, as well as the possibility of outdated results and data which may not be relevant to current economic trends, may also be an influencing factor.[77]

Contrary to these suggestions, it was indicated that takeovers act as major factors in the dismissal of poorly performing boards.[78] For example in the UK, the disciplinary effect of takeovers has been suggested to be caused by high level of leverage and low interest coverage in poorly performing firms.[79] Similarly, the disciplinary effect of takeovers is likely to occur in industries with overall poor performance, in light of the view that it is one of the suitable means of inducing management of public corporations to work towards shareholder value, amongst other reasons.[80]

Although there has not been a consensus that the disciplinary hypothesis is responsible for managerial turnover, the effect of takeover activities on target companies, especially its disciplinary role, cannot be denied. Whether the dismissal of managers of target companies is caused by poor performance prior to the takeover or by the initial rejection of bids by the managers to enhance the bid premiums, a takeover has a disciplinary character; it provides a profound opportunity for target shareholders to demonstrate that the property rights in their shares can be exercised in the way that the shareholders deem fit. The disciplinary nature of the exercise may extend to unsuccessful takeovers, since such threats could serve as incentives to managers to develop corporate policies towards enhancing shareholder value. This could be aimed at preventing the company from becoming or remaining a takeover target. The synergy hypothesis of takeovers is examined next.

3.4.2 *The synergy hypothesis*

The synergy hypothesis suggests that takeovers are motivated by the desire to create wealth through a combination of the resources of the acquiring and target

77 R. J. Limmack, *Takeovers as a Disciplinary Mechanism?* (Advances in Mergers and Acquisitions, 1: Emerald Group Publishing Limited, Bingley UK 2000) 108–111.

78 The study did not identify corporate takeovers as a definite effective disciplinary mechanism. Its findings revealed that takeovers could erroneously dismiss large numbers of managers in companies that are performing efficiently.

79 Julian Franks, Colin Mayer, and Luc Renneboog, 'Who Disciplines Management in Poorly Performing Companies?' (2001) 10 *Journal of Financial Intermediation* 209, 211. 245.

80 Rudolf Kerschbamer, 'Disciplinary Takeovers and Industry Effects' (1998) 7 *Journal of Economics & Management Strategy* 265, 269.

companies. This is done in such a way that the value of the combined entity is greater than the sum of the separate entity values.[81] This includes operating, managerial and financial synergies.[82]

The hypothesis identifies takeovers as an avenue for corporate expansion, and value creation, through negotiable mutual agreements engaged by managers to enhance the wealth of their shareholders. In view of this, there are certain assumptions about takeovers which are motivated by synergistic gains. First, since the synergistic hypothesis aims at enhancing the value of the combining companies, and since the combination of their resources can lead to a greater value than the sum of their separate values, it may imply that the target companies are performing well with regards to the return on investment. Second, by the nature of the synergistic motive which requires a combination of resources through series of negotiations, between the managements of the target and acquiring companies, takeovers with synergistic character may be termed as friendly rather than hostile.[83] Also, if companies which are targets in synergistic takeovers are economically stable prior to the takeover, it follows that such performance may well be attributed to managerial expertise. This is consistent with the analysis that the market disliked buyers that remove target management,[84] since such managers are able to achieve opportunities for economic growth.

It has been suggested that synergies would be more effective in enhancing value when the target and acquiring firms are in the same line of business.[85] This implies that the synergy hypothesis works more efficiently when firms with similar resource allocation patterns are combined.[86] However, conflicting evidence suggests that acquisitions between unrelated companies can lead to higher returns for the shareholders of both the acquired and acquiring companies than acquisitions of related companies.[87] From the foregoing, the findings on the effect of relatedness of post-acquisition performance are inconsistent. The inconsistency may sug-

81 Lynn Hodgkinson and Graham H. Partington, 'The Motivation for Takeovers in the UK' (2008) 35 *Journal of Business Finance & Accounting* 102. Even though takeovers appear to discipline 'non-performing managers', the quest for synergy remains the driving force for takeovers. Michael Jensen, 'Takeovers: Folklore and Science' in Peter J. Buckley and Pervez N. Ghauri (eds.), *International Mergers and Acquisitions: A Reader* (London, Thomson, 2002) 71.

82 Roberta Romano, 'A Guide to Takeovers: Theory, Evidence and Regulation' (1992) 19 *Yale Journal on Regulation* 119, 125–128.

83 See note 14, 120.

84 John G. Matsusaka, 'Takeover Motives during the Conglomerate Merger Wave' (1993) 24 *The Rand Journal of Economics* 357, 358, 373–376.

85 See generally H. Igor Ansoff, *Corporate Strategy: An Analytic Approach to Business Policy for Growth and Expansion* (New York, McGraw-Hill, 1965).

86 See generally Lois M. Shelton, 'Strategic Business Fits and Corporate Aquisition: Empirical Evidence' (1988) 9 *Strategic Management Journal* 297.

87 See Sayan Chatterjee, 'Types of Synergy and Economic Value: The Impact of Acquisitions on Merging and Rival Firms' (1986) 7 *Strategic Management Journal* 119, 129–130; P. RajanVaradarajan and Paulette Dubofsky, 'Diversification and Measures of Performance: Additional Empirical Evidence' (1987) 30 *The Academy of Management Journal* 597, 602.

gest that different factors may be responsible for the rate of success of corporate performance post-acquisitions. However, it has been contended that acquisitions involving companies with differences in resource allocation patterns may provide unique and valuable synergy,[88] in view of the fact that competitive bidders may be unaware of the potential synergy as a result of information asymmetry. This prevents the existence of an auction and a bid-up of price, which places acquiring firms in an advantageous position to extract value from the synergy which will be created with the target firm. Also, different resources may become complementary in a build-up to the synergy.[89] The complementary character of the synergy from acquisitions which involves companies with differences in resource allocation patterns discussed may lead to diversification soon after the acquisition if such synergy is not properly managed. The combined company may find it difficult to manage the demands of the different combined components, especially since these components are not related in business lines, and where there is an overlap in the existing operating structure. Also, where expected gains are not met, diversification may be needed to restructure the company to strengthen its financial position.[90]

The effect of synergy in a concluded takeover is that it leads to productivity and an expansion of the investments of shareholders. Since shareholders have property rights in shares, the role of managements in promoting the investment property in the shares shows that managements recognise the fact that the property rights in the shares resides with the shareholders. Also, it implies that managements understand that their responsibilities should be exercised in a way that should not infringe on the property rights of the shareholders. Generally, corporate takeovers have been vastly motivated by the synergy hypothesis. The disciplinary effect is merely an outcome which is not anticipated by the acquirers. While the synergy hypothesis seeks to promote corporate wealth through a combination of the resources of the target and acquiring companies,[91] the disciplinary hypothesis ultimately applies to correct managerial failures by dismissing poorly performing managers. However, irrespective of their different motives, the objectives of these hypotheses have the capacity to enhance the value of the shareholders of the acquiring and target companies.[92]

There are instances where takeovers may not promote value for shareholders; this may be attributable to managerial hubris.

3.4.3 The hubris hypothesis

Acquiring companies may record insignificant or zero gains post-takeover. This could be caused by different factors, including an overestimation of the bid price.

88 Jay B. Barney, 'Returns to Bidding Firms in Mergers and Acquisitions: Reconsidering the Relatedness Hypothesis' (1988) 9 *Strategic Management Journal* 71, 76.

89 Jeffrey S. Harrison et al., 'Synergies and Post-Acquisition Performance: Differences versus Similarities in Resource Allocations' (1991) 17 *Journal of Management* 173, 187.

90 This may indicate a failure of the acquisition strategy of managements.

91 Economies of scale.

92 Depending on the actual motives of managements of target and acquiring companies.

When this occurs, it may be referred to as the hubris hypothesis of takeover. It implies that the average increase in the target firm's market value should be more than offset by the average decrease in the value of the bidding firm, in such a way that the combined gain to the target and bidding firms is non-positive.[93] Since each acquisition is meant to increase the value of companies, corporate managers who pursue takeovers are expected to take measures towards ensuring that the process achieves positive gains for their companies and shareholders. When managers care less or when they develop ulterior motives, using synergy as a cloak to promote the idea of a takeover, the chances of recording large-scale losses post-takeovers becomes highly likely. Hence, it was contended that the arrogance and self-belief of managers as a result of past success may account for them taking less care in ensuring that takeover bids are properly examined and evaluated towards success.[94] This may cause managers to overestimate the synergistic benefit to be derived from a takeover, leading to hubris. Although the hubris hypothesis does not suggest that management deliberately make higher premiums,[95] the fact that managers can be influenced by pride, previous successes and their inability to focus on realistic gains by being overconfident[96] may suggest that some managers deliberately make costly acquisitions.

Loss of wealth by shareholders in takeovers may not necessarily affect the interests of managers; rather, it may lead to increase in remuneration by reason of increase in corporate size.[97] If managers invest significantly in companies in which they are employed, perhaps more care would be taken when they make investment decisions,[98] since any loss suffered by the shareholders would also be shared by the managers. Corporate managers whose takeover exercises are defeated by hubris may have negligently rather than deliberately paid higher premiums.

Consistent with this analysis is the view that managers of larger companies are much more likely to be involved in an empire-building exercise towards achieving

93 Richard Roll, 'The Hubris Hypothesis of Takeovers' (1986) 59 *The Journal of Business* 197, 201–203.

This may arise when management make costly acquisitions which leads to the transfer of wealth from the acquiring company to the target company. See Elazar Berkovitch and M. P. Narayanan, 'Motives for Takeovers: An Empirical Investigation' (1993) 28 *Journal of Finance and Quantitative Analysis* 347, 351.

94 Mahendra Raj and Michael Forsyth, 'Hubris amongst UK Bidders and Losses to Shareholders' (2003) 8 *International Journal of Business* 2, 8–15.

95 See note 93 (Roll), 213–214; Nejat H. Seyhun, 'Do Bidder Managers Knowingly Pay Too Much for Target Firms?' (1990) 63 *Journal of Business* 439, 453.

96 Ulrike Malmendier and Geoffrey Tate, 'Who Makes Acquisitions? CEO Overconfidence and the Market's Reaction' (2008) 89 *Journal of Financial Economics* 20, 36–42; Robert F. Bruner, 'Does M & A Pay? A Survey of Evidence for the Decision Maker' (2002) *Journal of Applied Finance* 48, 64–65; Gerald Vinten, 'Employee Relations in Mergers and Acquisitions' (1993) 15 *Employee Relations* 47, 48–50.

97 Michael Firth, 'Corporate Takeovers, Stockholder Returns and Executive Rewards' (1991) 12 *Managerial and Decision Economics* 421, 425–427.

98 Yakov Amihud, Baruch Lev, and Nicholaos G. Travlos, 'Corporate Control and the Choice of Investment Financing: The Case of Corporate Acquisitions' (1990) 45 *The Journal of Finance* 603, 611–615; Michael Firth, 'Takeovers, Shareholder Returns and the Theory of the Firm' (1980) 94 *The Quarterly Journal of Economics* 235, 255–258.

higher levels of perquisites. The acquisition ambitions of managers of larger companies appear to suggest that their acquisition-related activities are geared towards expanding the size of their companies with a negligibly corresponding increase in shareholder wealth. This may partly be caused by the view that the economic interests of the shareholders and managers of smaller firms are better aligned, since managers of smaller firms have a higher level of firm ownership than managers of larger firms.[99] The view that hubris is more of a factor for larger firms seems to be a reasonable assertion. Larger firms can engage in takeovers with high transaction costs,[100] such firms have access to huge financial resources among other reasons.

From the analysis of the hubris hypothesis of takeovers, it appears that losses to company shareholders as a result of managerial hubris may not have been contemplated by the managers themselves, since their takeover objectives would have been directed towards synergy. Some investment decisions may have been taken rather carelessly or negligently which may suggest that managers who are responsible for making these decisions have acted deliberately. However, more evidence may be needed to show that hubris is a deliberate act of managers. Also, since wealth can be transferred from the acquiring firm to target firms, which may indicate losses to the shareholders of the acquiring firm and gains to the shareholders of the target firms, it is thus indicative of zero gains to the combined company post-takeover.[101]

It may be observed that the synergy hypothesis of takeovers can be partly related to the disciplinary hypothesis through managerial synergy. The hubris hypothesis has no direct link with the disciplinary hypothesis, but it may indicate that managers are zero maximising agents of their firms. This could make such firms which have been combined with little or zero gains to be takeover targets with managerial discipline not necessarily a possible motive but an underlying effect.

While the motives of the managements that engage in acquisitions leading to hubris may not be clearly determined, the effects of hubris are that, among other things, the value in the property rights of shareholders can be diminished as a result of high takeover transaction costs. When managers engage in ambitious acquisitions without sufficient reasons to believe that the acquisition will lead to an increase in corporate value and consequently increased shareholder wealth, it undermines the value attached to property rights. It implies that the property rights of the shareholders were not put into consideration by the managers when the acquisition was contemplated. Motive may include any undisclosed objectives which form part of their personal benefits that may be derived from acquisitions. Personal benefits may include the salaries and bonuses that are related to the volume of business that a newly enlarged enterprise will generate rather than the business potentials in terms of returns to shareholders.[102] It may also include the

99 Harold Demsetz and Kenneth Lehn, 'The Structure of Corporate Ownership: Causes and Consequences' (1985) 93 *Journal of Political Economy* 1155, 1158.

100 Larger companies can make acquisitions to further expand their operations and to dominate the market.

101 See note 93, E. Berkovitch and M. P. Narayanan, 352.

102 Robert B. Reich, *The Next American Frontier* (New York, Times Books, 1983) 166.

prestige of managing 'a bigger company'. Shareholder vote on executive pay may restrict the ability of managements to use corporate acquisitions to raise their level of salaries and bonuses in the UK.[103] Even though managers may not be able to increase their salaries and allowances after an acquisition, they are likely to make subtle financial gains through outside directorship.[104] In light of these, managements can increase corporate size without a corresponding increase in wealth.

The effect of the hubris hypothesis shows that the problems of agency relationship can undermine the role of the market for corporate control. The problems persist because the conflicts between managers' and shareholders' interests derail managements from their agency responsibilities. Thus, there is the need to define the scope of the role of managements, to ensure that they perform their responsibilities in the ways that the property rights of shareholders are not only protected but preserved.

It was rightly suggested that managers should shun the habit of blindly increasing the size of their corporation.[105] Although managements may pursue acquisitions without value creation, nevertheless, a takeover remains an important investment decision through which the economic value of companies can be enhanced. The value-creation objective of takeovers can be promoted where managements are made to shun the practice of engaging in needless takeover transaction costs that can potentially undermine corporate value.

In the remaining sections, the challenges posed by conflict of interests in corporate takeovers are examined. A brief illustration of the devices that can be used by company management to frustrate takeovers is presented next.

3.5 Takeover defences

Takeover defences may be broadly classified as pre-bid defences and post-bid defences.[106] Pre-bid defences are actions taken by managements before an

103 *The Enterprise and Regulatory Reform Act 2013*, s 79, entitles shareholders to vote to reject a company's policy on executive remuneration. Also, the *UK Corporate Governance Code 2018* (5 Remuneration) recommends that executive remuneration should be appropriately linked to performance. This does not suggest that managers who pursue acquisitions should not be rewarded, but they should not be rewarded for merely making acquisitions. Rather, they should be rewarded based on the returns that the acquisitions have added to the firm.

104 The acquisitions that they have concluded may be a signal that they have the required skills and experience to manage a large enterprise, irrespective of whether the acquisitions actually led to an increase in corporate wealth. See generally Christopher Avery, Judith A. Chevalier, and Scott Schaefer, 'Why Do Managers Undertake Acquisitions? An Analysis of Internal and External Rewards for Acquisitiveness' (1998) 14 *The Journal of Law, Economics and Organisation* 24–43; Francis N. Botchway, 'Mergers and Acquisitions in Resource Industry: Implications for Africa' (2010–2011) 26 *Connecticut Journal of International Law* 51, 62.

105 Cyrus A. Ramezani, Luc Soenen, and Alan Jung, 'Growth, Corporate Profitability and Value Creation' (2002) 58 *Financial Analysts Journal* 56, 65.

106 See Richard S. Ruback, 'An Overview of Takeover Defenses' in Alan J. Auerbach (ed.), *Mergers and Acquisitions* (Chicago, University of Chicago Press, 1987) 49, 53–64.

actual takeover bid is made. These are meant to prevent the successful acquisition of the company, and they include but are not limited to: poison pills, staggered boards provision, fair price amendment, super majority provisions and golden parachutes. Some of these defences may be referred to as shark repellents.

Table 3.1 Pre-Bid Takeover Defences[107]

Pre-bid defence	*Meaning and Description*
1. Poison pill	Poison pills are strategies that are intended to make hostile takeover expensive and undesirable. They include the issuance of stock warrants or rights which allow shareholders (excluding acquiring shareholders) of a target company to buy shares (including those of the acquirer and the target) at a substantial discount from the market price. This right becomes exercisable when an acquirer buys more than a certain percentage of shares in the targets company preparatory to a takeover bid. These warrants or rights also allow the target's shareholders to purchase shares of the newly formed company at a discount, if the acquisition is successful. When the option is exercised before the acquisition, it is referred to as a *flip-in*, where it is exercised after the acquisition it is referred to as a *flip-over*.
2. Staggered Boards	It is a device that may be incorporated in a company's constitution, which ensures that the majority of members of the board of directors are not available for election during any election period. The board of directors may be classified into three groups, and only one of the three groups is elected annually. This makes it difficult for a hostile bidder to gain immediate control of the target company, since only one third of the board is elected at a time.
3. Super-Majority	This requires that the acquirer obtain certain percentage of shares before the merger or acquisition may be successful.
4. Fair Price	This defence is used when the super majority tactics is relaxed and the acquirer is required to pay all the shareholders of the company the same price per share.
5. Golden Parachutes	It is a device which is included in contractual arrangements between managements and their companies. It entitles the management to large forms of compensation in the event of loss of office, which may be caused be a takeover. The compensation to be paid could be so large that it may discourage an acquirer from taking over a company, especially where it would lead to the dismissal of the management.

107 See Thomas A Turk, Jeremy Goh and Candace E Ybarra, 'The Effect of Takeover Defenses on Long Term and Short Term Analysts' Earnings Forecasts: The Case of Poison Pills', (2007) 4 Corporate Ownership & Control, 127; Lucian A Bebchuk, John C Coates and Guhan Subramanian, 'The Power of Takeover Defenses', (Harvard: Harvard Law School Working Paper, 2007) 4. http://www.law.harvard.edu/programs/corp_gov/papers/2007sp_Subramanian.pdf Accessed 14th April 2018.

Table 3.2 Post-Bid Takeover Defences[108]

Post-bid defences	*Meaning and Description*
1. White knight and white squire	In the *white knight* defence strategy, the target company invites another friendly company to make a bid towards acquiring the company, to prevent the hostile acquirer from acquiring the company. White squire is a modified form of the white knight defence. Instead of taking over the control of the company, the friendly company is invited to acquire a large percentage of shares in the target company called 'a corner' which is used to vote against the takeover bid of the hostile acquirer.
2. Crown jewel	A target company sells its important assets to another company to become less attractive to the acquirer. Sometimes the assets are sold to a white knight for a possible repurchase on an agreed price after the acquirer withdraws its bid.
3. Greenmail and standstill agreement	A defence tactic in which the target company repurchases a certain number of shares from its shareholders, usually at a premium to prevent the hostile bidder from acquiring a major percentage of the companies' stocks. It is usually followed with a *standstill agreement* in which the shareholders agree not to rebuy any shares in the company for a given period of time. It can also be concluded without a repurchase and the shareholders agree not to buy any more shares. The shareholder(s) may be given some seats on the board to vote with management.
4. Pac-Man defence	The target company makes a counter move and starts acquiring shares in the company that has placed the bid.

After an acquirer signifies its interest to acquire the target company, certain measures may be implemented by the management to defeat the bid. Some of these include: crown jewel, white knight & white squire, Pac-Man defence, green mail and standstill agreement.

Managements may resist bids with a view towards increasing the bid price or to retain their positions in the company.[109] Despite the apparent conflict of interests between managers and shareholders, management's opposition to a takeover bid may increase shareholder value through competitive bids, leading to improved bid premiums, higher bargaining power and managerial incentives.[110] The higher

108 Note 106, 56–57.

109 Ibid. 50–53.

110 Peter Holl and Dimitris Kyriazis, 'Agency, Bid Resistance and the Market for Corporate Control' (1997) 24 *Journal of Business Finance & Accounting* 1037, 1060–1063; Gregg Jarrell, 'The Wealth Effects of Litigation by Targets: Do Interests Diverge in a Merger' (1985) 28 *Journal of Law and Economics* 151, 172–175; See generally Robert Comment and G. William Schwert, 'Poison or Placebo? Evidence on the Deterrence and Wealth Effects of Modern Antitakeover Measures' (1995) 39 *Journal of Financial Economics* 3; G. William Schwert, 'Hostility in Takeovers: In the Eyes of the Beholder?' (2000) 55 *The Journal of Finance* 2599, 2600.

premium may only be sustained if the bid is successful. Hence, considering the intensity of some of the defences, it may be thought that managements intend to prevent the success of takeover bids to entrench themselves in office.[111]

Although takeover defences may enhance the bargaining powers of the shareholders, through enhanced bid price it is also important to consider the sensitivity of such defences on the overall value of the company. The bargaining power which may enhance takeover premiums may appear to show minimal benefits or a decline in earning.[112] Some defences may not necessarily enhance takeover premiums,[113] but may serve as mediums through which inefficient managers entrench themselves in managerial positions. Thus, takeover defences may either be driven by conflict of interests between the managers and shareholders or a genuine attempt by managements to promote the overall corporate value.

3.6 Contractual relationships: agency conflicts and employment issues

3.6.1 Agency conflicts

The relationship between company management – directors and executive managers – and shareholders in the administration of the corporate entity as a going concern has been described as an agency relationship.[114] Managers are contractually employed to use their professional competence to manage companies. Since the contract of employment may not predict all possible outcomes, managers are left with a wide range of discretion in making certain decisions. These include decisions made during takeovers. In making such important decisions, some managers may be driven by self-interests rather than by a considered corporate interest, leading to a conflict of the interests of these managers with the interests of their shareholders.

Agency problems may have been caused by the meaning of 'agency' which has been ascribed to the relationship between company shareholders and managers. Managers are expected to use their professional competence in the day-to-day running of the firm. They are also expected to act as 'agents' in performing this function. Generally, the role of managers as agents does not appear to fit into

111 See generally Tilton L. Willcox, 'The Use and Abuse of Executive Powers in Warding Off Corporate Raiders' (1988) 7 *Journal of Business Ethics* 47; Donald M. DePamphilis, *Mergers, Acquisitions, and Other Restructuring Activities* (9th edn, London, UK, Elsevier, 2018) 106–117.

112 Guhan Subramanian, 'Takeover Defenses and Bargaining Power' (2005) 17 *Journal of Applied Corporate Finance* 85, 93–96.

113 Cathy M. Niden, 'An Empirical Examination of White Knight Corporate Takeovers: Synergy and Overbidding' (1993) 22 *Financial Management* 28, 42–44.

114 Michael C. Jensen and William H. Meckling, 'Theory of the Firm: Managerial Behaviour, Agency Cost and Ownership Structure' (1976) 3 *Journal of Financial Economics* 305, 308; Eugene F. Fama and Michael C. Jensen, 'Agency Problems and Residual Claims' (1983) 26 *Journal of Law and Economics* 327.

the 'legal agency relationship'. Agents are expected to carry out the instructions of principals, using their expert knowledge. Since managers do not actually take instructions from shareholders, they may not be referred to as agents strictly speaking. They are contracted to run the firm with a view towards productivity. Thus, legally, their services are essentially directed to the company as a going concern and not the shareholders.[115] As such, they perform fiduciary duties.[116]

However, managers may be regarded as agents to the extent that their investment decisions are informed by shareholder value. It is difficult to identify these intentions, except by the manifestations of the managers' investment decisions through corporate growth or decline in firms' value. The classification of a firm as a *nexus of contracts* appears to provide a better explanation of the relationship between corporate managers and shareholders; their agency relationship is only founded on economic grounds.[117]

Managerial incentives may mitigate the agency problems caused by conflict of interests. One such incentive is managers' stockholding in the target firm. There is much debate about managerial incentives in the form of rewards. For example, it is argued that when managers hold a certain percentage of stocks in target companies, the agency conflict may likely be mitigated by incentives – including stock options or executive pay as motivation for long-term corporate value – presented by the economic gains to be derived from the bid premium.[118]

115 See *Automatic Self-Cleansing Filter Syndicate Co. v Cunninghame* [1906] 2 Ch. 34 CA.

116 *UK Companies Act 2006, ss 171–173, 175–177;* Larry E. Ribstein, 'The Structure of the Fiduciary Relationship' No. LE03-003 *Illinois Law and Economics Working Papers Series* 1, 19.

117 See Brian R. Cheffins, *Company Law: Theory, Structure and Operation* (New York, Oxford University Press, 2000) 45. It is not economically viable for a principal to monitor all the activities of an agent because of imperfect information held by the principal and perfect information held by the agent. Thus, lack of access to the right information is a major element of agency problems. See Stephen A. Ross, 'The Economic Theory of Agency: The Principals Problem' (1973) 63 *American Economic Association* 134.

118 Ali R. Maleqadeh and Victoria B. Mcwilliams, 'Managerial Efficiency and Share Ownership: The Market Reaction to Takeover Defenses' (1995) 11 *Journal of Applied Business Research* 48, 49.

Conflicting results have been presented on the extent to which incentives align with performance. See generally Luian A. Bebchuk and Jesse M. Fried, 'Paying for Long-Term Performance' (2010) 158 *University of Pennsylvania Law Review* 1915; Lucian A. Bebchuk and Jesse M. Fried, *Pay without Performance: The Unfulfilled Promise of Executive Compensation* (Cambridge, MA, Harvard University Press, 2006); Stephen Bryan, Lee Seok Hwang, and Steven Lilien, 'CEO Stock-Based Compensation: An Empirical Analysis of Incentive-Intensity, Relative Mix and Economic Determinants' (2000) 73 *The Journal of Business* 661; Martin J. Conyon, 'Executive Compensation and Incentives' (2006) *Academy of Management Perspectives* 25; Brian R. Cheffins, 'Will Executive Pay Globalise along American Lines?' (2003) 11 *Corporate Governance* 8; Kevin J. Murphy, 'Corporate Performance and Managerial Remuneration an Empirical Analysis' (1985) 7 *Journal of Accounting and Economics* 11; Cynthia E. Devers et al., 'Executive Compensation: A Multidisciplinary Review of Recent Developments' (2007) 33 *Journal of Management* 1016; Michel A. Habib and Alexander Ljungqvist, 'Firm Value and Managerial Incentives: A Stochastic Frontier Approach' (2005) 78 *The Journal of Business* 2053; Shane A. Johnson, Harley E. Ryan, Jr., and Yisong S. Tian, 'Managerial Incentives and Corporate Fraud:

Consequently, it is suggested that managers with higher stockholding may show little resistance to acquisition bids, since they may be less interested in seeking to entrench themselves in management functions.[119] This is mainly encouraged if the benefit to be derived from the sale of their stocks to the bidders will enhance their economic interests. Alternatively, managerial incentives can be caused by agency problems.[120] This can occur when firms have weak governance structures which encourage managements to extract incentives.

The importance to be attached to takeovers is determined by the extent that the interests of the key corporate constituents – the shareholders, creditors, employees, directors and managers[121] – are integrated. These key corporate constituents are actively involved in promoting the success of a company as a going concern. As such, they are largely interested in the investment decisions of companies, including takeovers. Company directors and managers have the capacity to negotiate for the protection of their interests during takeovers; this applies to target or acquiring companies. Also, creditors may not likely be negatively affected by takeovers, in view of the fact that the combination of companies' assets provides a higher level of securities for their debt capital, except unsecured creditors. For shareholders – especially shareholder of acquiring companies – and employees, the protection of their interests is not guaranteed, except they are specifically protected by statute, or they rely on company directors and managers to protect their interests.

In view of this, the likelihood of conflict of interests is present, since managers could undertake low or non-value-yielding acquisitions for the purpose of enhancing managerial gains. Shareholders and employees may be regarded as forming a distinct class of corporate constituents during takeovers in view of the fact that they do not have the capacity to protect their interests during takeovers when compared to other active participants. As such, they may be regarded as having a collective interest in this regard. It may not be possible to devise a single mechanism through which their interests may be protected in view of the differences in their status. Shareholders are financial stakeholders in a company, employees are not; unlike shareholders, they are non-financial stakeholders.

The Sources of Incentives Matter' (2009) 13 *Review of Finance* 115; Bengt Holmstrom, 'Pay without Performance and the Managerial Power Hypothesis: A Comment' (2005) 30 *Journal of Corporation Law* 703; Wilbur Lewellen, Claudio Loderer, and Kenneth Martin, 'Executive Compensation and Executive Incentive Problems: An Empirical Analysis' (1987) 9 *Journal of Accounting and Economics* 287; Brian G. M. Main, Charles A. O'Reilly III, and James Wade, 'The CEO, the Board of Directors and Executive Compensation: Economic and Psychological Perspectives' (1995) 4 *Industrial and Corporate Change* 293.

119 See Moon H. Song and Ralph A. Walkling, 'The Impact of Managerial Ownership on Acquisition Attempts and Target Sharegholder Wealth' (1993) 28 *The Journal of Finance and Quantitative Analysis* 439, 453–456; David P. Baron, 'Tender Offers and Management Resistance' (1983) 38 *The Journal of Finance* 331, 340.

120 John E. Core, Robert W. Holthausen, and David F. Larcker, 'Corporate Governance, Chief Executive Officer Compensation, and Firm Performance' (1999) 51 *Journal of Financial Economics* 371; Lucian A. Bebchuk and Jesse M. Fried, 'Executive Compensation as an Agency Problem' (2003) 17/3 *Journal of Economic Perspectives* 71–92.

121 See note 117 B R Cheffins, 47.

Managers of acquiring companies may be motivated by factors which may not create value for their firms. They could be motivated to expand the corporate investment by building empires using free cash flow to increase the size of their firms.[122] They may also seek to expand the investment of their firm to decrease their employment risks, among other reasons.[123] Also, agency conflict may prompt managers to acquire assets through takeovers to increase the level of their firm's dependence on their management skills.[124] They may be inclined to acquire investments which clearly relate to their managerial competence, whether or not these investments will enhance the value of the corporation. Apart from increasing the level of the firm's dependence on their managerial skills, these investment decisions are likely to increase their salaries and allowances in view of the large business empire which they subsequently control post-takeovers. It was observed that such managerial decisions can exploit this dependence to increase their prerequisite consumption or defeat rivals who are better than them in running some of the operations of the firm. This can lead to agency costs which inevitably reduce the total value of the combined firm available to shareholders.[125] Thus, despite the fact that takeovers can be an efficient mechanism for corporate control, the challenges posed by agency conflict between the managers and shareholders may influence managers to make acquisitions which are geared towards the maximisation of their personal interests[126] at the expense of shareholders and other corporate constituents.

Also, managers of target companies may oppose takeover bids from acquirers, even though it may be advantageous to the firm's economic value. While some acquisition bids may be opposed by management for purposes related to shareholder value, such as enhancing the bid premium, others may be done with the intention of promoting the interests of management. Managers may resist a takeover bid for fear of being considered as having failed in their managerial responsibilities in promoting the economic value of the company, which may likely lead to their dismissal post-takeover, especially where they have only little incentive to endorse the bid,[127] such as absence of or inadequate compensation policy, or other gains which may mitigate their loss of employment and reputation.

Although, the agency problem of conflict of interests, as illustrated with regards to the target and acquiring companies, may not always influence managers during takeovers, however, its occurrence is likely. Conflict of interests may be present in

122 Note 47 Jensen, 328; Lucian Bebchuk and Yaniv Grinstein, 'Firm Expansion and CEO Pay' (2005) *Harvard Law School* Discussion Paper No. 533, 111–133.

123 See generally Yakov Amihud and Baruch Lev, 'Risk Reduction as a Managerial Motive for Conglomerate Merger' (1981) 12 *The Bell Journal of Economics* 605.

124 Andrei Shleifer and Robert W. Vishny, 'Management Entrenchment: The Case of Manager-Specific Investments' (1989) 25 *Journal of Financial Economics* 123, 134–136.

125 Note 93 Berkovitch and Narayanan, 350.

126 See Randall Morck, Andrei Shleifer, and Robert Vishny, 'Do Managerial Objectives Drive Bad Acquisitions?' (1990) 45 *The Journal of Finance* 31, 46–47.

127 Note 106, 52.

the decision of the target company to accept or reject a bid, as well as the decision of the acquiring company to bid for a takeover. The problem persists because shareholders cannot personally manage their property rights in shares; they require the services of managements. Managements may not always realise that the property rights in the investments that they control resides with their shareholders, even though their fiduciary duty is owed to the company.

An important justification for takeover regulations that protect the interests of shareholders from the challenges caused by agency conflicts is to ensure that the property rights of shareholders are protected. One of the major reasons that company managements are appointed is to manage the investments of their shareholders. Property rights in these investments reside in the investors – shareholders. One of the ways of ensuring that managements act in the interests of their shareholders is to establish effective institutional structures that can determine the scope of the responsibilities of managements. In a bid to ensure that the property rights of shareholders are protected, efforts have been made to restrict the role of managements by takeover regulations. Their level of discretion in opposing takeover bids has been largely curtailed,[128] to ensure that the contractual relationship between managers and shareholders enhances corporate value in a way that can be directly beneficial to shareholders.

3.6.2 Employment issues

Company employees are also parties to a contractual relationship. They are parties to contracts of employment. Employer-employee contractual relationships exist between employees and corporate entities. Employees are another category of corporate constituents that do not have the capacity to protect their interests during takeovers. The interests of company employees may not be derived from an agency relationship like shareholders, but the interests of management may conflict with the interests of employees. The decision to make acquisitions or to oppose or accept a bid is often made without due regard to the interests of company employees. In light of the threat which takeovers pose to employment, it may be indicative that employees should look elsewhere to protect their interests.

The concerns that have been elicited towards the impact of takeovers on employment show that there is indeed a link between takeovers and general employment levels. This may not necessarily imply that all takeovers lead to employee dismissal; there is an indication that the higher the number of takeovers that are concluded, the higher the number of employees that are likely to be disengaged. For example, even though the *EU Takeover Directive* was mainly established for the protection of shareholders of target companies, it nevertheless recognises the impact that takeovers can have on employment. It requires managements of target companies to set out their opinions on how a takeover would

128 Especially in the UK. See: *The City Code on Takeovers*, 2 (a), *EU Takeover Directive* art. 9.

affect employment, the acquirers' strategic plan for the target company and their likely effects on employment.[129] The establishment of employment protection regulation in the UK[130] also show that takeovers are threats to employment. Despite the establishment of employment protection regulation, the Business Innovation and Skills Committee of the UK House of Commons have shown interest in the impact of takeovers on employment, by inquiring into the extent to which jobs may be affected by takeovers: this included takeovers involving AstraZeneca – Pfizer and Kraft – Cadbury.

The problems of integration post-takeovers have been a recurrent disadvantage of mergers and takeovers. It was observed that every merger creates as many problems, especially of people-related problems, more than it would if the business were developed from within.[131] One of the main causes of this problem is the level of uncertainty that arises when acquisition is imminent. The uncertainty appears to work in the favour of managements because it enables managements to exercise their discretion. The manner in which the discretion is exercised may not be in the interests of the corporate value generally, shareholders specifically or other stakeholders such as employees. The incompleteness of employment contract makes it unclear and uncertain whether employees will be retained post-takeovers. This means that managements can exercise their discretion in the determination of whether employees should be dismissed or not. This is largely because company managements do not consider themselves as owing any duty to the employees of their company. Proponents of shareholder value suggest that the only objective of managements is to make profit and enhance the economic value of investors without regards to any external objective.[132]

The ability of company managements to 'freely' disengage employees post-takeover suggest that managements can engage in large and unproductive acquisitions. Losses to acquiring shareholders caused by high costs of acquisitions can be mitigated by a reduction of the corporate costs in the form of employee disengagement. High transaction costs can potentially reduce corporate value and shareholder wealth. The transaction cost economics suggest that transactions should be conducted in the least possible costs. Effective institutional arrangements can be used to ensure that transaction costs are mitigated towards

129 *EU Takeover Directive* 2004 art. 9(5).

130 *'The Transfer of Undertakings Protection of Employment Regulations' (TUPE) CAP 46 (2006).*

131 Conflict of interests among the different corporate constituents during takeovers could be difficult to manage see: T. M. Fapohunda, 'The Human Resources Management Challenges of Post Consolidation Mergers and Acquisitions in Nigeria's Banking Industry' (2012) 6 *International Business Management* 68, 71, citing Peter Drucker, *Management Challenges for the 21st Century* (New York, Harper Business, 1999); see also Michael R. Patrone, 'Sour Chocolate: The UK Takeover Panel's Improper Reaction to Kraft's Acquisition of Cadbury' (2001) 8 *Brigham Young University International Law and Management Review* 64.

132 See generally Milton Friedman, *Capitalism and Freedom* (Chicago, University of Chicago Press, 1962).

strengthening the role of the market. Since employees play active roles in promoting the success of a company as a going concern, it is important to consider their interests, being investors of human capital to the extent that they may obtain skills that are less valuable to other employers,[133] but particularly valuable to the company. Protecting employee interests may be of beneficial value to shareholders and the general corporate interests.[134]

The challenges of takeovers are clearly beyond the conflict of interest issues between managements and their shareholders. Employment issues are among the biggest challenges to takeovers in modern times; this poses a further challenge to governments and social institutions. It remains to be seen whether sufficient efforts have been made towards the strengthening of takeover institutional frameworks to address these problems.

The relationships between shareholders and managements and employees and managements are largely determined by reference to contracts; agency relationships with respect to shareholders and employment contracts with respect to employees. Thus, the extent to which shareholders and employees can be protected during takeovers may be determined by reference to whether a company can be considered to have evolved through the contractual theory of the firm and the extent of the limitations of the contractual theory, if any.

3.6.3 The contractual theory of the corporation

The contractual theory[135] of the corporation identifies a company as an organisation that is characterised by a 'nexus of contracts' amongst the company's major participants.[136] The relationship of these participants is determined by reference to the existing contracts among the corporate constituents without state intervention. The state may intervene for the purpose of enforcement of the contracts since the parties to the intra-firm relationships may not have the capacity to enforce the contracts. Even though the relationships amongst the corporate constituents may be determined by reference to their contracts, it may not always be possible to determine the rights and liabilities of all the parties in every

133 Frank H. Easterbrook and Daniel R. Fischel, 'Corporate Control Transactions' (1982) 91 *The Yale Law Journal* 698, 703.

134 See the analysis in Chapter 7.

135 See Henry N. Butler, 'The Contractual Theory of the Corporation' (1988) 11 *George Mason Law Review* 99–123; note 114; Frank H. Easterbrook and Daniel R. Fischel, 'The Corporate Contract' (1989) 89 *Columbia Law Review* 1416, 1429. See generally Charles W. L. Hill and Thomas M. Jones, 'Stakeholder-Agency Theory' (1992) 29 *Journal of Management Studies* 131.

136 Directors/managers, shareholders, creditors and employees. See note 117; Caspar Rose, 'Stakeholder Orientation vs. Shareholder Value: A Matter of Contractual Failures' (2004) 18 *European Journal of Law and Economics* 77; Stephen M. Bainbridge, 'Director Primacy: The Means and Ends of Corporate Governance' (2003) 97 *North-Western University Law Review* 547, 552–558.

situation,[137] especially in unforeseen situations, such as takeovers. Hence, when a company becomes the subject of a takeover, negotiations leading to the takeovers may become characterised by conflicts of interest. The interests of some corporate participants may be 'traded', especially when they do not have the capacity to negotiate and protect their interests.

Shareholders appear to rank higher than employees in protecting and enforcing their contracts. Apart from the protection that may be provided by company law,[138] an important objective of takeover regulation is to protect shareholders.[139] Although shareholder protection is limited in scope, it is generally more extensive when compared with the form of employment protection during takeovers.[140] Thus, even though the interests of shareholders and employees are capable of being undermined during takeovers, employees are more exposed to risks than shareholders.

Company employees lack the capacity to negotiate for the protection of their interests during takeovers. Hence, by reference to the contractual theory of the firm, it is a major challenge for company employees to protect their interests, especially the employees of target companies.

The contractual theory considers a firm to be an entity through which the collective objectives of individuals are brought into equilibrium within a framework of contractual relations.[141] However, the extent to which the rights of the contractual parties can be clearly determined is not clear. Contracts within a company may be viewed from two perspectives: 'an originating contract' and an 'operational contract'.[142] The former includes contracts that led to the establishment of a company, with defined rights and responsibilities. The latter refers to the contract that defines the applicable relationships among the parties in the originating contract and other subsequent parties in the pursuit of the objectives of the company. Obviously, the 'nexus of contracts' definition disregards this distinction. It merely classifies a corporation as a private contract which does not require state intervention except for the purposes of enforcement.[143] One of the

137 This problem, among others, challenges the contractual theory. See Michael Klausner, 'The Contractarian Theory of Corporate Law: A Generation Later' (2006) *The Journal of Corporation Law* 779.

138 These are examined in Chapter 4, section 4.4 and Chapter 5, section 5.5.

139 The objective of *The UK City Code on Takeovers 2016* and the *EU Takeover Directive* 2004 are stated to be for the protection of the interests of shareholders (shareholders of target companies specifically). See *UK Takeover Code*, s 2(a), see generally, *EU Takeover Directive* 2004.

140 The extent to which employees are protected during takeovers in the UK and the United States (Delaware) is examined in Chapter 4, section 4.4 and Chapter 5, section 5.5.

141 Note 114, 311; William W. Bratton, 'The Nexus of Contracts Corporation: A Critical Appraisal' (1989) 74 *Cornell Law Review* 406, 415–423.

142 Ige O. Bolodeoku, 'Economic Theories of the Corporation and Corporate Governance: A Critique' (2002) *Journal of Business Law* 411, 417.

143 Henry N. Butler and Larry E. Ribstein, 'The Contract Clause and the Corporation' (1989–1990) 55 *Brooklyn Law Review* 767, 769.

challenges of this contract is that the corporate constituents have different rights and responsibilities attached to their interests.

These rights and responsibilities are not evenly assigned to the constituents – such as the contractual rights and responsibilities of shareholders and employees. Hence, the nexus of contracts theoretical framework would not encourage any attempt to investigate the extent to which these rights and responsibilities are shared and vested.[144] The nexus of contracts dwells more on the originating contract which contains pre-defined rights and responsibilities subsequent to the operational contract. Since the modern corporation as a going concern is mainly established for economic reasons, it can be argued that emphasis should be accorded to the operational contract. Within the operational contract are other corporate constituents – such as company employees – who may not be parties to the originating contract of the firm, whereas, they make important contributions in promoting the economic objective of firms.

This operating contract generally enables parties to be able to determine their rights and responsibilities outside the originating contract.

This may not always apply in practice because parties such as employees may not have the capacity[145] to conclude contracts. They may not have the same bargaining powers as a company in obtaining a fair bargain,[146] among other reasons. It was suggested that the contractual theory does not reside with stockholders; it is not logically tied to any set of rights for shareholders, and that corporate constituents including employees should be able to obtain a bargain with reference to the contractual theory of the firm.[147] However, employees are not empowered to enforce this contract since their contract of employment limits the extent to which the contractual theory of the firm can operate to their advantage. Hence external intervention through legal institutions[148] may be necessary to define their basic rights and rewards, to ensure that employees are not unfairly treated. This explains the need for regulation to determine the minimum wage for employees, even though employees and employers are free to enter into contracts of employment. This form of legal institutions can be established through the instrument of the state, by reference to the entity theory of the firm.

144 Note 142, 418.

145 Employees usually do not have a strong negotiating capacity, especially in situations of 'economic downturn' where the urgent need to find a job can undermine the capacity of employees to make well-considered decisions as to the terms of their employment contracts.

146 Katherine V. W. Stone, 'Employees as Stakeholders under State Non-Shareholder Constituency Statutes' (1991–1992) 21 *Stetson Law Review* 45, 55.

147 John Boatright, 'Contractors as Stakeholders: Reconciling Stakeholder Theory with the Nexus-of-Contracts Firm' (2002) 26 *Journal of Banking & Finance* 1837, 1841.

148 It has been suggested that implicit contracts between employees and companies are not contracts in the legal sense, but mere unilateral promises from employers that are generally unenforceable see John E. Parkinson, 'The Contractual Theory of the Company and the Protection of Non-Shareholder Interests' in David Feldman and Franklin Meisel (eds.), *Corporate and Commercial Law: Modern Developments* (London, Lloyd's of London Press Ltd, 1996) 133.

3.6.4 The entity theory of the corporation

The entity theory of the corporation is based on the view that a corporation exists at the pleasure of the state. It supports direct intervention by the state through regulations, since the state created the corporation by granting it a charter[149] – to acquire the status of artificial personality. State intervention appears to negate the contractual theory of the firm. It was observed that statutes that permit company managements to consider the welfare of non-shareholder interests when making corporate decisions cannot be reasonably justified.[150] This view may not have considered that every private contract requires the state to enforce its terms. Also, a contract is deemed valid by reference to the standard that has been set by the state, for example offer, acceptance and the intention to create a legal relationship.

Even though state intervention may not be encouraged in every situation, corporate contracts cannot be 'entirely' private. Hence, it is important that a balance should be created to ensure that the corporate contract is not used to promote unfair arrangements, especially when the parties do not have equal negotiating powers and capacities. In light of this, the entity theory of a corporation is as important as the contractual theory especially in investment decisions such as takeovers.

The objective of the entity theory is not to displace the contractual theory of the firm; rather it aims at preserving it by ensuring that parties are not treated unfairly as a result of any uncertain event(s) which may occur during the pendency of their contracts. This can be achieved with the establishment of effective institutions. It is actually relevant because it helps to provide the default solution to those circumstances which may not have been contemplated in the contract. The inability of contracting parties to determine future possible matters that may occur signifies that uncertainties are likely to characterise contractual relationships, including corporate contracts. The incompleteness of these contracts which causes uncertainties can be present in takeovers. This can lead to increased transaction costs of takeovers. The absence of an effective institutional framework for takeover regulation can create a high level of uncertainty in relation to employment post-takeovers. The costs that are associated with the uncertainties are also indirectly borne by the shareholders of acquiring companies, since large premiums are paid to the target shareholders in pursuit of the acquisition. This can undermine the synergistic objective of takeovers. Even though employees are disengaged and large amounts of the future wage bill is saved in the short term, it does not actually enhance shareholder or corporate value. It merely prevents further costs. The relevance and importance of the entity theory is to mitigate this problem that can be caused by uncertainty.

The entity theory objective is more extensively applied by the new institutional economics theory. The entity theory merely recognises the need for state intervention to ensure that contracting parties are protected without identifying

149 Note 135 H. Butler, 100.
150 Note 143, 800.

the process towards achieving this objective. However, the new institutional economics not only identifies the need for the state to use institutions to strengthen the process of interactions and exchange, it is also concerned with how the institutions are created and the process of change of these institutions.

The 'nexus of contract theory' may not actually characterise a corporation in the absence of state recognition. As rightly observed, an entity can only assume the status of a corporation and be recognised as such only if it acts in a legally authorised way, or is legally recognised.[151] Hence, even though certain individuals agree to transact by entering a contract, legal personality cannot be obtained *simpliciter*. It can only be conferred at the pleasure of the state. This same state intervention which confers individual status of legal personality is also used to restrict the use to which the legal personality can be put.[152] This is necessarily to protect vulnerable parties and ensure that the corporation operates in a responsible way. Thus, effective institutional mechanisms can be used to moderate the relationship amongst the different corporate constituents. The objective of the established institutions is not meant to replace the market functions and free market competition, rather, it is meant to strengthen the role of the market as a medium for exchange of resources. This is consistent with the objective of the new institutional economics theory, especially in relation to providing an appropriate framework for coordinating contractual relationships. This can be successfully applied to prevent conflict of interests and market expropriation as it affects the interests of shareholders and employees during takeovers.[153]

The need to protect company employees during takeovers has not featured as much as the clamour for the protection of the interest of shareholders. Apparently, this is because the interests of shareholders appear to rank higher than those of employees, since shareholders are financial stakeholders in companies. Apart from the fact that shareholders have certain rights attached to their shares by which they may constrain management to act in their favour, regulatory measures are being developed to protect shareholders' interests during takeovers. For employees that do not have tangible rights in shares like shareholders, not much has been done to protect their interests during takeovers. For example, the regulation that appears to protect employee interests in the UK is severely limited;[154] employees remain threatened by takeovers.

3.7 Conclusion

This chapter has examined the theoretical framework of takeovers and a brief illustration of the effects of takeovers on shareholder and employee interests. It

151 Jan Dejnozka, 'Corporate Entity' 2007 1, 23 www.members.tripod.com/~Jan_Dejnozka/corporate_entity_book.pdf accessed 11 April 2018.

152 George F. Canfield, 'The Scope and Limits of the Corporate Entity Theory' (1917) 17 *Columbia Law Review* 128, 133–143.

153 See Chapter 2, section 2.6.

154 This is examined in Chapter 4.

was shown that hostile takeovers have managerial disciplinary character. Managers are believed to be generally hostile towards bids for fear of losing their positions. Managerial hostilities towards bids may emerge from lack of incentives to promote shareholder interests; hence managers tend to seek the path of entrenchment. It was also shown that takeovers which are actually directed towards corporate synergy are generally not hostile, but rather friendly. This is because of the fact that managers negotiate their contracts and the fusion of the firms may lead to the continuous employment of managers who may otherwise have been dismissed post-takeovers. Importantly, it emerged that the disciplinary function of takeovers is only relevant to the target company and not the acquiring company. It is the objective of the acquiring company to enhance their corporate investment and not to actually aid the investors of the target company in the pursuit of good corporate management. Also, it was observed that the disciplinary effect of takeovers does not apply to successful takeovers only; it may extend to unsuccessful acquisitions. The threat of dismissal post-takeovers may serve as an incentive to managements to enhance the value of their firms.

The hubris hypothesis of takeovers was suggested to be caused by 'careless' investment decisions of managers. Although managerial hubris may be a deliberate act of managers, evidence is required to justify this view, since acquisitions are also leading to synergistic gains.

Meanwhile, since takeovers do not often lead to negotiated agreements amongst the different corporate interests, managers often oppose takeover bids. The oppositions to takeover bids by corporate managers are prompted by reasons best known to them. These reasons may not be far-fetched. In the analysis of the takeover defences that are adopted by managers to frustrate takeovers, it emerged that managerial oppositions to takeover bids could serve certain purposes. These include: to prevent a successful takeover or to increase the bid price in favour of their shareholders. While the former operates to promote their personal objectives, the latter is aimed at conferring benefit on their shareholders. However, as earlier noted, the latter purpose may be defeated if the bidder is not able to meet the higher bid-premium prices.

It can be observed that takeovers can be a medium for value creation for shareholders and the corporate entity generally. This can be achieved when managers actually promote synergy through takeovers. Also, takeovers can be used to either redistribute or destroy corporate value. This can occur in those takeovers that are influenced by overestimation of bid prices, by overambitious managers, leading to costly acquisitions. This can lead to a mere increase in the size of corporate entity without a corresponding increase in the economic value of the combined entities. Managerial hubris can promote the value-redistributing effect of takeovers, especially where the role of managements during takeovers is not restricted and challenged.

Generally, takeovers affect the same web of interests in the target and acquiring companies in essentially the same way in different jurisdictions. It emerged that shareholders and employees can be easily short-changed during takeovers relative to other corporate constituents. It was shown that the identified problems may

have been caused by conflict of interests between corporate management and investors, as well as incomplete contracts and uncertainties in employer-employee relationships. The entity theory of the corporation was shown to justify state intervention in regulating the relationship amongst the corporate constituents. The relevance of the entity theory was identified as a response to the limitations of the contractual theory of the firm. Since the entity theory supports state intervention, the establishment of effective institutions to administer and regulate takeovers was identified as an important way to address the challenges of takeovers. The new institutional economics was thus identified as fulfilling the important objectives of the entity theory of the firm, through effective regulatory and administrative institutions.

In the next chapter, the takeover regulatory mechanism which is applicable in the United Kingdom is examined in relation to shareholder and employee interests.

References

Amihud, Y. and Baruch Lev, 'Risk Reduction as a Managerial Motive for Conglomerate Merger' (1981) 12 *The Bell Journal of Economics* 605.

Amihud, Y., Baruch Lev, and Nicholaos G. Travlos, 'Corporate Control and the Choice of Investment Financing: The Case of Corporate Acquisitions' (1990) 45 *The Journal of Finance* 603.

Ansoff, H. I., *Corporate Strategy: An Analytic Approach to Business Policy for Growth and Expansion* (New York, McGraw-Hill, 1965).

Arcot, S., Valentina Bruno, and Antoine Faure-Grimaud, 'Corporate Governance in the UK: Is the Comply or Explain Approach Working?' (2010) 30 *International Review of Law and Economics* 193.

Avery, C., Judith A. Chevalier, and Scott Schaefer, 'Why Do Managers Undertake Acquisitions? An Analysis of Internal and External Rewards for Acquisitiveness' (1998) 14 *The Journal of Law, Economics and Organisation* 24.

Bainbridge, S. M., 'Director Primacy: The Means and Ends of Corporate Governance' (2003) 97 *North-western University Law Review* 547, 552.

Barney, J. B., 'Returns to Bidding Firms in Mergers and Acquisitions: Reconsidering the Relatedness Hypothesis' (1988) 9 *Strategic Management Journal* 71, 76.

Baron, D. P., 'Tender Offers and Management Resistance' (1983) 38 *The Journal of Finance* 331.

Bebchuk, A K. and Marcel Kahan, 'A Framework for Analyzing Legal Policy Towards Proxy Contests' (1990) 78 *California Law Review* 1071, 1102.

Bebchuk, L. A., 'The Case for Facilitating Competing Tender Offers' (1982) 95 *Harvard Law Review* 1028.

Bebchuk, L. A., John C. Coates, and Guhan Subramanian, *The Power of Takeover Defenses* (Harvard, Harvard Law School Working Paper, 2007) www.law.harvard.edu/programs/corp_gov/papers/2007sp_Subramanian.pdf accessed 14 April 2018.

Bebchuk, L. A. and Jesse M. Fried, 'Executive Compensation as an Agency Problem' (2003) 17/3 *Journal of Economic Perspectives*.

Bebchuk, L. A. and Jesse M. Fried, 'Paying for Long-Term Performance' (2010) 158 *University of Pennsylvania Law Review* 1915.

Bebchuk, L. A. and Jesse M. Fried, *Pay without Performance: The Unfulfilled Promise of Executive Compensation* (Cambridge, MA, Harvard University Press, 2006).

Bebchuk, L. A. and Yaniv Grinstein, 'Firm Expansion and CEO Pay' (2005) *Harvard Law School* Discussion Paper No. 533, 111.

Berkovitch, E. and M. P. Narayanan, 'Motives for Takeovers: An Empirical Investigation' (1993) 28 *Journal of Finance and Quantitative Analysis* 347.

Boatright, J., 'Contractors as Stakeholders: Reconciling Stakeholder Theory with the Nexus-of-Contracts Firm' (2002) 26 *Journal of Banking & Finance* 1837.

Bolodeoku, I. O., 'Economic Theories of the Corporation and Corporate Governance: A Critique' (2002) *Journal of Business Law* 411.

Botchway, F. N., 'Mergers and Acquisitions in Resource Industry: Implications for Africa' (2010–2011) 26 *Connecticut Journal of International Law* 51.

Bradford, S. C., 'Stampeding Shareholders and Other Myths: Target Shareholders and Hostile Tender Offers' (1989–1990) 15 *Journal of Corporation Law* 417.

Bratton, W. W., 'The Nexus of Contracts Corporation: A Critical Appraisal' (1989) 74 *Cornell Law Review* 406, 415.

Brealey, R. A., Stewart C. Myers, and Franklin Allen, *Principles of Corporate Finance* (New York, McGraw-Hill/Irwin, 2008).

Brown, P., Andrew Ferguson, and Peter Lam, 'What's in a Shell? Analysing the Gain to Shareholders from Reverse Takeovers' (2010) *Social Science Research Network* 1, 5 file:///C:/Users/user/Downloads/SSRN-id1896004.pdf accessed 20 April 2018.

Bruner, R. F., 'Does M & A Pay? A Survey of Evidence for the Decision Maker' (2002) *Journal of Applied Finance* 48, 64.

Bryan, S., Lee Seok Hwang, and Steven Lilien, 'CEO Stock-Based Compensation: An Empirical Analysis of Incentive-Intensity, Relative Mix and Economic Determinants' (2000) 73 *The Journal of Business* 661.

Butler, Henry N., 'The Contractual Theory of the Corporation' (1988) 11 *George Mason Law Review* 99.

Butler, Henry N. and Larry E. Ribstein, 'The Contract Clause and the Corporation' (1989–1990) 55 *Brooklyn Law Review* 767.

Canfield, G. F., 'The Scope and Limits of the Corporate Entity Theory' (1917) 17 *Columbia Law Review*.

Chatterjee, S., 'Types of Synergy and Economic Value: The Impact of Acquisitions on Merging and Rival Firms' (1986) 7 *Strategic Management Journal* 119.

Cheffins, Brian R., *Company Law: Theory, Structure and Operation* (New York, Oxford University Press, 2000).

Cheffins, Brian R., 'Will Executive Pay Globalise along American Lines?' (2003) 11 *Corporate Governance* 8.

Christie, A. and Jerold L. Zimmerman, 'Efficiency and Opportunistic Choices of Accounting Procedures: Corporate Control Contests' (1994) 69 *The Accounting Review* 539.

Coffee, J. C., Jr., 'Regulating the Market for Corporate Control: A Critical Assessment of the Tender Offer's Role in Corporate Governance' (1984) 84 *Columbia Law Review* 1145.

Comment, R. and G. William Schwert, 'Poison or Placebo? Evidence on the Deterrence and Wealth Effects of Modern Antitakeover Measures' (1995) 39 *Journal of Financial Economics* 3.

Conyon, Martin J., 'Executive Compensation and Incentives' (2006) *Academy of Management Perspectives* 25.

for opportunistic bids and such bids may be resisted by managers initially to achieve higher share price premiums.[66]

There is a contention that little empirical evidence exists to support the claim that the disciplinary nature of takeovers is to be found only in hostile takeovers. It has been asserted that the post-takeover CEO turnover associated with a hostile takeover is not related to past performance, but that such CEO removal, by way of resignation or dismissal, is likely due to disagreements about the bid price of the takeover and/or future expected performance of the target company.[67] This conclusion was reached because the study found no positive relationship between CEO turnover and past performance in certain corporate takeovers.

By implication, takeovers could have no disciplinary motive. It also implies that if there is any disciplinary effect of takeovers, such can be found both in hostile or friendly takeovers and not exclusively to hostile takeovers. It was suggested that there is little evidence to show that takeovers leading to changes in power of control results from acts of past poor performance. Accordingly, it was argued that the targets of hostile takeovers do not necessarily perform any more poorly than the targets of accepted bids; this implies that some hostile takeovers may not necessarily perform a disciplinary function.[68]

While it may be right to assert that takeovers have no disciplinary motive from the perspective of the acquirers, it is different when viewed from the perspective of the acquired company.[69] First, takeovers can be influenced by the inefficiency of the management team of the acquired company.[70] This includes poor managerial decisions that lead to a value-decreasing acquisition which subsequently reduces the value of the company to the level of a target company.[71] Hence, such managers are not expected to be retained post-takeover. Second, because of the series of negotiations which characterise friendly takeovers, it may not be regarded as performing a disciplinary role, since managers can be compensated if they negotiate their exit or if their employment contracts require that they should be compensated.

A study which examined the role of takeovers in managerial discipline did not establish any difference between hostile and friendly takeovers with regards to

66 Raveeja Sinha, 'The Role of Hostile Takeovers in Corporate Governance' (2004) 14 *Applied Financial Economics* 1291, 1292, 95.

67 See generally Omesh Kini, William Kracaw, and Shehzad Mian, 'The Nature of Discipline by Corporate Takeovers' (2004) 59 *The Journal of Finance* 1511, 1549.

68 Julian Franks and Colin Mayer, 'Hostile Takeovers and the Correction of Managerial Failure' (1996) 40 *Journal of Financial Economics* 163, 177. See John C. Coffee, Jr., 'Regulating the Market for Corporate Control: A Critical Assessment of the Tender Offer's Role in Corporate Governance' (1984) 84 *Columbia Law Review* 1145, 1163.

69 Acquiring companies do not deliberately seek to 'discipline' managements of target companies through takeovers. The dismissal of managements of target companies is a necessary incidence since the managements of the acquiring company would take control of the newly acquired company.

70 See generally Michael S. Weisbach, 'Corporate Governance and Hostile Takeovers' (1993) 16 *Journal of Accounting and Economics* 199.

71 Mark L. Mitchell and Kenneth Lehn, 'Do Bad Bidders become Good Targets?' (1990) 98 *Journal of Political Economy* 372, 376.

dismissal of top managers. It further reported that, on average, all takeover targets come from industries that are performing well, relative to the market, and while the targets of disciplinary takeovers are performing poorly within their industry, the targets of non-disciplinary takeovers are performing well as the average firm in their industry. This implies that the disciplinary effect of a takeover is dependent on the benchmark of the *industry peer group* rather than the *market*. Also, in its analysis, it contended that the dismissal of top managers is not exclusively related to either hostile or friendly takeovers. However, it rightly emphasised that takeovers play a role in managerial discipline in view of the fact that targets of takeovers in which there is a change in top managers soon after the takeover are on the average performing significantly worse than those target firms in which there is no change in top manager.[72]

Meanwhile, it has been suggested that acquisitions which are value-decreasing are mainly attempted by managers of larger firms than those of smaller firms. This is because managers of larger companies pay more for acquisition, since they have more resources and perhaps fewer obstacles, and are influenced by managerial hubris which they believe to be more socially important.[73] Impliedly, it was thus hypothesised that managers are much more likely to indulge in value-destroying, empire-building acquisitions, when they are in the positions that they would be less likely disciplined by the market for corporate control.[74]

From the foregoing it is indicative that the market for corporate control is less effective as a disciplinary mechanism for managers of larger companies than those of smaller companies. Alternatively, it was suggested that managers of larger firms are more likely to be disciplined by the market for corporate control – apparently they are easily spotted by the market because of their size. Nonetheless, they are more inclined to indulge in value-destroying, empire-building acquisitions than managers of smaller companies,[75] apparently because of prestige and the access to capital. Going by the latter analysis, it implies that different incentives make managers act in the way they do, including the view that managers make acquisitions as a means towards defending the company from being taken over.[76] Alternatively, the disciplinary effect of the market for

72 See generally Kenneth J. Martin and John J. Mcconnell, 'Corporate Performance, Corporate Takeovers and Management Turnover' (1991) 46 *The Journal of Finance* 671, 672, 680.

73 Sara B. Moeller, Frederik P. Schlingemann, and René M. Stulz, 'Firm Size and the Gains from Acquisitions' (2004) 73 *Journal of Financial Economics* 201, 203–204, 26.

74 See Ronald W. Masulis, Cong Wang, and Fei Xie, 'Corporate Governance and Acquirer Returns' (2007) 62 *The Journal of Finance* 1851, 1853.

75 David Offenberg, 'Firm Size and the Effectiveness of the Market for Corporte Control' (2009) 15 *Journal of Corporate Finance* 66, 67, 78.

76 Gary Gorton, Matthias Kahl, and Richard Rosen, 'Eat or Be Eaten: A Theory of Mergers and Firm Size', *Working Paper* (University of Pennsylvania, 2009) 1, 3–4, 36 http://papers.ssrn.com/sol3/papers.cfm?abstract_id=713769 accessed 29 March 2018; Ajit Singh, 'Takeovers, Economic Natural Selection, and the Theory of the Firm: Evidence from the Post-War United Kingdom Experience' (1975) 85 *The Economic Journal* 497, 513.

Conyon, Martin J., et al., 'Do Hostile Mergers Destroy Jobs?' (2001) 45 *Journal of Economic Behaviour & Organization* 427.

Core, J. E., Robert W. Holthausen, and David F. Larcker, 'Corporate Governance, Chief Executive Officer Compensation, and Firm Performance' (1999) 51 *Journal of Financial Economics.*

Cotter, J. F., Ani Shivdasani, and Marc Zenner, 'Do Independent Directors Enhance Target Shareholder Wealth during Tender Offers?' (1997) 43 *Journal of Financial Economics* 195.

Cotter, J. F. and Marc Zenner, 'How Managerial Wealth Affects the Tender Offer Process' (1994) 35 *Journal of Financial Economics* 63.

Cuervo, A., 'Corporate Governance Mechanisms: A Plea for Less Code of Good Governance and More Market Control' (2002) 10 *Blackwell Publishers* 84.

Deangelo, H. and Linda Deangelo, 'Proxy Contests and the Governance of Publicly Held Corporations' (1989) 23 *Journal of Financial Economics* 29.

Deangelo, L. E., 'Managerial Competition, Information Costs and Corporate Governance: The Use of Accounting Performance Measures in Proxy Contests' (1988) 10 *Journal of Accounting and Economics* 3.

Dejnozka, J., 'Corporate Entity' 2007 1, 23 www.members.tripod.com/~Jan_Dejnozka/corporate_entity_book.pdf accessed 11 April 2018.

Demsetz, H. and Kenneth Lehn, 'The Structure of Corporate Ownership: Causes and Consequences' (1985) 93 *Journal of Political Economy* 1155.

DePamphilis, D. M., *Mergers, Acquisitions, and Other Restructuring Activities* (9th edn, London, UK, Elsevier, 2018).

Devers, C. E., et al., 'Executive Compensation: A Multidisciplinary Review of Recent Developments' (2007) 33 *Journal of Management* 1016.

Dobson, J., 'Size Matters: Why Managers Should Pursue Corporate Growth, Even at the Expense of Shareholder Value' (2004) 23 *Business and Professional Ethics Journal* 45.

Drucker, P., *Management Challenges for the 21st Century* (New York, Harper Business, 1999).

Easterwood, Cintia M., 'Takeovers and Incentives for Earnings Management: An Empirical Analysis' (1998) 14 *Journal of Applied Business Research* 29.

Easterbrook, F. H. and Daniel R. Fischel, 'The Corporate Contract' (1989) 89 *Columbia Law Review* 1416.

Easterbrook, F. H. and Daniel R. Fischel, 'Corporate Control Transactions' (1982) 91 *The Yale Law Journal* 698.

Easterbrook, F. H. and Daniel R. Fischel, *The Economic Structure of Corporate Law* (Cambridge, MA, Harvard University Press, 1991).

Fama, E. F., 'Agency Problems and the Theory of the Firm' (1980) 88 *Journal of Political Economy* 288.

Fama, E. F. and Michael C. Jensen, 'Agency Problems and Residual Claims' (1983) 26 *Journal of Law and Economics* 327.

Fapohunda, T. M., 'The Human Resources Management Challenges of Post Consolidation Mergers and Acquisitions in Nigeria's Banking Industry' (2012) 6 *International Business Management* 68.

Firth, M., 'Corporate Takeovers, Stockholder Returns and Executive Rewards' (1991) 12 *Managerial and Decision Economics* 421.

Firth, M., 'Takeovers, Shareholder Returns and the Theory of the Firm' (1980) 94 *The Quarterly Journal of Economics* 235.

Fischel, D. R., 'Efficient Capital Market Theory, the Market for Corporate Control and the Regulation of Cash Tender Offers' (1978) 57 *Texas Law Review* 1.

Fos, V., 'The Disciplinary Effects of Proxy Contests' (2011) 1 *Social Science Research Network* 17–19 http://ssrn.com/abstract=1705707 accessed 11 March 2018.

Franks, J. and Colin Mayer, 'Hostile Takeovers and the Correction of Managerial Failure' (1996) 40 *Journal of Financial Economics* 163.

Franks, J., Colin Mayer, and Luc Renneboog, 'Who Disciplines Management in Poorly Performing Companies?' (2001) 10 *Journal of Financial Intermediation* 209.

Friedman, M., *Capitalism and Freedom* (Chicago, University of Chicago Press, 1962).

Gleason, K. C., Leonard Rosenthal, and Roy A. Wiggins, III, 'Backing into Being Public: An Explanatory Analysis of Reverse Take-Overs' (2005) 12 *Journal of Corporate Finance* 54.

Gorton, G., Matthias Kahl, and Richard Rosen, 'Eat or Be Eaten: A Theory of Mergers and Firm Size', *Working Paper* (University of Pennsylvania, 2009) 1, 3–4 & 36 http://papers.ssrn.com/sol3/papers.cfm?abstract_id=713769 accessed 29 March 2018.

Grossman, Sanford J. and Oliver D. Hart, 'Takeover Bids, the Free-Rider Problem and the Theory of the Corporation' (1980) 11 *The Bell Journal of Economics* 42.

Habib, M. A. and Alexander Ljungqvist, 'Firm Value and Managerial Incentives: A Stochastic Frontier Approach' (2005) 78 *The Journal of Business* 2053.

Hamilton, R. W., 'Some Reflections on Cash Tender Offer Legislation' (1969) 15 *New York Law Forum* 269, 270.

Hancock, G. D., 'Battles for Control: An Overview of Proxy Contests' (1992) 18 *Managerial Finance* 59.

Hancock, G. D. and Mbodja Mougoue, 'The Impact of Financial Factors on Proxy Contest Outcomes' (1991) 18 *Journal of Business Finance & Accounting* 541.

Harris, M. and Artur Raviv, 'Corporate Control Contests and Capital Structure' (1986) 20 *Journal of Financial Economics* 55.

Harrison, J. S., et al., 'Synergies and Post-Acquisition Performance: Differences versus Similarities in Resource Allocations' (1991) 17 *Journal of Management* 173.

Hayes, S. L. and Russell A. Taussi, 'Tactics of Cash Takeover Bids' (1967) 45 *Harvard Business Review* 135.

Hill, C. W. L. and Thomas M. Jones, 'Stakeholder-Agency Theory' (1992) 29 *Journal of Management Studies* 131.

Hodgkinson, L. and Graham H. Partington, 'The Motivation for Takeovers in the UK' (2008) 35 *Journal of Business Finance & Accounting* 102.

Holl, P. and Dimitris Kyriazis, 'Agency, Bid Resistance and the Market for Corporate Control' (1997) 24 *Journal of Business Finance & Accounting* 1037.

Holmstrom, B., 'Pay without Performance and the Managerial Power Hypothesis: A Comment' (2005) 30 *Journal of Corporation Law* 703.

Ikenberry, D. and Josef Lakonishok, 'Corporate Governance through Proxy Contests: Evidence and Implications' (1993) 66 *The Journal of Business* 405.

Jarrell, G. A., 'The Wealth Effects of Litigation by Targets: Do Interests Diverge in a Merger' (1985) 28 *Journal of Law and Economics* 151.

Jarrell, G. A., James A. Brickley, and Jeffry M. Netter, 'The Market for Corporate Control: The Empirical Evidence since 1980' (1988) 2 *The Journal of Economic Perspectives* 49.

Jenkinson, T. and Colin Mayer, 'The Assessment: Corporate Governance and Corporate Control' (1992) 8 *Oxford Review of Economic Policy* 1.

Jensen, M. C., 'Agency Costs of Free Cash Flow, Corporate Finance, and Takeovers' (1986) 76 *The American Economic Review* 323.

Jensen, M. C., 'Takeovers: Folklore and Science' in Peter J. Buckley and Pervez N. Ghauri (eds.), *International Mergers and Acquisitions: A Reader* (London, Thomson, 2002) 71.

Jensen, M. C., 'Takeovers: Their Causes and Consequences' (1988) 2 *The Journal of Economic Perspectives* 21, 24.

Jensen, M. C. and William H. Meckling, 'Theory of the Firm: Managerial Behaviour, Agency Cost and Ownership Structure' (1976) 3 *Journal of Financial Economics* 305, 308.

Jenson, M. C. and Richard S. Ruback, 'The Market for Corporate Control: The Scientific Evidence' (1983) 11 *Journal of Financial Economics* 5.

Johnson, S. A., Harley E. Ryan, Jr., and Yisong S. Tian, 'Managerial Incentives and Corporate Fraud: The Sources of Incentives Matter' (2009) 13 *Review of Finance* 115.

Kerschbamer, R., 'Disciplinary Takeovers and Industry Effects' (1998) 7 *Journal of Economics & Management Strategy* 265.

Kini, O., William Kracaw, and Shehzad Mian, 'The Nature of Discipline by Corporate Takeovers' (2004) 59 *The Journal of Finance* 1511.

Klausner, M., 'The Contractarian Theory of Corporate Law: A Generation Later' (2006) *The Journal of Corporation Law* 779.

Knoeber, C. R., 'Golden Parachutes, Shark Repellents, and Hostile Tender Offers' (1986) 76 *The American Economic Review* 155.

Laudano, E., 'One Man's Junk Mail Is Another Man's Treasure: Proxy Contests and Corporate Governance' (2004) 3 *Connecticut Public Interest Law Journal* 430.

Lewellen, W., Claudio Loderer, and Kenneth Martin, 'Executive Compensation and Executive Incentive Problems: An Empirical Analysis' (1987) 9 *Journal of Accounting and Economics* 287.

Limmack, R. J., *Takeovers as a Disciplinary Mechanism?* (Advances in Mergers and Acquisitions, 1: Emerald Group Publishing Limited, Bingley UK 2000) 108.

Main, B. G. M., Charles A. O'Reilly, III, and James Wade, 'The CEO, the Board of Directors and Executive Compensation: Economic and Psychological Perspectives' (1995) 4 *Industrial and Corporate Change* 293.

Maleqadeh, A. R. and Victoria B. Mcwilliams, 'Managerial Efficiency and Share Ownership: The Market Reaction to Takeover Defenses' (1995) 11 *Journal of Applied Business Research* 48.

Malmendier, U. and Geoffrey Tate, 'Who Makes Acquisitions? CEO Overconfidence and the Market's Reaction' (2008) 89 *Journal of Financial Economics* 20.

Manne, H. G., 'Cash Tender Offers for Shares: A Reply to Chairman Cohen' (1967) *Duke Law Journal* 231.

Marquez, R. and Bilge Yilmaz, 'Information and Efficiency in Tender Offers' (2008) 76 *Journal of the Econometric Society* 1075.

Martin, K. J. and John J. Mcconnell, 'Corporate Performance, Corporate Takeovers and Management Turnover' (1991) 46 *The Journal of Finance* 671.

Masulis, R. W., Cong Wang, and Fei Xie, 'Corporate Governance and Acquirer Returns' (2007) 62 *The Journal of Finance* 1851.

Matsusaka, J. G., 'Takeover Motives during the Conglomerate Merger Wave' (1993) 24 *The Rand Journal of Economics* 357.

Mitchell, M. L. and Kenneth Lehn, 'Do Bad Bidders become Good Targets?' (1990) 98 *Journal of Political Economy* 372.

Moeller, S. B., Frederik P. Schlingemann, and René M. Stulz, 'Firm Size and the Gains from Acquisitions' (2004) 73 *Journal of Financial Economics* 201.

Moerland, P. W., 'Alternative Disciplinary Mechanisms in Different Corporate Systems' (1995) 26 *Journal of Economic Beghaviour and Organisation* 17.

Morck, R., Andrei Shleifer, and Robert W. Vishny, 'Alternative Mechanisms for Corporate Control' (1989) 79 *The American Economic Review* 842.

Morck, R., Andrei Shleifer, and Robert W. Vishny, 'Characteristics of Targets of Hostile and Friendly Takeovers' in Alan J. Auerbach (ed.), *Corporate Takeovers: Causes and Consequences* (Chicago, University of Chicago Press, 1988) 102.

Morck, R., Andrei Shleifer, and Robert W. Vishny, 'Do Managerial Objectives Drive Bad Acquisitions?' (1990) 45 *The Journal of Finance* 31.

Mulherin, H. J. and Annette B. Poulsen, 'Proxy Contests and Corporate Change: Implications for Shareholder Wealth' (1998) 47 *Journal of Financial Economics* 279.

Murphy, K. J., 'Corporate Performance and Managerial Remuneration an Empirical Analysis' (1985) 7 *Journal of Accounting and Economics* 11.

Niden, C. M., 'An Empirical Examination of White Knight Corporate Takeovers: Synergy and Overbidding' (1993) 22 *Financial Management* 28.

Offenberg, D., 'Firm Size and the Effectiveness of the Market for Corporte Control' (2009) 15 *Journal of Corporate Finance* 66.

Parkinson, J. E., 'The Contractual Theory of the Company and the Protection of Non-Shareholder Interests' in David Feldman and Franklin Meisel (eds.), *Corporate and Commercial Law: Modern Developments* (London, Lloyd's of London Press Ltd, 1996).

Patrone, M. R., 'Sour Chocolate: The UK Takeover Panel's Improper Reaction to Kraft's Acquisition of Cadbury' (2001) 8 *Brigham Young University International Law and Management Review* 64.

Pound, J., 'Proxy Contests and the Efficiency of Shareholder Oversight' (1988) 20 *Journal of Financial Economics* 237.

Queenan, J., 'The Proxy Wars: There Are More of Them and They Are Meaner' (1988) *Barrons.*

Raj, M. and Michael Forsyth, 'Hubris amongst UK Bidders and Losses to Shareholders' (2003) 8 *International Journal of Business* 2.

Ramezani, C. A., Luc Soenen, and Alan Jung, 'Growth, Corporate Profitability and Value Creation' (2002) 58 *Financial Analysts Journal* 56.

Reich, R. B., *The Next American Frontier* (New York, Times Books, 1983).

Ribstein, L. E., 'The Structure of the Fiduciary Relationship' No. LE03-003 *Illinois Law and Economics Working Papers Series* 19.

Richard, R. S., 'An Overview of Takeover Defenses' in Alan J. Auerbach (ed.), *Mergers and Acquisitions* (Chicago, University of Chicago Press, 1987).

Roll, R., 'The Hubris Hypothesis of Takeovers' (1986) 59 *The Journal of Business* 197.

Romano, R., 'A Guide to Takeovers: Theory, Evidence and Regulation' (1992) 19 *Yale Journal on Regulation* 119.

Rose, C., 'Stakeholder Orientation vs. Shareholder Value: A Matter of Contractual Failures' (2004) 18 *European Journal of Law and Economics* 77.

Ross, S. A., 'The Economic Theory of Agency: The Principals Problem' (1973) 63 *American Economic Association* 134.

Safieddine, A. and Sheridan Titman, 'Leverage and Corporate Performance: Evidence from Unsuccesful Takeovers' (1999) 54 *The Journal of Finance* 547.

Scharfstein, D., 'The Disciplinary Role of Takeovers' (1988) 55 *The Review of Economic Studies* 185.

Schwert, G. W., 'Hostility in Takeovers: In the Eyes of the Beholder?' (2000) 55 *The Journal of Finance* 2599, 2600.

Seidl, D., Paul Sanderson, and John Roberts, *Applying 'Comply or Explain': Conformance with Codes of Corporate Governance in the UK and Germany* (Cambridge, Centre for Business Research, University of Cambridge, 2009) 2 www.cbr.cam.ac.uk/fileadmin/user_upload/centre-for-business-research/downloads/working-papers/wp389.pdf accessed 12 March 2018.

Seyhun, N. H., 'Do Bidder Managers Knowingly Pay Too Much for Target Firms?' (1990) 63 *Journal of Business* 439.

Shelton, L. M., 'Strategic Business Fits and Corporate Aquisition: Empirical Evidence' (1988) 9 *Strategic Management Journal* 297.

Shleifer, A. and Lawrence H. Summers, 'Breach of Trust in Hostile Takeovers' in Alan J. Auerbach (ed.), *Corporate Takeovers: Causes and Consequences* (Chicago, University of Chicago Press, 1988) 34–35.

Shleifer, A. and Robert W. Vishny, 'Management Entrenchment: The Case of Manager-Specific Investments' (1989) 25 *Journal of Financial Economics* 123.

Shleifer, A. and Robert W. Vishny, 'Value Maximization and the Acquisition Process' (1988) 2 *Journal of Economic Perspectives* 7.

Singh, A., 'Takeovers, Economic Natural Selection, and the Theory of the Firm: Evidence from the Post-War United Kingdom Experience' (1975) 85 *The Economic Journal* 497.

Sinha, R., 'The Role of Hostile Takeovers in Corporate Governance' (2004) 14 *Applied Financial Economics* 1291.

Song, M. H. and Ralph A. Walkling, 'The Impact of Managerial Ownership on Acquisition Attempts and Target Sharegholder Wealth' (1993) 28 *The Journal of Finance and Quantitative Analysis* 439.

Stein, J. C., 'Takeover Threats and Managerial Myopia' (1988) 96 *Journal of Political Economy* 62, 63, 71.

Stone, K. V. W., 'Employees as Stakeholders under State Non-Shareholder Constituency Statutes' (1991–1992) 21 *Stetson Law Review* 45.

Subramanian, G., 'Takeover Defenses and Bargaining Power' (2005) 17 *Journal of Applied Corporate Finance* 85.

Turk, T. A., Jeremy Goh, and Candace E. Ybarra, 'The Effect of Takeover Defenses on Long Term and Short Term Analysts' Earnings Forecasts: The Case of Poison Pills' (2007) 4 *Corporate Ownership & Control* 127.

Varadarajan, P. R. and Paulette Dubofsky, 'Diversification and Measures of Performance: Additional Empirical Evidence' (1987) 30 *The Academy of Management Journal* 597.

Vinten, G., 'Employee Relations in Mergers and Acquisitions' (1993) 15 *Employee Relations* 47.

Walkling, R. A., 'Predicting Tender Offer Success: A Logistic Analysis' (1985) 20 *Journal of Financial and Quantitative Analysis* 461.
Walsh, J. P. and James K. Seward, 'On the Efficiency of Internal and External Corporate Control Mechanisms' (1990) 15 *Academy of Management Review* 421.
Weir, C., David Laing, and Phillip J. Mcknight, 'Internal and External Governance Mechanisms: Their Impact on the Performance of Large UK Public Companies' (2002) 29 *Journal of Business, Finance & Accounting* 579.
Weisbach, M. S., 'Corporate Governance and Hostile Takeovers' (1993) 16 *Journal of Accounting and Economics* 199.
Willcox, T. L., 'The Use and Abuse of Executive Powers in Warding Off Corporate Raiders' (1988) 7 *Journal of Business Ethics* 47.
Williamson, O. E., *The Economics of Discretionary Behaviour: Managerial Objective in a Theory of the Firm* (Chicago, Markham Publishing Company, 1964).

Part II

4 Takeover regulation in the United Kingdom

4.1 Introduction

This chapter examines the regulatory framework for takeovers in the United Kingdom, in relation to shareholder and employee interests. It identifies the extent to which shareholders are involved in decision-making during takeovers and the extent to which employee interests are incorporated into takeover arrangements.

First, the historical development of takeover regulation in the United Kingdom is examined, to ascertain the factors that led to the development of the takeover legal framework. Next, the regulatory mechanism for shareholder protection is evaluated. This is done by reference to the effects of takeovers on shareholders of acquiring and target companies. The objective is to determine the extent to which there is a difference in the scope of protection available to shareholders of acquiring and target companies. Then, the effects of takeovers on the employees of the combined company post-takeovers are examined before the conclusion.

4.2 The historical development of takeover regulation in the United Kingdom

During the nineteenth century, industries in Britain were mainly controlled and dominated by partnership and family-owned firms, which had the nature of a private entity. Afterwards, during the mid-twentieth century, there was a transformation of this ownership structure into a more competitive ownership structure, with a reduction in the concentration of ownership. This led to a greater level of control with ownership powers residing in larger corporations.[1] Despite the transformation of ownership structure which led to a rapid growth in the size of firms, the market for corporate control did not show much significant effect.

The post-war economic effects that heralded the need for investment opportunities led to the beginning of takeovers in the United Kingdom. The first

1 P. Sargant Florence, *Ownership, Control and Success of Large Corporations: An Analysis of English Industrial Structure and Policy 1936–1951* (London, Sweet & Maxwell Limited, 1961) 70–77.

takeover occurred in Britain in the early period of the 1950s. Before this period, the fusion of companies was known to occur only through amalgamation.[2] This scheme was essentially not a takeover because of the series of negotiations which lead to agreements between companies. However, if they were takeovers, they were generally not hostile.

The emergence of hostile takeovers in the United Kingdom was influenced by certain factors which created the opportunity for investors to access the value of the corporate assets of companies as against the properties of these companies. One such factor was the level of dividend payment. After the war, the government imposed a voluntary dividend restraint, whereby companies were prevented from paying dividends except in accordance with the rise in profit of the companies.[3] During this period, company managements did not consider it important to pay higher dividends as profits increased. The payments received as dividend did not generally reflect the rate of increase in company profits. Another factor which encouraged the emergence of hostile takeovers was the high undervaluation of corporate assets, including freehold and leasehold property, as well as quoted investments. Certain businessmen who had knowledge of the prevailing financial status of these companies took advantage of the situation. Knowing that the companies were grossly undervalued, they attempted to acquire control to reap the gains of the true value of the corporate assets of these companies.[4] The practise of restricted dividend payments and the economic downturn as an aftermath of the war caused a dwindling effect on the portfolio of a shoe company.[5] Its share price was substantially undervalued, but this did not reflect in the market share price because the value of corporate investment was determined by investors through dividend yields, rather than by share prices. In view of this, an investor[6] who had knowledge of the undervaluation made a tender offer directly to the shareholders of the company. The company's board attempted to convince shareholders to reject the bid by increasing the rate of dividend payment.[7] The majority of shareholders accepted the bid. This led to the first successful hostile takeover in the United Kingdom.

2 Known as 'the Scheme of Arrangement', under the *Companies Act, CAP 38* (1948). Sections 206 & 208 (as was applicable), now *Companies Act, CAP 46* (2006). S. 900.
3 Companies at that time were encouraged to reinvest their profits. See John Armour, Jack B. Jacobs, and Curtis J. Milhaupt, 'The Evolution of Hostile Takeover Regimes in Developed and Emerging Markets: An Analytical Framework' (2011) 52 *Harvard International Law Journal* 219, 233. Citing Edward Stamp and Christopher Marley, *Accounting Principles and the City Code: The Case for Reform* (London, Butterworth, 1970).
4 Ronald W. Moon, *Business Mergers and Takeover Bids* (5th edn, London, Gee & Co, 1976) 9–10.
5 The 'J. Sears Holdings'.
6 Charles Clore.
7 Higher dividend payment and re-valuation of the value of the firm was reported to have been successfully used by managements to gain shareholder support in an earlier hostile bid by Charles Clore. See John Armour and David A Skeel, 'Who Writes the Rules for Hostile Takeovers, and Why? The Peculiar Divergence of US and UK Takeover Regulation' (2006–2007) 95 *The GeorgeTown Law Journal* 1727, 1757.

Later in the same year, another corporate control contest occurred. An investment financial specialist[8] initiated a takeover bid. He commenced the purchase of a large number of shares in a company[9] which he intended to convert to commercial offices. In response to the bid, the board of directors of the company arranged that the company be sold to another company[10] and leased back to the directors, on the agreement that the company building should be used only for the purpose of a hotel business. Such terms were meant to frustrate the move of the investor since he intended to convert the hotel to commercial offices.

In the later part of 1958, two different investors[11] made separate bids to take over a British company.[12] Without the knowledge and input of the shareholders of the company, the company board rejected one of the bids and accepted the other bid. The company board effectively issued new shares which amounted to one-third of the shares in the company to the accepted bidder investor. The board of directors publicly revealed the deal only when the other investor whose bid was rejected by the board disclosed their intentions to deal directly with the shareholders of the company. The shareholders were furious and felt short-changed by the decisions of the management of the company. Efforts by the company board to appeal to the shareholders with dividends-increase failed. The shareholders sold their stocks to the opposing bidder. Just like other earlier takeovers, the shareholders were not consulted by managements. The problems which occurred during this period include: the unequal treatment of shareholders, information asymmetries, the inadequacy of shareholder remedies and asset-stripping activities by bidders.[13]

The incidents that led to these takeovers showed that company shareholders have not been generally treated fairly. In the first three hostile takeovers in the United Kingdom, shareholders had to oppose the decisions of management. Shareholder disenchantment appears to originate from the fact that when managers are meant to act with absolute discretion, there is no guarantee that their discretion will be exercised in favour of shareholders. Hence, in the United Kingdom, the market for corporate control from the early period has been characterised with a contest; first, between company managements and bidders and, second, between managements and their shareholders.

From the early period of takeovers, it appears that the interests of company employees were not incorporated into takeover arrangements. In one of the takeover attempts, the bidders sought to take over a hotel with the intention of converting the hotel premises into commercial offices – Savoy Hotel Limited. If the bid was successful, several employees may have been disengaged since the

8 'Harold Samuel'.
9 'Savoy Hotel Limited'.
10 'Worcester (London) Co. Ltd.'
11 Reynolds Metal Company in partnership with U.K.-based Tube Investments. ('TI-Reynolds') and the Aluminium Company of America (ALCOA).
12 'British Aluminium Ltd'.
13 John H. Farrar, *Takeovers, Institutional Investors and Modernization of Corporate Laws* (Oxford, University Press, 1993) 6.

office spaces would be offered for rent. It is not clear whether the management of the hotel defended the bid in the interest of the employees or for their own personal interest since their services would not also be needed post-takeover. The conduct of company management during corporate control contests, as shown in the early periods of takeovers in the UK, informed the need for takeovers to be regulated.[14] A committee was inaugurated to administer takeovers. However, further conflicts between managements and shareholders necessitated the need for a more effective regulatory mechanism. Thus, the Takeover Panel was inaugurated to administer takeovers in the United Kingdom.[15]

4.3 Shareholder protection

Much of the conflicts which arise during corporate takeovers are between shareholders and corporate managements. The decision of company shareholders to accept or reject a takeover bid from outside investors may be impeded by company managements.[16] Also, the decision to commence a takeover bid may be made without a high prospect of enhancing the economic value of acquiring companies.

4.3.1 Shareholders of target companies

From the time of the early development of takeovers in the UK, decisions of company management to accept or reject takeover bids have conflicted largely with the interests of their shareholders. This led to the establishment of the non-frustration rule.[17] The rule seeks to exclude managements from interfering with a bid or making any decision on a bid without the prior authorisation of the general meeting of the shareholders. It is aimed at ensuring board neutrality when a takeover bid crystallises. Although, this is aimed at protecting the property rights of shareholders during takeovers, the agency problems of conflict of interests may still persist.

The non-frustration rule of takeovers as embodied in the *EU Takeover Directive* and *The City Code on Takeovers* prohibits managerial positive actions when a bid is made. The management board of a company is required not to do anything which may indicate that a bid is accepted or rejected without the authority of the shareholders of the company. They are also not required to do anything to enhance the interests of shareholders, except to the extent of outsourcing independent advice on the fairness of a bid which should be communicated to shareholders.[18] The

14 See note 7, 1758.

15 The authority of the Takeover Panel to administer takeovers and other related matters in the UK is derived from the *Companies Act 2006*, ss 942–943.

16 In The UK, management cannot make any final decision to accept or reject a bid without the approval of shareholders. See *The City Code on Takeovers and Mergers, 2016*, Rule 21, section A1, B1 General Principles 2 and 3; Directive 2004/25/EC of the European Parliament and of the Council of 21 April 2004 on takeover bids (*EU Takeover Directive*) art. 9.

17 Ibid. See also the mandatory bid rule, which seeks to ensure that shareholders in target companies are generally treated fairly when a takeover is made in certain circumstances – *UK Takeover Code*, Rule 9.

18 *UK Takeover Code*, Rule 3.1.

objective of this approach is to restrict the functions of management during takeovers to advisory roles to prevent managements from influencing the outcomes of bids. However, since management is merely required to advise shareholders on the implications of accepting or rejecting a bid, without any independent mechanism for determining the value of such advice, it is difficult to assess the value of such advice. Thus, advice on takeover bids that is provided by management may be influenced by personal interests since they are aware that such advice is not subject to review. This is capable of misleading shareholders in view of the fact that managerial recommendations[19] of whether to accept or reject a takeover bid may largely determine the outcome of takeovers.[20] It was observed that the substance of such independent advice may not be free from managerial influence.[21] This is an indication that restricting the role of company management to advisory roles for the purpose of limiting their influence over takeovers is not an absolute guarantee that they would not influence takeover decisions.

The non-frustration rule may not apply to pre-bid defences.[22] The objective of the rule is that the target board should refrain from taking any action as soon as the takeover bids have been made.[23] This means that managements of target companies are not prevented from taking or omitting to take any action which may determine the effects of takeover bids. Provided that, such act or omission occurred before any takeover bid has actually been made or before any bid is even imminent. Imminent bids can arguably be defined as bids that have not yet been made but are based on speculations that an investor may likely make an attempt to acquire the company. Management of target companies can undermine the effect of this rule by establishing mechanisms which preexist bids. Some of the mechanisms that may be adopted include employment contracts which provide for lucrative compensation packages if there is a change in control leading to termination of their appointment. Although corporate governance rules recommend that payment of remuneration should be linked to performance, it also recommended that adequate payments should be made to attract the best persons for the job.[24]

19 The recommendation could be based on the characteristics and composition of boards. See generally Noel O'sullivan and Pauline Wong, 'Board Composition, Ownership Structure and Hostile Takeovers: Some UK Evidence' (1999) 29 *Accounting and Business Research* 139. See James F. Cotter, Ani Shivdasani, and Marc Zenner, 'Do Independent Directors Enhance Target Shareholder Wealth During Tender Offers?' (1997) 43 *Journal of Financial Economics* 195, 196.

20 See Blanaid Clarke, 'The Takeover Directive: Is a Little Regulation Better Than No Regulation?' (2009) 15 *European Law Journal* 174, 188. Citing Peter Holl and Dimitris Kyriazis, 'The Determinants of Outcome in UK Takeover Bids' (1996) *International Journal of Economics and Business* 165.

21 See generally Darren Henry, 'Directors' Recommendations in Takeovers: An Agency and Governance Analysis' (2005) 32 *Journal of Business Finance & Accounting* 129.

22 The *EU Takeover Directive*, art. 9(3) may not apply to pre bid defences in light of the provisions of art 6(1).

23 See particularly The *EU Takeover Directive*, para 2, and art. 9(2); *UK Takeover Code* B1 General Principles 3.

24 See *UK Corporate Governance Code 2018* (5 Remuneration). This provision can encourage shareholders to vote against 'unreasonable' remuneration policies. However, binding

Other measures include adopting a staggered board appointment procedure or issuance of dual class voting stock. It appears that most of the managerial entrenchment techniques outlined have been largely restricted by company law and corporate governance principles.[25] The restrictions may not be very effective, in view of the fact that they are only generally applicable to regulate the relationship between the board and company shareholders as agents and principals respectively.[26] For example, the requirement to publish directors' remuneration may not meet the desired objective, since it has no effect on the validity of the already concluded contracts between the company and director. Since companies cannot be compelled to reduce levels of compensations, this has the effect of making takeovers much more expensive for the acquiring companies. Also, negotiation for remuneration is usually held between the company hierarchy and the prospective executive. The company executive must convince the shareholders to vote in support of the remuneration or risk losing the services of the executive to a rival company.

Operative rules which are aimed at preserving the interests of shareholders may nevertheless give the target management the opportunity to influence takeover bids. Rules which require companies to disclose the identities of the beneficial owners of voting shares have been suggested to be capable of giving management extended time to devise accepted means of opposing bids.[27] One such means is the use of white knights[28] which is permissible by the rules. The use of white knight may indicate that managements are interfering with the property rights of shareholders to decide on the merit of the bid. The first bidder may be frustrated by competition despite having incurred certain costs in furtherance of the bid, as a result of the white knight that is sought by the target board. It was suggested[29] that the use of white knights by target boards may be controlled by making directors enter into contracts 'not to seek' white knights, followed by a commitment from the target company by way of an agreed fee for compensation for costs incurred if defeated by the rival. This may undermine competition and free market. It implies that the emergence of a genuine competitor which may not actually be a white knight would require the payment of compensation to the first

---

shareholder votes on executive pay are limited to listed companies only. See *The Enterprise and Regulatory Reforms Act 2013*, s 79.

25 Shareholders' approval is required to issue new shares, dual-class voting stock is largely unsupported by institutional shareholders and staggered boards mechanisms are rendered ineffective in view of the fact that shareholders can remove directors at any time. See *Companies Act 2006*, s 168. Also, it is required that companies publish remuneration of directors and other executives for shareholder scrutiny. See note 7, 1736–1737.

26 Reinier Kraakman et al., *The Anatomy of Corporate Law: A Comparative and Functional Approach* (2nd edn, New York, Oxford University Press, 2009) 247.

27 Ibid. 236.

28 Han-Wei Liu, 'The Non-Frustration Rule of the UK City Code on Takeover and Mergers and Related Agency Problems: What Are the Implications for the EC Takeover Directive' (2010–2011) 17 *The Columbia Journal of European Law* 5, 9.

29 See note 26, 237–238.

bidder. Once the offeror announces their bid, other potential acquirers become aware of the target's identity, which may lead to competitive bids in the same way as if a white knight has been sought.[30]

The non-frustration rule, which seeks to give decision-making powers to company shareholders, can mitigate the agency problems. The view that company directors should contract not to seek white knights to protect first bidders and shareholders' interests may not achieve the desired objective. This could make takeovers more expensive. Investors should not expect to succeed in a bid merely because they were the first bidders. Competition is a market characteristic. Also, shareholder value can be enhanced where competition for their shares is allowed to thrive since it can lead to enhanced premiums. The presence or invitation of white knights has the same effects as genuine bid competitors who become aware of the existence of a target company by virtue of the announcement of a bid. Thus, the use of white knights remains an ideal option for management of the target company to frustrate takeover attempts from unwanted bidders.

The underlying objective of takeover regulations in the UK – under the *EU Takeover Directive* and the *UK Takeover Code* – is to protect the property rights of shareholders. This also forms the basis for regulating takeovers in some other jurisdictions, including the EU countries which are expected to apply the *EU Takeover Directive.* This objective applies to different regulatory frameworks because takeovers can have similar challenges in different jurisdictions. The same categories of corporate interests are largely affected: shareholders, employees, managements, amongst others. Also, takeovers in any of these jurisdictions, including the UK, can lead to either one or more of synergistic gains, disciplinary functions or hubris. Thus, the regulatory functions of takeovers in different jurisdictions can have similar functions since they generally seek to ensure that an efficient market where property rights in shares can be freely exercised.

The non-frustration rule seeks to ensure that shareholders of target companies determine how control over their property rights in shares can be exercised, free from managerial manipulation and control. This can strengthen the role of the market for corporate control by ensuring that the disciplinary role of takeovers and synergistic gains are not impeded by managements. From the account of the historical development of takeovers in the UK, it can be observed that the main challenges that were experienced during takeovers were caused by agency relationship between shareholders and managements. The agency problems were manifested in the form of conflict of interests. This influenced the creation of the non-frustration rule, to ensure that managements are confined to the objective of their roles. It also shows that even though company managements owe their duty to their company directly, the importance of the property rights of shareholders cannot be denied when managements exercise this duty, especially during

30 Frank H. Easterbrook and Daniel R. Fischel, 'The Proper Role of a Target's Management in Responding to a Tender Offer' (1981) 94 *Harvard Law Review* 1161, 1178.

takeovers. Thus, the property rights of shareholders can largely be protected and preserved where the agency conflicts that are caused by agency relationship are mitigated by takeover regulations such as the 'non-frustration rule'.

Meanwhile, the decision to make a bid is as important as the decision to accept or reject a bid. Companies make acquisitions for several reasons; it is not clear whether shareholders of acquiring companies are actively involved in the decision to make bids. This is examined next.

4.3.2 Shareholders of acquiring companies

Shareholders of acquiring companies face nearly as many challenges as those of target companies. It is not clear whether there are sufficient measures for protecting their interests during takeovers.[31]

In certain exceptional circumstances, the approval of the shareholders of acquiring companies may be required. Where a listed company with premium listing[32] seeks to acquire another company, by issuing securities as consideration, shareholder approval must be sought and obtained if the takeover transaction is considered as a 'class 1' transaction.[33] 'Class 1' transactions are those transactions in which any of the following ratios, expressed as a percentage, is 25% or more:[34]

a) the gross assets of the offeree divided by the gross assets of the offeror;
b) the net pre-tax profits of the offeree divided by the net pre-tax profits of the offeror;
c) the consideration divided by the aggregate market value of all of the offeror's ordinary shares; and
d) the gross capital of the offeree divided by the gross capital of the offeror.

Also, shareholder approval is required where a listed company acquires a business, an unlisted company or assets where any of the above percentage ratios is 100% or more or where such acquisition would result in a fundamental change in the business or in a change in board or voting control of the offeror.[35]

This requirement for shareholder approval is limited to transactions of the volumes indicated and this means that the size of the target company should be

31 Offerors may include individual investors and corporate entities. This book is concerned with offerors as corporate entities during takeovers.

32 Premium listing is one of the routes to trading on the main market in the Official List of the UK Listing authority. Companies trading on the London Stock Exchange with premium listings comply with the UK highest standards of regulation and corporate governance beyond the requirement of the EU regulations. The premium listing segment is open to commercial companies and investment entities wishing to list equity shares only.

33 The *United Kingdom Listing Rules 10.5*. See Slaughter and May, 'A Guide to Takeovers in the United Kingdom' www.slaughterandmay.com/media/39320/a-guide-to-takeovers-in-the-united-kingdom.pdf accessed 10 December 2018, 45.

34 *UK Listing Rules 10.2 (3), R 10 (annex 1.1) (1G).*

35 See *UK Listing Rules 5.6.3, 5.6.4.*

at least 25% smaller than the size of the acquiring company. It implies that target companies in these kinds of transactions are relatively medium-sized companies. This means that the requirement for shareholder approval is restricted. The approval is not generally required when a listed company is involved in a takeover. What is required is that, first, the acquiring company must be a listed company with a premium listing; second, the size of the acquirer should exceed the target company by at least 25% or more,[36] or 100% in reverse takeovers.[37]

This requirement for shareholder approval may not sufficiently challenge the roles of management of acquiring companies during takeovers. It applies to those categories of takeovers that would ordinarily draw the attention of the shareholders of acquiring companies in view of the size of the target. Also, since takeovers that fall into these categories do not occur frequently, it appears to indicate that takeovers generally should be considered to be a usual investment decision for which managements should be responsible for making.

During negotiations for the takeover of *Cadbury* by *Kraft*, one of the shareholders of *Kraft* indicated his opposition to the deal, but because of the inability of the shareholder to vote on the issue, he could not successfully challenge the acquisition.[38] The growing concern that shareholders of acquiring companies should be made to approve takeovers have not been given the needed consideration.[39] The Takeover Panel suggested that protection is not extended to the shareholders of the acquiring companies mainly because of the following reasons. First, shareholders can avail themselves of the protection offered by company law and other regulatory rules (such as contract law). Second, the code would be made to apply to foreign acquirers. Third, some acquirers may be single investors with no shareholders and finally that it might provide offerors who subsequently wished to avoid an offer the opportunity to delay the bid without having to prove materiality as required under r. 13.4(a).[40]

In response to the concerns outlined, first, the extent to which shareholders of acquiring companies can rely on company law and other regulatory mechanisms to protect their interests is limited. A reference to such remedies would be by way of a response to unproductive acquisitions by seeking remedies, rather than preventing such acquisitions. Second, the application of the code to foreign acquirers would not likely create problems because the approval from the panel

36 Note 33 Slaughter And May, 5.

37 *UK Listing Rules 5.6.3.*

38 Warren Buffet who owned 9.4% stakes in Kraft indicated that he would block the deal if he could. See: *The Guardian* report www.theguardian.com/business/2010/jan/20/warren-buffett-blasts-kraft-cadbury accessed 19 April 2018.

39 The Institute of Directors recommended that significant takeover transactions should be preceded by shareholder approval, partly because many takeovers do not lead to expected synergies. See the Institute of Directors 'Review of Certain Aspects of the Regulation of Takeover Bids' July 2010 www.iod.com/mainwebsite/resources/Document/Takeover_Panel_Review_0710.pdf accessed 11 January 2018.

40 See Blanaid Clarke, 'Reviewing Takeover Regulation in the Wake of Cadbury Acquisition: Regulation in a Twirl' (2011) 3 *Journal of Business Law* 298, 307–308.

would simply be based on the fact that the acquisition has been approved by the shareholders and it is not meant to serve managerial interests. Third, where an acquirer is a single investor, the approval of the investor would suffice. Last, delays that are not related to materiality can be avoided when provision is made for shareholder approval to be obtained within a specific time. Thus, the case for protecting acquiring shareholders remains valid despite the reasons stated by the Takeover Panel.

Takeover regulation is mainly focused on protecting the property rights of target company shareholders. Gains to acquirers are neither certain nor immediate, apparently because of the high costs of acquisitions. Shareholders of acquiring companies must retain their shares in the company until such a time that synergy from the acquisition materialises.[41] In view of the fact that the existing takeover regulations in the United Kingdom are mainly designed for the protection of the shareholders of target companies,[42] certain assumptions are inevitable.

i) Are shareholders of acquiring companies protected from opportunistic behaviour of management?

The standard required for the conduct of company boards of acquiring companies is not specifically outlined in the *Takeover Code*, thus reference may be made to the general duties of directors.[43] Some of the duties that may apply are briefly examined.

The assumption that shareholders of acquiring companies have adequate protective measures may be derived from the duties of company directors. Only a few of these duties are arguably applicable to takeovers, and these include: the duty to promote the success of the company, the duty to exercise reasonable care, skill and diligence and more specifically the duty to avoid conflict of interests.[44]

A) THE DUTY TO PROMOTE THE SUCCESS OF THE COMPANY

In the discharge of their responsibilities, company directors are required to act in the way that they consider in good faith would promote the success of the company for the benefit of the members as a whole.[45] For purposes of takeovers, it

41 Tiernan Fitzgibbon, 'An Analysis of the Takeover Code's Treatment of an Acquiring Company's Shareholders: Stealing from the Rich to Give to the Already Wealthy?' (2010) 2 *King's Student Law Review* 51, 58. See also, Marina Martynova and Luc Renneboog, 'Mergers and Acquisitions in Europe' *Finance Working Paper*, No. 114 (2006) 1–83.

42 This is clearly indicated in these regulations. See the *EU Takeover Directive*, para (2), the *City Code on Takeover*, s A (1) 2 (a).

43 *Companies Act 2006*, ss 171–177.

44 *Companies Act 2006*, ss 172, 174, 175.

45 Their role is to be observed by reference to the enlightened shareholder value. They are required to consider the interests of certain stakeholders. However, this duty is required to be performed to the extent that it confers benefit on the members of the company. It is unlikely to include non-shareholder interests, except a winding-up is imminent. See Leonard Sealy,

may be contended that this duty requires the board to engage in acquisitions that would enhance the economic interests of the company and their shareholders. This means that corporate management should not merely focus on expanding corporate investments while making acquisitions, they should engage in acquisitions for the purposes of expanding corporate investments as well as ensuring a corresponding increase in corporate wealth.[46] It would likely be challenging to rely on this duty to hold directors to account for unproductive takeovers in view of the fact that the duty is defined by reference to *what the directors* consider to be in good faith. The ways in which the directors are to go about their duties in promoting the interests of their shareholders is relative. Although *what the directors consider to be in good faith* may be judged by reference to what a reasonable director of similar company would do in the circumstance, the duty would likely be dependent on the ways the directors themselves consider to be ideal in their own judgement. It is expected that the extent to which an investment decision will enhance the interests of the company members should be largely reflected on the effectiveness of the decision and the likelihood of added value. This is different from what the directors may merely consider to be ideal as provided in the Act. In light of this, recourse to this duty may not be helpful.

B) THE DUTY TO EXERCISE REASONABLE CARE, SKILL AND DILIGENCE

The duty to exercise reasonable care, skill and diligence requires company boards to exhibit a certain level of standard in the performance of their duties. Earlier, this duty was required to be interpreted subjectively. The level of duty of care and skill which was to be expected from company directors was limited to the knowledge and experience that directors could reasonably be expected to exhibit and no more.[47] The standard of the duty has been extended from subjective application to include objective interpretation. A director is required to exhibit the care, skill and diligence that would be exercised by a reasonable and diligent person. This means that a director is expected to have the general knowledge, skill and experience that may reasonably be expected of someone carrying out the same functions as the particular director in relation to the company. Also, the general knowledge, skill and experience that the director actually has may also be relevant. It has been suggested that the standard of these forms of duty – the general knowledge, skill or experience of a usual director or the director's actual skill – apply to the one that is higher.[48] Since the level of diligence which is required

'"Bona Fides" and "Proper Purposes" in Corporate Decisions' (1989) 15 *Monash University Law Review* 265, 269–271.

46 David Kershaw, *Principles of Takeover Regulation* (Oxford, Oxford University Press, 2016) 302–303. More corporate investments can lead to larger corporate size. This may not necessarily enhance the value of shareholders.

47 *City Equitable Fire Insurance Co. Re* (1925) *Ch.* 407. *Romer J.*

48 Peter Loose, Michael Griffiths, and David Impey, *The Company Director: Powers, Duties and Liabilities* (11th edn, Bristol, Jordan Publishing Limited, 2011) 24.

from company directors is determined by reference to objective standard, the absence of objectivity in the discharge of their responsibilities as directors may be considered as negligent conduct. In *D'Jan of London Ltd*,[49] a director who signed an insurance proposal form without checking its contents was regarded as negligent. Also, in *Westlowe Storage and Distribution Ltd*,[50] a director who failed to ensure that the company benefited properly from a transaction it was engaged in when it was his responsibility to ensure that a proper accounting system was in place was held to have been negligent. This means that directors are expected to exhibit the standard which is expected of an objective director, whether or not they have such skill or experience and they may be held liable for negligence where they fail to act accordingly.[51]

Whether company directors may be held liable in breach of this duty during takeovers is unclear. Since they are expected to perform their functions as directors according to a higher objective standard, it is imperative that directors of acquiring companies ensure that the decision to expand corporate investment through acquisitions is done prudently. In complying with the requirement of this duty, the board should make acquisition decisions that may reasonably be adjudged as the best decision taken in the interests of the company and its shareholders.[52] This duty does not only apply to negligent conduct of directors, it also applies to omissions that amount to failing to act to protect the interests of the company. For example, a director can be held liable for failing to demonstrate sufficient attention to the affairs of the company, especially where such attention could potentially have prevented losses suffered by the conduct of other member(s) of the board.[53] But a director who makes a decision to the best of his ability by acting on appropriate legal advice may not be regarded as having acted negligently.[54] However, where directors breach their duty by failing to act reasonably and lawfully, any advice obtained in the process of their decision would not justify their misconduct.[55] Despite the extensive scope of this duty, it is unlikely for directors who negligently cause loses by virtue of needless and unproductive acquisitions to be held liable. First, the duty is owed to the company.[56] Second, the specific negligent conduct may be difficult to establish against the board after the acquisition has been concluded.

For example, it would have to be proved that directors intentionally set out to make acquisitions for purposes that would not promote corporate value.[57]

49 *D'Jan of London Ltd*, [1993] BCC 646.
50 *Westlowe Storage and Distribution Ltd*, [2000], BCC 851.
51 Stephen Girvin, Sandra Frisby, and Alastair Hudson, *Charlesworth's Company Law* (18th edn, London, Sweet & Maxwell, 2010) 336.
52 Losses to offeror companies post-takeover can be avoided or mitigated if this duty applies in relation to takeovers.
53 *Lexi Holdings Plc. v Luqman* [2009] EWHC Civ 117.
54 *Green v Walkling* [2007] EWHC 3251.
55 *John Bairstow v Queens Moat Houses Plc* [2000] BCC 1025.
56 *Companies Act 2006*, s 170(1).
57 Such as 'empire building' acquisition objectives, to expand the control size of the managers.

The major problem of takeovers that undermine the interests of shareholders of acquiring companies is associated with high costs of acquisitions. The high costs that are expended on takeovers can increase target shareholder value while acquiring shareholders may experience losses, zero or insignificant gains. It is unclear whether managements anticipate the high costs that they expend on acquisitions, especially as they are expected to manage corporate investments in the manner that would mitigate transaction costs. Since transaction cost economics suggest that transactions should be conducted in the least possible costs, managements should ideally consider the costs of acquisitions relative to the expected gains that can be made towards enhancing corporate value. Because of the challenge of conflicts of interest which characterises agency relationships between shareholders and managements, the role of managements can be largely unpredictable. Hence, it may be practicable to prevent directors from making unproductive acquisitions rather than making directors accountable for unproductive acquisitions by reference to the duty of care, skill and diligence.

C) THE DUTY TO AVOID CONFLICT OF INTERESTS

This duty applies to all aspects of decision-making by the board, including takeovers. The duty is particularly important when applied to acquisitions made by company management. Managers may pursue acquisitions even when such acquisitions are only capable of ensuring long-term gains, irrespective of whether or not the management have any special expertise in running the acquired businesses.[58] This has the capacity of depriving the immediate shareholders of the expected gains from their investments. In *Aberdeen Railway Co. v Blaikie Bros*,[59] it was observed that no one having – fiduciary – duties to discharge shall be allowed to enter into engagements in which he has or can have personal interest conflicting with or which may possibly conflict with the interests of those of whom he is bound to protect.

Restricting certain management functions may stifle entrepreneurial activities in a company,[60] however, managements can engage in conducts that are opportunistic.[61] In light of the potentials for conflict of interests, it is reasonable to review managerial decisions relating to takeovers. Even though this may not eliminate the chances of management pursuing their own objective, it has the capacity to strengthen the duty to avoid conflict of interests.[62]

58 Andrei Shleifer and Robert W Vishny, 'Value Maximization and the Acquisition Process' (1988) 2 *Journal of Economic Perspectives* 7, 14.
59 [1854] 1 Macq H.L. 461, 471.
60 Company Law Review Steering Group, Modern Company Law for a Competitive Economy (Final Report vol 1 2001) Para 3.23.
61 Brenda Hannigan, 'Reconfiguring the No Conflict Rule: Judicial Strictures, a Statutory Restatement and the Opportunistic Director' (2011) 23 *Singapore Academy of Law Journal* 714, 743.
62 Brenda Hannigan, *Company Law* (5th edn, Oxford, Oxford University Press, 2018) 274–278.

The relevant directors' duties that have been examined only provide apparent guarantee to shareholders that acquisitions made by managements would enhance corporate value and ultimately promote shareholder interests. The general duties of directors are stated to be owed to the company, not to shareholders.[63] Also, the extent to which the duty may be distinguished for the purpose of determining whether the duty in a particular circumstance is owed to the company or to shareholders was considered in *Peskin v Anderson*.[64] The fiduciary duties which are owed by directors to a company were distinguished from the fiduciary duties which are owed to shareholders which arise out of a 'special factual relationship' between the directors and the shareholders. It was stated that directors duties which are owed to individual shareholders and not to the company would have to arise where directors place themselves as against shareholders individually in one of the established legal relationships to which fiduciary duties are attached.[65] This includes agency relationship,[66] in which directors are authorised to sell shares in a takeover bid.[67] Despite the 'special relationship' exception, which operates to make directors' duties in particular circumstances to be owed to shareholders rather than the company, the scope of application of such special relationship is unclear. There are no clear parameters for determining when such relationship arises, and each case may be decided based on its specific facts. It has been suggested to apply in cases where the company is small or family-owned rather than companies with large shareholding.[68] Alternatively, such relationship has been stated to exist in companies with large shareholding in circumstances where advice is given by directors in the course of a takeover bid. In *a Company*,[69] it was observed that where directors offer advice to shareholders on a bid, they must do so with a view to enabling the shareholders to obtain the best bargain which is obtainable and not to promote the bids which the directors themselves are favourable to. Although these cases dealt with the relationship between directors and shareholders in a target company, they nevertheless apply *mutatis mutandis* to acquiring companies. The underlying objective of the declared relationship is that the decisions of directors during takeovers have direct impact on the economic interests of the shareholders of their companies, whether target or acquiring companies.

Meanwhile, in the event of a significant loss leading to divestitures, the duties can only be enforced on behalf of the company after the losses may have occurred since personal interests cannot be anticipated but only detected afterwards. Also, it is doubtful whether the court would allow itself to be drawn into such dispute. Courts

63 *Companies Act 2006*, s 170. *Percival v Wright* [1902] 2 Ch 421. *Towcester Racecourse Co. Ltd v The Racecourse Association Ltd* [2003] 1 BCLR 260. Leonard Sealy and Sarah Worthington, *Sealy and Worthington's Cases and Materials in Company Law* (11th edn, Oxford, Oxford University Press, 2016) 336–341.

64 *Peskin v Anderson* [2001] 1 BCLC 372. at 379, Mummery L.J.

65 See also *Bank v Sharp* [2015] EWHC 3220 (ch).

66 Paul Davies (ed.), *Gower and Davies Principles of Modern Company Law* (10th edn, London, Sweet and Maxwell, 2016) Chapter 16 generally.

67 *Briess v Woolley* [1954] A.C. 333, HL; *Allen v Hyett* [1914] 30 T.L.R. 444, PC.

68 Note 62, 183. See *Coleman v Myers* [1977] 2 N.Z.L.R. 225 CA (NZ).

69 *Re a Company* [1986] BCLC 382 Hoffmann J.

are reluctant in second-guessing investment decisions of managers.[70] It is particularly difficult where such decisions were made in the discharge of their duties in the ordinary course of enforcing the business objectives of the company as a going concern.

From the foregoing, it appears that shareholders of acquiring companies are not protected from managerial domineering roles during takeovers. By reference to the general duties of directors under the Act, it is doubtful whether shareholders can be protected. Hence, the extent to which corporate acquisitions can enhance the value of shareholders of acquiring companies is largely dependent on the objectives of managements. Since the role of managements can be influenced by agency conflicts, there is the need for effective takeover regulations to protect the property rights of acquiring shareholders.

ii) Do shareholders of acquiring companies always record gains from takeovers?

The effects of a takeover[71] may determine the actual motives or objectives that influenced the takeover. Generally, hostile takeovers have disciplinary character,[72] in view of the fact that the management board of target companies are less likely to be retained post-takeover. Although the disciplinary function of takeovers has been largely mooted,[73] the benefit of this function may not be shared by the shareholders of acquiring companies. The disciplinary role of takeovers is primarily beneficial to the shareholders of the target companies, since their 'poorly performing' management board are often dismissed post-takeover and their anticipated exit enhances the opportunity of shareholders to sell their shares to the acquirer.

Although, synergistic gains in takeovers are expected when a combination of the resources of the acquiring and target companies form a pool of resources,[74] it is not guaranteed.

Figures 4.1 and 4.2 show the relative levels of M&A activities in the United Kingdom. They indicate that M&A were at their highest points during the periods of 1998–2001.

70 *ARB International Ltd v Baillie* [2013] EWHC 2060 (Comm), *Regentcrest Plc v Cohen* [2001] BCC 494, *Moxon v Litchfield* [2013] EWHC 3957. The attitude of the courts towards the rights and duties of corporate participants is to defer to the contract terms and related arrangements which the participants have made. See Brian R Cheffins, *Company Law: Theory, Structure and Operation* (New York, Oxford University Press, 2000) 322.

71 These have been examined in details in Chapter 3, section 3.4. When managers make acquisitions, they often indicate that the acquisition is influenced by synergy. However, the extent to which an acquisition is actually influenced by synergy can only be determined post-takeovers; when the added value to shareholder and corporate wealth is determined.

72 Randall Morck, Andrei Shleifer, and Robert W. Vishny, 'Characteristics of Targets of Hostile and Friendly Takeovers' in Alan J. Auerbach (ed.), *Corporate Takeovers: Causes and Consequences* (Chicago, IL, University of Chicago Press, 1988) 102.

73 R. A. Brealey, S. C. Myers, and F. Allen, *Principles of Corporate Finance* (New York: McGraw-Hill/Irwin, 2008) 887; David Scharfstein, 'The Disciplinary Role of Takeovers' (1988) 55 *The Review of Economic Studies* 185, 192.

74 See generally Michael Bradley, Anand Desai, and E. Han Kim, 'Synergistic Gains from Corporate Acquisitions and Their Division between the Stockholders of Target and Acquiring Firms' (1988) 21 *Journal of Financial Economics* 3.

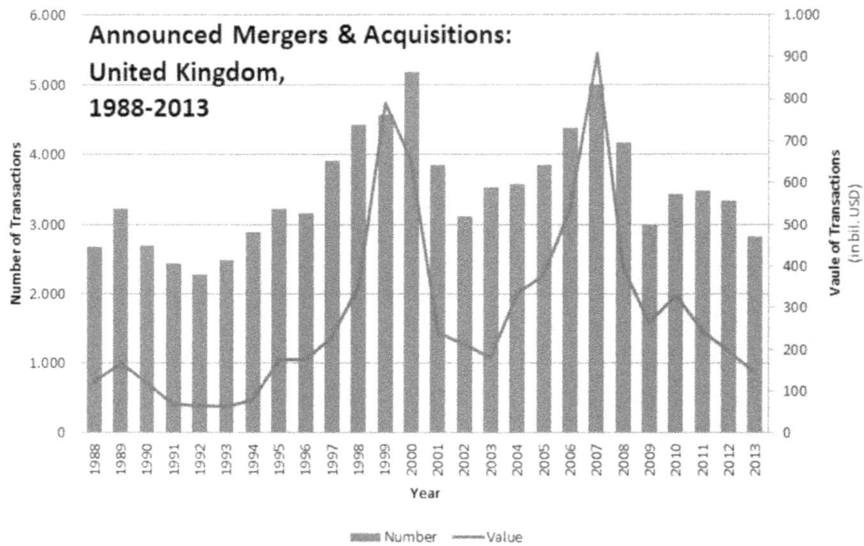

Figure 4.1 Statistics of Announced Mergers and Acquisitions in the United Kingdom 1988–2013[75]

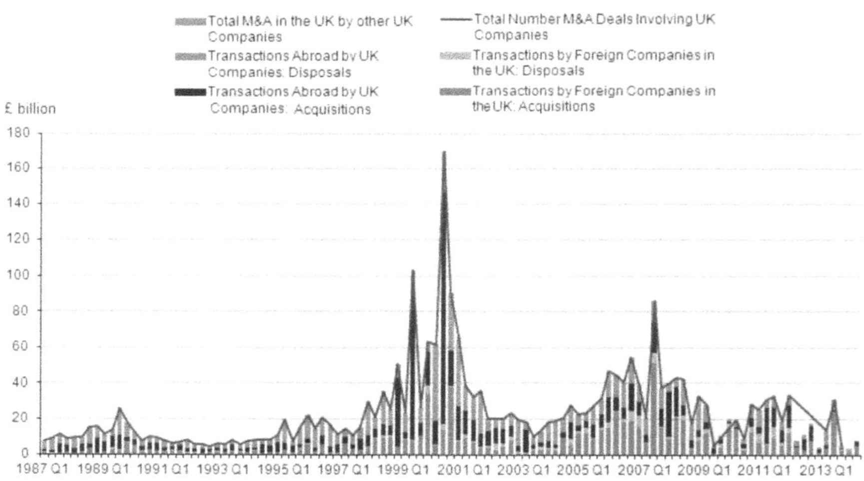

Figure 4.2 Levels of Corporate Acquisitions in the UK from 1987–2013[76]

75 Source: Institute of Mergers, Acquisitions and Alliances data www.imaa-institute.org/statistics-mergers-acquisitions.html#MergersAcquisitions_United Kingdom accessed 28 April 2018.

76 Data on Mergers and Acquisitions in the UK between Q1 1987 to Q1 2014; source: Office of National Statistics United Kingdom www.ons.gov.uk/ons/rel/international-transactions/mergers-and-acquisitions-involving-uk-companies/q1-2014/sty-m-a-uk-companies.html accessed 28 April 2018.

It has been shown that acquirers of listed companies record negative returns relative to acquirers of private companies.[77] One of the studies covered a period of 1981–2001.[78] This is within the period of 1998–2001 (as indicated in the figures) which accounted for one of the highest levels of acquisitions in the UK. The combined effects of Figures 4.1 and 4.2 and the studies show that managers that are driven by ambitious acquisitions are inclined to ignore challenges of post-acquisition effects and managers that are prudent and concerned with improved corporate value are more likely to be cautious when they make acquisitions. High levels of acquisitions may show that the market for corporate control is active, but it may not necessarily depict effectiveness and efficiency of the market for corporate control.

The hubris hypothesis of takeovers has also been identified as an underlying effect of takeovers. This hypothesis is based on the premise that the management of acquiring firms overestimate the benefit to be derived from synergistic gains. This makes managers pay higher premiums, as a result of overestimation of the bid price, leading to non-positive gains post-takeover. Arguably, the overpayment which leads to hubris occurs as a result of managerial error in their bid to maximise shareholder value. Whether or not the overpayment leading to hubris occurs as a result of honest mistakes of the managers, the shareholders of the acquiring firms can make zero gains from acquisitions. When shareholders of an acquiring company do not record gains post-takeovers, wealth is deemed to have been effectively transferred to the shareholders of acquired companies. Despite this challenge, the extent to which shareholders can successfully make managements accountable for unproductive acquisitions is unclear. The derivative action procedure is examined next.

iii) Derivative action and personal actions by shareholders of acquiring companies

One of the changes introduced by the *Companies Act 2006* is the codification of the derivative action procedure.[79] Through a derivative action, a company shareholder can file a claim against a director on behalf of the company, where

77 Paul Draper and Krishna Paudyal, 'Acquisitions: Private Versus Public' (2006) 12 *European Financial Management* 57, 71–73; Mahendra Raj and Michael Forsyth, 'Hubris amongst UK Bidders and Losses to Shareholders' (2003) 8 *International Journal of Business* 9; Marco Becht, Patrick Bolton, and Ailsa Roell, 'Corporate Governance and Control' (2005) *Finance Working Paper* 2/2002 1, 72. See also Robert Conn et al., 'The Impact on UK Acquirers of Domestic, Cross-Border, Public and Private Acquisitions' (2005) 32 *Journal of Business Finance and Accounting* 815; Mara Faccio, John J. McConnell and David Stolin, 'Returns to Acquirers of Listed and Unlisted Targets' (2006) 41 *The Journal of Financial and Quantitative Analysis* 197; Alan Gregory, 'An Examination of the Long Run Performance of UK Acquiring Firms' (1997) 24 *Journal of Business Finance & Accounting*, 971.

78 Note 77, P. Draper and K. Paudyal.

79 *Companies Act 2006*, ss 260–269.

the acts of the director include negligence, default and breach of duty or trust. The derivative action procedure shows that the importance which is attached to the duties that the directors owe to the company is related to the extent that the duties ultimately affect the interests of shareholders as residual claimants.[80] The *Companies Act* recognises the need to balance managerial expertise with the protection of the company from negligent and careless investment decisions by requiring that the permission of the court must be obtained before a derivative action can be instituted.[81] The general duties of directors apply to general investment and managerial decisions and the derivative action procedure applies to all acts that involve negligence, default and breach of duty or trust. It is doubtful whether shareholders of acquiring companies can successfully commence derivative actions against directors in relation to takeovers because derivative action is meant to remedy a wrong or fraudulent act on a minority by those in control of the affairs of the company.[82] Even though a *prima facie* case existed, it has to be shown that the majority of the shareholders independent of the wrongdoers support the claim.[83] Also, the importance to be attached to derivative actions for the purpose of protecting the interests of the shareholders of acquiring companies may not be significant after all. If shareholders succeed in derivative actions against company management for loss caused by unproductive and needless acquisitions, the success of the action will not lead to the revocation of the acquisition. Also, derivative claims are usually instituted on behalf of a company, the proceeds from the successful claim goes directly to the company. Successful actions may only indicate that shareholders can have redress on behalf of the company against managements' investment policies that undermine corporate values during takeovers, without any actual benefit to shareholders.

While a derivative claim may not be appropriate, it is also doubtful whether a shareholder of an acquiring company can succeed in a claim for personal loss. It has been held that the losses to shareholders as a result of the reduction in the value of their shares are only reflective of the loss of company.[84] This means that shareholders may only recover losses when such losses are independent of the losses that are suffered by the company, provided that the losses that they suffer occur as a result of the breach of a duty that is owed to them by managements specifically. Since losses to shareholders are merely reflective of the company's loss, shareholders may not recover in respect of the loss of the value of their shares. Importantly, whether or not the loss to shareholders is reflective of the company's loss, shareholders actually suffer losses when the value of their shares is reduced by 'poor' investment decisions of management. It is difficult to measure

80 This is apparently stated in s 172.

81 *Companies Act*, ss 261–262.

82 *Foss v Harbottle 1843 2 Hare 461.*

83 *Smith v Croft (No2) [1987] 3 All ER 909.*

84 *Prudential Assurance Co. Ltd v Newman Industries Ltd* (No. 2) [1981] Ch 257. See also, *Stein v Blake* (No. 2) [1998] BCC 316 (CA) at 318; *Johnson v Gore Wood & Co.* [2002] 2 AC 1 (HL).

gains or losses of a company without reference to the value of the shares of a company, especially in view of the fact that the market capitalisation of a company is determined by the value of its outstanding shares.

Apparently, the 'no reflective loss' principle is meant to prevent multiple and frivolous action by shareholders and to ensure that company managements are unencumbered in making discretionary investment decisions within their expertise as they reasonably deem fit. Thus, it was observed that the principle is justified to curtail excessive shareholder litigation, to protect the separate personality status of companies, by treating companies as the primary victims of the alleged wrong as the appropriate claimant.[85] This principle effectively distinguishes losses that may be said to have been suffered by the company and losses to shareholders. It preserves shareholders' right of action to losses that directly affect them as shareholders.[86] As such, shareholders of acquiring companies may only succeed in a personal claim for loss caused by needless acquisitions, if it can be proved that the loss specifically applies to the shareholder(s).

The derivative claim procedure and personal actions do not appear to be appropriate remedies for shareholders of acquiring companies in relation to losses caused by needless acquisition. As indicated in *Johnson v Gore Wood & Co.*,[87] shareholders must establish that the breach of the directors' duty which led to the losses that they have suffered was owed specifically to the shareholders and not to the company generally. Also, in view of the requirements of obtaining the permission of the court before continuing a derivative action, it is doubtful whether the hurdles created by the Act can be surmounted by derivative actions that are founded on takeovers. The court has hardly granted the permission to continue derivative actions.[88]

While it remains a difficult task for shareholders to influence the motives of managers when they make acquisitions, the challenges of employees during takeovers may be more enormous. Whether the interests of company employees are actually protected during takeovers is largely unclear, in view of the fact that the takeover objectives of managers may not guarantee such protection. The extent

85 It is also meant to guard against the risk of double jeopardy for the defendant who might be exposed to parallel claims from both the company and the shareholder. See David Milman, 'Shareholder Remedies and the Scope of the Reflective Loss (or No Reflective Loss) Principle' (2005) 4 *Company Law Newsletter* (Sweet & Maxwell) 1, 3.

86 *Heron International Ltd v Lord Grade* [1983] BCLC 244 at 262, Lawton L.J. However, in certain circumstances, the 'no reflective loss' principle may not apply if a company is unable to pursue its own cause of action precisely because of the acts of the wrongdoer. Personal losses that arise from the same wrong that was done to the company may be recovered by a shareholder. See *Giles v Rhind* [2002] EWCA Civ 1428.

87 [2002] 2 AC 1 (HL).

88 See *Franbar Holding Ltd v Patel and Ors.* [2008] EWHC 1534 (Ch); *Mission Capital v Sinclair* [2008], EWHC 1339 (Ch); *Stimpson v Southern Private Landlords Association* [2009] EWHC 2072 (Ch); *Iesini v Westrip Holdings Ltd* [2009] EWHC 2526 (Ch). In certain circumstances, approval to continue derivative action have been granted. See *Kiani v Cooper* [2000] EWHC 577 (Ch); *Stainer v Lee* [2010] EWHC 1539 (Ch).

to which the interests of company employees are incorporated into takeovers is examined next.

4.4 Employment protection

As soon as a company becomes a target of a takeover, threats of employee dismissal become apparent. As indicated earlier, this problem exists because managements engage in costly acquisitions and they can dismiss employees to mitigate the costs of the acquisitions that have been concluded. This shows that there is a high level of uncertainty which characterises the interests of employees when a takeover becomes imminent; since their employment contract does not provide for all possible situations or outcomes during the pendency of their employment.

This is one of the challenges of takeovers in the UK and the world over. Although, corporate laws make provisions for some level of consultations in relation to the interests of corporate constituents including employees, there appears to be no real protection for the interests of employees.[89] This may partly be caused by the view that employees should look beyond the corporation[90] to protect their interests.

In the United Kingdom, the general duties of company directors have been extended to include a *consideration* of the interests of employees, in promoting the success of the company.[91] UK company law recognises the need to promote the success of the company as it affects the company stakeholders. Directors are required to consider the effect of their policies on the interests of other corporate constituents, including company employees. This enlightened shareholder value approach recognises the fact that the corporate entity is embedded with multiplicity of interests. Nonetheless, it appears that directors are to focus on the interests of their shareholders. They are required to promote the success of the company for the benefit of its members as a whole.

Company employees may not rely on this provision in view of the fact that the duty is stated to be owed by the directors to the company. Although, directors are required to consider the interests of the employees in this regard, they do not owe the duty to employees. Employees may not successfully enforce the provisions of this duty to their particular advantage because this duty is a fiduciary duty, and it may only be enforced by the company.[92]

89 Hugh C. Collins, Paul Davies, and Roger W. Rideout, *Legal Regulation of the Employment Relation* (London, Kluwer Law International, 2002) 597–599. Cited in Lord Wedderburn of Charlton, 'Employees, Partnership and Company Law' (2002) 31 *Industrial Law Journal* 99, 102.

90 Such as Labour/Employment Laws and Contract Laws.

91 *Companies Act 2006*, s 172.

92 Note 48, 287. The extent to which directors may consider the interests of other stakeholders such as company employees is limited to the extent to which such consideration would promote the interests of the company and shareholders. See *Parke v Daily News* [1963] 2 All E. R. 929. It was held that generosity to employees can only be lawful where it can be justified by reference to the long-term interest of the company. Thus, the similar position of

Employees appear to be in the same position as if their interests have not been actually considered. The duty is owed to the company and not to the employees. As such, it was observed that by reference to the provision concerning this duty, it may be misleading to refer to it as a duty owed by the directors to company employees. Rather, it may be appropriate to refer to the provision as a defence which may avail company directors, where they are criticised by shareholders for acting with social responsibilities towards employees.[93] This view strongly represents the classical interpretation of the duty; directors are to 'have regard to' the interests of the company employees in their 'duty towards promoting the success of the company'.

The interests of company employees may not be genuinely considered by directors in their duty to promote the success of a company. Although the duty is owed to the company, nevertheless, the duty is expected to be carried out for the benefit of the members of the company.[94] A company is an abstraction; it may not *personally* enjoy any benefit or suffer any detriment, except to the extent that the interests of members are affected. In pursuance of this objective, it is stated that the duty should be discharged for the benefit of the members of the company.

While company law recognises that stakeholders contribute to the success of a corporation as a going concern, this duty does not appear to accord with the stakeholders, particularly employees any special position in the corporation. Where directors are of the view that certain investment decisions would enhance the interests of the shareholders of the company, nothing in this duty prevents them from implementing such decisions, even though the decision may have negative consequences on the interests of the company employees.[95]

Specifically, the extent to which the interests of company employees may be considered by directors in promoting the success of a company appears to be given a limited application. Company employees have not been given exclusive protection as of right; their interests are only to be considered in such a way as to promote the interests of the shareholders of the company.[96] This means that employees do not enjoy any significant level of protection; their interests may only serve as an appendage to those of the shareholders.

---

the old *Companies Act 1985*, s 309, which requires directors to have regards to the interests of company employees in general when performing their duties, applies under the *Companies Act 2006*, s 172.

93 Note 48, 288.

94 *Companies Act 2006*, s 170. Thus, as rightly observed, s 172 appears to maintain the traditional shareholder-value approach. Andrew Keay, 'Tackling the Issue of the Corporate Objective: An Analysis of the United Kingdom's Enlightened Shareholder Value Approach' (2007) 29 *Sydney Law Review* 577; Andrew Keay, 'The Duty to Promote the Success of The Company: Is It Fit for Purpose?' (2010) 1–36 http://papers.ssrn.com/sol3/papers.cfm?abstract_id=1662411 accessed 11 June 2018.

95 See John Birds et al. (eds.), *Boyle and Bird's Company Law* (8th edn, Bristol, Jordan Publishing Limited, 2011) 637.

96 Derek French, Stephen W. Mayson, and Christopher L. Ryan, *Company Law* (34th edn, Oxford, Oxford University Press, 2017–2018) 483–492.

By virtue of the fact that company employees were merely included for consideration by directors, it is expected that their interests should be given less consideration to those of the shareholders. The Company Law Review Steering Group (CLRSG) explained the reason for this approach. The pluralist approach as against the enlightened shareholder value approach was reasoned to be capable of diluting the obligations which the directors owed to shareholders among other things. It would enable directors to frustrate takeovers against the wishes of the shareholders and to distort the operation of the market for corporate control.[97] It was thought reasonable to give mere recognition to the interests of stakeholders. The pluralist approach recognises the genuine concerns and interests of company shareholders and stakeholders in pursuit of corporate objectives. The objective of this approach is to ensure that the interests of company shareholders or stakeholders are not promoted or enhanced in disregard to the other. This means that they would have an equal claim to the benefits which may accrue from a corporate entity as a going concern. In view of this, the CLRSG considered that the pluralist approach would not be appropriate in the circumstance, especially with regards to the scope of the directors' duties. Apparently, directors' duties were thus codified to provide certainty to the scope of their functions and this was particularly meant to define their roles which are to be directed towards the interests of their shareholders. Thus, the CLRSG was not prepared to deviate from the underlying objective of directors' duties; rather it introduced the enlightened shareholder value which appears to incorporate the interests of company stakeholders including employees into the scope of directors' duties.

It may be reasonable to assert that enlightened shareholder approach was never intended for directors to promote the interests of company stakeholders or employees. It can also be reasonably inferred that the interests of stakeholders are to be considered only to the extent that the shareholders' value is not eroded or possibly to consider the interests of stakeholders to the extent that it actually enhances shareholder value. If this reasoning does not capture the objective of the CLRSG in the introduction of the enlightened shareholder value, it will be difficult to support the argument that the purpose for which it was introduced was for the actual enhancement of the interests of the company stakeholders. Having regard to the statutory provision under consideration, these stakeholders do not have the legal right to challenge directors in pursuit of their interests within the company. In light of the fact that employees as stakeholders cannot compel directors to defend their interests, arguably, the enlightened shareholder value – which presently characterises directors' duty to promote the success of the company – does not seem to serve any useful purpose as far as employees are concerned -. There is no indication that directors can slightly enhance the interests of company employees by relying on this duty, particularly when such an attempt may conflict with the interests of shareholders. Thus, employees may have to look elsewhere to protect their interest, especially in relation to takeovers.

97 Note 62, 226.

Meanwhile, in certain circumstances, the duty may not be enforceable against directors by shareholders, if the directors decide to consider employee interests. The duty is to be carried out in the way that *the directors consider* in good faith would be most likely to promote the success of the company. Arguably, what the directors consider in good faith can be determined by reference to what a reasonable director acting in the same position would consider. In light of this, a slight amendment of *section 172* can be done to require directors to actually consider the interests of employees. Thus, it was rightly suggested that the 'shackles' which prevent employees from approaching the courts to protect their interests by reference to the duties of directors to consider employee interests should be reformed to deter frivolous and unthinkable actions by company directors.[98] One of the areas where 'frivolous and unthinkable' actions of directors can be manifested is in corporate takeovers, where employee dismissal can be used to promote needless acquisitions.

The duty to promote the success of the company is the responsibility of the directors of the acquiring company post-takeover. However, it may appear that the directors of target companies are not entirely excluded from the responsibility of their employees. They can incorporate the interests of their employees into the negotiations leading to takeovers. But the extent to which they can protect employee's interests may be limited to the extent to which the interests of shareholders conflict with the interests of the employees as well as the interests of the corporate management themselves. The possibility of negotiating for the interests of the employees is highly unlikely in view of the fact that the managements do not have the incentive to engage in such negotiations. The higher bid premium which may be sought from the bidder company to enable them gain control and the negotiations for compensation for the management of the target company are impediments to the interests of employees. Demands from the target company to the acquirers that employees should be retained or adequately compensated post-takeovers as part of the negotiations may encourage the acquirers to demand a variation of other aspects of the negotiation.

The *EU Takeover Directive* appears to incorporate the interests of employees into takeover arrangements.[99] The board of the target company is required to give its opinion on the effects of the bid on the welfare of the employees of the company. This should also include the acquirer's strategic plans for the target company and the repercussions on employment. This opinion is to be published by the board of the target company apparently for the purpose of raising concerns about the effect of the bid on the welfare of the employees of the target company. Even

98 The reform was suggested to be made in relation to the *Companies Act 1985*, s 309, which is currently reflected in the *Companies Act 2006*, s 172 (1) (b). See David Milman, 'From Servant to Stakeholder: Protecting the Employee Interest in Company Law' in David Feldman and Franklin Meisel (eds.), *Corporate and Commercial Law: Modern Developments* (London, Lloyd's of London Press Ltd, 1996) 170.

99 See *EU Takeover Directive* art. 9(5). Also, the *Fair Trading Act 1973*, s 84, apparently recognises the need to protect employee interests as part of public interest consideration during mergers.

though the *EU Takeover Directive* recognises the need for the interests of company employees to be protected during takeovers, it is not clear whether the objective of the directive in this regard is to actually protect the interests of company employees. The objective of the directive is stated to be for the protection of the interests of holders of securities[100] and employees[101] of target companies among other reasons. While the interests of holders of securities are further strengthened in the directive,[102] employees do not enjoy the same protection. The directive may be conceived of as a regulation which recognises the need for protecting the interests of company employees during takeovers without any actual protection.

The combined effects of these provisions – the duties of company directors as it affects employees as contained in the *Companies Act* and the relevant provisions of the *Takeover Directive* – may not have any significant effect on the interests of company employees during takeovers in the United Kingdom.

Although, the regulations may have recognised the need to protect company employees during takeovers, the relevant provisions in these regulations do not indicate how this should be achieved. The mere recognition of the need to protect employees would not likely be acted upon by company management. More so, the position of company shareholders as the focal point of the directors' responsibilities is not shared by other constituent groups such as employees. Thus, it was rightly suggested that shareholder primacy has been further reiterated.[103] In view of the fact that the framework for takeover regulations and the duties of directors under company law does not provide any protective measure for company employees during takeovers, recourse may be had to employment regulations which are established for the purpose of employment protection. In the United Kingdom, the EC Directive[104] for safeguarding employees' rights in circumstances similar to takeovers has been implemented.[105] This regulation is examined next.

4.4.1 *The Transfer of Undertakings (Protection of Employment) Regulations* (TUPE)

Until the introduction of TUPE,[106] employees were not protected from dismissal when a takeover is made. The objective of TUPE is to protect employees in

100 Introductory Para (2).

101 Introductory Para (17).

102 See art. 9(2).

103 P. L. Davies (ed.), *Gower and Davies' Principles of Modern Company Law* (9th edn, London, Sweet & Maxwell, 2012) 542.

104 *European Council, 'Council Directive on the Approximation of the Laws of the Member States Relating to the Safeguarding of Employees' Rights in the Event of Transfers of Undertakings, Business or Parts of Undertakings or Business', 2001/23/EC (European Community, 2001). (Acquired Rights Directive).*

105 The Directive has been domesticated in the United Kingdom; *'The Transfer of Undertakings Protection of Employment Regulations', (TUPE) CAP 46 (2006).*

106 *The Transfer of Undertakings (Protection of Employment) Regulations 1981.* Amended in 2006 pursuance to Council Directive 77/187 of 14 February 1977, which aims at 'the

the event of a change of employer where there has been a transfer of a business or undertaking. It applies to a transfer of undertaking, business or part of an undertaking or business situated immediately before the transfer in the United Kingdom to another person, where there is a transfer of an economic entity.[107] The effect of its application is to ensure that such transfers do not operate to terminate contracts of employment during takeovers. With regards to contracts of employment which affect the employees and the acquirer, the rights, duties and liabilities which are connected with the contract of employment are deemed to be transferred from the acquired company to the acquirer.[108] Where a contract of employment is varied by reasons of the transfer, such variation will be void and of no effect.[109] Also, all collective agreements and trade union recognition agreements which had been concluded prior to the transfer are deemed to have effect as if the acquirer were a party to the agreements. However, agreements that are concluded after the transfer may be renegotiated by the incoming employers.[110]

TUPE appears to fill the needed gap in takeover regulation in relation to employees. It aims at addressing the uncertainty in employment contracts which enables managers to dismiss employees post-takeover. It seeks to ensure that even though employment contract may not make provisions for all possible outcomes, the interests of employees should not be determined by reference to managerial preferences. This means that TUPE seeks to prevent employees from being dismissed by reason of takeovers.

However, the extent to which it can actually protect employees from dismissal relating to takeovers is not clear. While the regulation considers dismissal of employees on grounds related to the transfer to be unfair dismissal,[111] the scope of this protection is restricted to such dismissals which are not connected to economic, technical or organisational reasons entailing changes in the workforce.[112] This means that an employer cannot dismiss employees as a result of a takeover except such dismissal is based on economic, technical or organisational reasons. This exception appears to 'take away' the protection which is provided for company employees by the regulation. Employee dismissal as a result of takeovers is

---

approximation of the laws of the Member States relating to the safeguarding of employees' rights in the event of transfers of undertakings, businesses or parts of businesses' (as amended by Directive 98/50/EC of 29 June 1998; consolidated in Directive 2001/23 of 12 March 2001).

107 See Regulation 3(1)(a). *The Transfer of Undertakings (Protection of Employment) Regulations 2006* (TUPE).

108 Regulation 4(2).

109 Regulation 4(4).

110 Regulations 5 and 6 preserve collective agreements that have been concluded before a transfer. See the amended Regulation 4A, which provides that TUPE does not operate to transfer any rights under collective agreements as long as the provisions of the collective agreement has been agreed after the transfer date and that the transferee (new employer) did not take part in the collective bargaining.

111 In the UK, employees are generally protected from unfair dismissal. See *Employment Rights Act 1996*, s 94.

112 Regulation 7 (1).

largely caused by economic, technical or organisational reasons. The combined company post-takeover may likely carry out a re-organisation, especially where there is duplicity of employee positions.[113] For the purpose of positioning the company towards the implementation of its new objective framework, it has been suggested that divestments may be adopted to reduce costs and enhance the economic value of the corporate entity post-takeover.[114] Also, the costs of acquisitions has often contributed to diversification, which implies that costs would have to be cut through re-organisation for economic reasons, and employee dismissal is one of the ways of achieving this.[115] Hence the objective of this regulation can be undermined because an acquirer can rely on one or more of the exceptions as a reason for staff dismissal post-takeover to avoid liabilities under the regulation. Also, the pension rights of employees who have been transferred to the new employees are limited or largely excluded.[116]

Unlike other regulatory frameworks, TUPE specifically deals with the rights and interests of company employees during takeovers and it set out to ensure that employees are not unfairly dismissed during takeovers. However, like other regulations, it can hardly protect employees from dismissal relating to takeovers. While other regulatory frameworks merely recognise the need to consider the interests of company employees,[117] this regulation recognises and is set out to protect their interests. However, in light of the limitations in TUPE, it is doubtful whether it can actually achieve its objective. The exemptions which allow company employees to be dismissed based on economic, organisational or technical reasons as well as their exclusion from pension-related agreements largely undermine the protective capacity of TUPE.

Clearly, effort has been made to address the uncertainty which characterises employee interests by establishing TUPE. This is to ensure that employees are not dismissed by reasons of takeovers. However, the level of uncertainty has not been effectively addressed by TUPE. Managements can dismiss employees post-takeovers for reasons relating to economic and organisational reasons. They can achieve their employment-dismissal objective, which can indirectly influence

113 See K. C. O'Shaughnessy and David J. Flanagan, 'Determinants of Layoff Announcements Following M & As: An Empirical Investigation' (1998) 19 *Strategic Management Journal* 989, 990–991.

114 See generally Luis H. R. Alvarez and Rune Stenbacka, 'Takeover Timing, Implementation, Uncertainty and Embedded Divestment Options' (2006) 10 *Review of Finance* 1.

115 Hema A. Krishnan, Michael A. Hitt, and Daewoo Park, 'Acquisition Premiums, Subsequent Workforce Reductions and Post-Acquisition Performance' (2007) 44 *Journal of Management Studies* 709, 711–713. See also, Randall Morck, Andrei Shleifer, and Robert W. Vishny, 'Alternative Mechanisms for Corporate Control' (1989) 79 *The American Economic Review* 842, 852.

116 Regulation 10, TUPE. The regulation may not preserve occupational pension schemes which may be applicable before the takeover occurred, except it is in relation to benefits for old age.

117 *Companies Act*, s 172 on duties of directors to consider the interests of stakeholders including employees, *EU Takeover Directive* 2004 art. 9 (5), the *UK City Code on Takeovers and Mergers 2013*, r 24.2 and 25.2.

takeovers, especially costly takeovers. This means that high transaction costs can continue to characterise takeovers, since employees can be dismissed to mitigate the high costs associated with takeovers. Transaction cost economics seeks to enhance productivity and the economic value of transactions, by mitigating costs that are associated with transactions. When the high costs of corporate acquisitions are mitigated, the possibility of gains to acquiring shareholders would be highly likely and the need to dismiss employees post-takeovers can be dispensed with or largely mitigated. This can ensure that managements are prevented from interfering with the actual role of the market for corporate control, leading to the 'free' occurrence of synergy and the disciplinary role of takeovers and it can prevent or mitigate the occurrence of hubris.

TUPE as an employment protection regulation has not successfully protected the interests of employees in some takeovers that have been concluded in the UK. As long as company managements can wilfully dismiss employees during takeovers, they may influence the role of takeovers as an important element of the market for corporate control. The failure of TUPE to protect employees has been demonstrated in the dismissal of employees after the enactment of TUPE, and takeovers have continued to have negative effects on employment. For example, a study indicates that the negative effect of acquisitions on employees has not been addressed by TUPE.[118] It shows that acquisitions in the UK can reduce the need for labour demand by 12.4%. The data and result of the study pre-dates 2006, before the current TUPE was amended. The post-2006 acquisition period does not indicate that employees are better off than they were in the pre-2006 period. For example, Kraft-Cadbury takeover led to the disengagement of over 400 employees of Cadbury, after the closure of Somerdale plant.[119] This occurred post-2006. Also, the Pfizer-AstraZeneca proposed takeover appeared to confirm job losses, even during negotiation stages. During negotiations for the takeovers, concerns were raised for the interests of the employees of AstraZeneca. The Chief Executive of Pfizer stated (while appearing before the House of Commons *Business, Innovation and Skills Committee*) that Pfizer cannot guarantee that the jobs in AstraZeneca would be 'safe'.[120] These indicate that employees in the United Kingdom are not actually protected by TUPE. Nevertheless, TUPE provides sufficient awareness that takeovers are a threat to employment and the need to protect the interest of employees is desirable.

118 Klaus Gugler and B Burcin Yurtoglu, 'The Effects of Mergers on Company Employment in the USA and Europe' (2004) 22 *International Journal of Industrial Organisation* 481, 494–495.

119 See the *Telegraph Report* of 24 May 2011 www.telegraph.co.uk/finance/newsbysector/epic/cbry/8531542/Kraft-acted-irresponsibly-in-Cadbury-takeover-say-MPs.html accessed 11 June 2018.

120 Rupert Neate *and* Jennifer Rankin, 'Pfizer Admits Takeover of AstraZeneca Would Lead to Cuts in UK Jobs and R&D' *The Guardian* Tuesday 13 May 2014 www.theguardian.com/business/2014/may/13/pfizer-astrazeneca-uk-job-cuts-mps-hostile accessed 19 November 2018.

4.5 Conclusion

The effect of corporate takeovers on company shareholders and other corporate constituents is largely a function of the regulatory framework which governs takeovers. The regulatory framework determines the extent to which the interests of corporate constituents are promoted during takeovers. In the United Kingdom, the development of takeover regulations has been directed towards achieving this purpose, amongst other reasons. In light of this, this chapter sought an examination of the regulatory framework for takeovers in the United Kingdom with particular focus on the extent to which the interests of company shareholders and employees are protected.

Takeover regulation in the United Kingdom emerged as a result of the need to limit the domineering influence of corporate management on takeovers. This was identified following the examination of the historical development of takeovers. Also, it was observed that the emergence of takeover regulation was mainly directed at protecting the interests of company shareholders, since the regulation is aimed at empowering shareholders to make independent decisions whether to accept or reject a takeover bid. This is generally meant to protect the property rights of shareholders; to ensure that shareholders determine how control over their property rights in the shares can be exercised.

Although the emergence and the continuous development of takeover regulations tend to promote shareholder value, it remains to be seen whether it has actually achieved this purpose. This is in view of the fact that management may still be able to assert their influence over takeovers with a view towards determining the outcome of takeover bids. Particularly, it was revealed that certain pre-bid defences may be adopted by management to achieve this purpose. It was argued that shareholders of acquiring companies are hardly protected from managerial excesses. This includes decisions to engage in acquisitions which may not show any reasonable prospect of enhancing the economic value of shareholders particularly and the company in general. It was observed that this problem can persist because the current takeover regulation was designed specifically to protect the interests of the shareholders of target companies.[121]

The derivative action procedure and the option of personal action by shareholders which were briefly examined may not actually provide remedies to shareholders of acquiring companies. They are only generally protected in very restricted circumstances. Enhanced economic value of shareholders of acquiring companies may be dependent on the discretion of company managements.

Further, it was revealed that the importance of employment protection during takeovers has been recognised by various regulations. However, the extent to which employees are actually protected was shown to be doubtful, especially in light of the limitations of TUPE.

121 See generally Francis Okanigbuan, 'Corporate Takeovers and Shareholder Protection: UK Takeover Regulation in Perspective' (2013) 2 *Manchester Law Review* 268.

The main conflicts which occur during takeovers are among company management, shareholders and employees. While takeover regulation was envisaged to address these problems, it may not have actually achieved the desired objective. Although the current regulatory framework is not actually a perfect solution to the takeover problems of conflict of interests, it is expected that future developments in the area of takeover regulation would address these problems. Also, it is expected that employees' protection during takeovers will be given a more meaningful effect when the regulation for that purpose is reviewed.

The development of takeover regulation in the United Kingdom as it affects company shareholders and employees continues to evolve. From the periods of early development of takeover to recent times, many improvements have been made to protect this vulnerable group of corporate constituents. This shows that there is the possibility of a greater level of protection for this group as takeovers develop further in the United Kingdom. The next chapter examines the regulatory framework for takeovers in the United States, with particular reference to the state of Delaware.

References

Alvarez, L. H. R. and Rune Stenbacka, 'Takeover Timing, Implementation, Uncertainty and Embedded Divestment Options' (2006) 10 *Review of Finance* 1.

Armour, J., Jack B. Jacobs, and Curtis J. Milhaupt, 'The Evolution of Hostile Takeover Regimes in Developed and Emerging Markets: An Analytical Framework' (2011) 52 *Harvard International Law Journal* 219, 233.

Armour, J. and David A. Skeel, 'Who Writes the Rules for Hostile Takeovers, and Why? The Peculiar Divergence of US and UK Takeover Regulation' (2006–2007) 95 *The GeorgeTown Law Journal* 1727, 1757.

Becht, M., Patrick Bolton, and Ailsa Roell, 'Corporate Governance and Control' (2005) *Finance Working Paper* 2/2002 1.

Birds, J., et al. (eds.), *Boyle and Bird's Company Law* (8th edn, Bristol, Jordan Publishing Limited, 2011) 637.

Bradley, M., Anand Desai, and E. Han Kim, 'Synergistic Gains from Corporate Acquisitions and Their Division between the Stockholders of Target and Acquiring Firms' (1988) 21 *Journal of Financial Economics* 3.

Brealey, R. A., S. C. Myers, and F. Allen, *Principles of Corporate Finance* (New York, McGraw-Hill/Irwin, 2008).

Cheffins, B. R., *Company Law: Theory, Structure and Operation* (New York, Oxford University Press, 2000).

Clarke, B., 'Reviewing Takeover Regulation in the Wake of Cadbury Acquisition: Regulation in a Twirl' (2011) 3 *Journal of Business Law* 298.

Clarke, B., 'The Takeover Directive: Is a Little Regulation Better Than No Regulation?' (2009) 15 *European Law Journal* 174, 188.

Collins, H. C., Paul Davies, and Roger W. Rideout, *Legal Regulation of the Employment Relation* (London, Kluwer Law International, 2002) 597–599.

Conn, Robert, et al., 'The Impact on UK Acquirers of Domestic, Cross-Border, Public and Private Acquisitions' (2005) 32 *Journal of Business Finance and Accounting*.

Cotter, J. F., Ani Shivdasani, and Marc Zenner, 'Do Independent Directors Enhance Target Shareholder Wealth during Tender Offers?' (1997) 43 *Journal of Financial Economics* 195, 196.

Davies, P. (ed.), *Gower and Davies Principles of Modern Company Law* (10th edn, London, Sweet and Maxwell, 2016).

Draper, P. and Krishna Paudyal, 'Acquisitions: Private Versus Public' (2006) 12 *European Financial Management* 57, 71–73.

Easterbrook, F. H. and Daniel R. Fischel, 'The Proper Role of a Target's Management in Responding to a Tender Offer' (1981) 94 *Harvard Law Review* 1161.

Faccio, Mara, John J. McConnell and David Stolin, 'Returns to Acquirers of Listed and Unlisted Targets' (2006) 41 *The Journal of Financial and Quantitative Analysis* 197.

Farrar, J. H., *Takeovers, Institutional Investors and Modernization of Corporate Laws* (Oxford, Oxford University Press, 1993) 6.

Fitzgibbon, T., 'An Analysis of the Takeover Code's Treatment of an Acquiring Company's Shareholders: Stealing from the Rich to Give to the Already Wealthy?' (2010) 2 *King's Student Law Review* 51, 58.

Florence, P. S., *Ownership, Control and Success of Large Corporations: An Analysis of English Industrial Structure and Policy 1936–1951* (London, Sweet & Maxwell Limited, 1961).

French, D., Stephen W. Mayson, and Christopher L. Ryan, *Company Law* (34th edn, Oxford, Oxford University Press, 2017–2018).

Girvin, S., Sandra Frisby, and Alastair Hudson, *Charlesworth's Company Law* (18th edn, London, Sweet & Maxwell, 2010) 336.

Gregory, Alan, 'An Examination of The Long Run Performance of UK Acquiring Firms' (1997) 24 *Journal of Business Finance & Accounting* 971.

Gugler, K. and B. Burcin Yurtoglu, 'The Effects of Mergers on Company Employment in the USA and Europe' (2004) 22 *International Journal of Industrial Organisation* 481, 494–495.

Hannigan, B., *Company Law* (5th edn, Oxford, Oxford University Press, 2018) 274–278.

Hannigan, B., 'Reconfiguring the No Conflict Rule: Judicial Strictures, a Statutory Restatement and the Opportunistic Director' (2011) 23 *Singapore Academy of Law Journal* 714, 743.

Henry, D., 'Directors' Recommendations in Takeovers: An Agency and Governance Analysis' (2005) 32 *Journal of Business Finance & Accounting* 129.

Holl, P. and Dimitris Kyriazis, 'The Determinants of Outcome in UK Takeover Bids' (1996) *International Journal of Economics and Business* 165.

Keay, A., 'The Duty to Promote the Success of The Company: Is It Fit for Purpose?' 2010 1 http://papers.ssrn.com/sol3/papers.cfm?abstract_id=1662411 accessed 11 June 2018.

Keay, A., 'Tackling the Issue of the Corporate Objective: An Analysis of the United Kingdom's Enlightened Shareholder Value Approach' (2007) 29 *Sydney Law Review* 577.

Kershaw, D., *Principles of Takeover Regulation* (Oxford, Oxford University Press, 2016).

Kraakman, R., et al., *The Anatomy of Corporate Law: A Comparative and Functional Approach* (2nd edn, New York, Oxford University Press, 2009) 247.

Krishnan, H. A., Michael A. Hitt, and Daewoo Park, 'Acquisition Premiums, Subsequent Workforce Reductions and Post-Acquisition Performance' (2007) 44 *Journal of Management Studies* 709, 711–713.

Liu, Han-Wei, 'The Non-Frustration Rule of the UK City Code on Takeover and Mergers and Related Agency Problems: What Are the Implications for the EC Takeover Directive' (2010–2011) 17 *The Columbia Journal of European Law* 5, 9.

Loose, P., Michael Griffiths, and David Impey, *The Company Director: Powers, Duties and Liabilities* (11th edn, Bristol, Jordan Publishing Limited, 2011).

Lord Wedderburn of Charlton, 'Employees, Partnership and Company Law' (2002) 31 *Industrial Law Journal* 99.

Martynova, M. and Luc Renneboog, 'Mergers and Acquisitions in Europe' (2006) *Finance Working Paper* No. 114, 1–83.

Milman, D., 'From Servant to Stakeholder: Protecting the Employee Interest in Company Law' in David Feldman and Franklin Meisel (eds.), *Corporate and Commercial Law: Modern Developments* (London, Lloyd's of London Press Ltd, 1996) 170.

Milman, D., 'Shareholder Remedies and the Scope of the Reflective loss (or No Reflective Loss) Principle' (2005) 4 *Company Law Newsletter* (Sweet & Maxwell) 1.

Moon, R. W., *Business Mergers and Takeover Bids* (5th edn, London, Gee & Co., 1976) 9–10.

Morck, R., Andrei Shleifer, and Robert W. Vishny, 'Alternative Mechanisms for Corporate Control' (1989) 79 *The American Economic Review* 842, 852.

Morck, R., Andrei Shleifer, and Robert W. Vishny, 'Characteristics of Targets of Hostile and Friendly Takeovers' in Alan J. Auerbach (ed.), *Corporate Takeovers: Causes and Consequences* (Chicago, University of Chicago Press, 1988).

Okanigbuan, F., 'Corporate Takeovers and Shareholder Protection: UK Takeover Regulation in Perspective' (2013) 2 *Manchester Law Review* 268.

O'shaughnessy, K. C. and David J. Flanagan, 'Determinants of Layoff Announcements Following M & as an Empirical Investigation' (1998) 19 *Strategic Management Journal* 989.

O'sullivan, N. and Pauline Wong, 'Board Composition, Ownership Structure and Hostile Takeovers: Some UK Evidence' (1999) 29 *Accounting and Business Research* 139.

Raj, M. and Michael Forsyth, 'Hubris amongst UK Bidders and Losses to Shareholders' (2003) 8 *International Journal of Business* 9.

Scharfstein, David, 'The Disciplinary Role of Takeovers' (1988) 55 *The Review of Economic Studies* 185, 192.

Sealy, L., '"Bona Fides" and "Proper Purposes" in Corporate Decisions' (1989) 15 *Monash University Law Review* 265, 269–271.

Sealy, L. and Sarah Worthington, *Sealy and Worthington's Cases and Materials in Company Law* (11th edn, Oxford, Oxford University Press, 2016).

Shleifer, A. and Robert W. Vishny, 'Value Maximization and the Acquisition Process' (1988) 2 *Journal of Economic Perspectives* 7, 14.

Stamp, E. and Christopher Marley, *Accounting Principles and the City Code: The Case for Reform* (London, Butterworth, 1970).

5 The regulatory framework for takeovers in the United States (Delaware)

5.1 Introduction

In view of the federal system of government that applies in the United States, takeovers are regulated by the combined effects of federal and state laws. While federal laws regulate the sale and transfer of company securities through the *Securities and Exchange Commission*, individual state regulation applies in the states where acquired companies are registered.

This chapter examines the relevant regulatory mechanisms for takeovers at the federal level and, particularly, the state of Delaware. The examination is done in relation to the interests of shareholders of target and acquiring companies. Also, the extent to which the interests of employees are protected during takeovers is examined. At the core of these examinations is an identification of the scope of the statutory role of corporate management during takeovers and the effect of their roles on shareholders, employees and the overall corporate interest.

First, the historical development of takeover regulation in the United States is illustrated to ascertain the factors that led to the emergence of the regulatory framework. Next, the regulatory mechanisms for shareholder protection are examined. This will identify the scope of the protection available to shareholders of target and acquiring companies. Then, the role of takeover regulation in relation to employee interests is examined before the conclusion.

5.2 The historical development of takeover regulation

During the early periods of takeover activities in the United States, the interests of shareholders were largely undermined, especially shareholders of target companies. Acquirers adopted different tactics to acquire shares to enable them to gain control over target companies, this includes private or public purchase of shares. Acquirers intimidated shareholders in target companies by offering to pay what appeared to be an exorbitant amount of money to a limited number of shareholders that are willing to sell their shares on 'first come, first served' basis.[1]

1 Alistair Alcock, 'The Regulation of Takeovers' (2001) 5 *Journal of International Financial Markets* 163, 166.

This method of acquisition was essentially tender offers which replaced the previous widely used proxy contests.[2] Acquirers sought to pay premium prices over the market value of shares. This was meant to trigger panic sale, so that target shareholders would be threatened to sell their shares immediately, to avoid becoming minority shareholders and being forced to sell at lower prizes if 'squeeze out' is activated.[3] During this period, acquirers had little restrictions, their acquisition activities were largely unregulated. For example, acquirers presented different types of consideration to conclude deals, such as cash that they expected to obtain in the future. Also, when shares of acquiring companies are used as consideration, only a minimum disclosure requirement under the applicable *Securities Exchange Act*[4] had to be complied with. The disclosure was necessary because the Act required company securities to be registered before they are sold. Thus, the disclosures were apparently only made when shares were used as part of the consideration. The disclosures were not actually made in relation to the acquisition obligation of acquirers; they acted with significant level of freedom when making acquisitions.

There were also challenges relating to target companies. Management boards of target companies devised different means of frustrating bids and the acquirers did not have the opportunity to engage with the shareholders. The defensive attitude of managements of target companies towards takeover bids partly led to the emergence of the short-term, high-price bids by acquirers that were offered to target shareholders on a 'first come, first served' basis as this ensured that management of target companies had little time to respond to the acquisition tactics that were adopted by the acquirers. Thus, the scope of the takeover challenges in the early period mainly undermined the interests of shareholders in target companies, and these problems were caused by acquirers' activities and the role of management of target companies. It became necessary to challenge the acquisition tactics of acquirers and the defensive tactics of management of target companies.

In a bid to address the challenges, the US Congress enacted the *Williams Act*[5] which effectively amended the *Securities Exchange Act*. The Act was a response to the actions of acquiring investors and the tactics they adopted in intimidating target shareholders to sell their shares. It imposed new disclosure and procedural requirements that must be complied with when tender offers are made. For example, investors who obtain certain threshold of ownership of the shares of target companies must disclose certain information about their identity.[6] Other

2 Proxy context and tender offers were examined in Chapter 3. See Samuel L. Hayes III, and Russell A. Taussig, 'Tactics of Cash Takeover Bids' (1967) 45 *Harvard Business Review* 135, 136–137.

3 John Armour, Jack B. Jacobs, and Curtis J. Milhaupt, 'The Evolution of Hostile Takeover Regimes in Developed and Emerging Markets: An Analytical Framework' (2011) 52 *Harvard International Law Journal* 219, 241. See also, Stephen Kenyon-Slade, *Mergers and Takeovers in the US and UK* (Oxford, Oxford University Press, 2004) 333.

4 *The Securities Exchange Act 1934.*

5 *The Williams Act 1968.*

6 Ibid., s 13(d).

changes include; shares deposited by shareholders' pursuance to a tender offer can be withdrawn within seven days; the offer from the acquirer is required to be kept open for a certain period; and shareholders that tender their shares are to be treated equally.[7] This is meant to avoid panic sale whereby shareholders were coerced into selling their shares because of threats that their shares could be sold at lower prices if they failed to sell their shares immediately. The *Williams Act* only addressed the challenges of target shareholders that were caused by the attitude of acquiring investors. The Act did not resolve the challenges caused by managements of target companies when they defend takeovers without the concurrence of their shareholders. It was suggested that the scope of intervention of the Act excluded the challenges caused by managerial defence to bids because corporation law in the United States is the residual responsibility of individual states. Hence, the responsibility of the management of target companies to their companies and shareholders and the validity of their defensive tactics was a matter for state regulation.[8]

The state of Delaware has the vast majority of the United States public incorporated corporations; as such, it has attempted to respond to the challenges caused by management of target companies when they defend bids. The Delaware Supreme Court has established some minimal guidelines to determine acceptable defence tactics in an attempt to restrict the role of managements of target companies in deciding whether a bid should be accepted.[9] The guidelines are determined by reference to the fiduciary obligations of corporate boards.

Generally, the scope of the responses to the challenges affecting shareholders of target companies extends to the acquisition tactics of acquiring investors and the defensive measures adopted by managements of target companies. While federal laws have responded to the problems caused by the tactics of acquirers, the state of Delaware has attempted to challenge the defensive mechanisms of target management. Although these responses have challenged unfavourable treatment of shareholders in target companies, the extent to which federal and state regulatory controls have actually enhanced the interests of shareholders is unclear. First, managements of target companies are not completely barred from engaging in managerial defences without the concurrence of their shareholders; Delaware courts regulate the defences on a case-by-case basis. Second, the scope of protection to shareholders of target companies appears limited. There is no provision for mandatory bid to be made; to give minority shareholders the opportunity to tender their shares at a similar value that the shares of other shareholders were purchased. This would provide minority shareholders with the opportunity to exit the company.[10]

It can be observed that the development of the regulatory framework for takeovers in the United States has been influenced by the need to protect the interests

7 Ibid., s 14(d).

8 Note 1; 166; William B. Chandler, III, 'Hostile M&A and the Poison Pill in Japan: A Judicial Perspective' (2004) *Columbia Business Law Review* 45, 49–50.

9 These are examined in section 5.3.2.

10 See note 3, J Armour, J B Jacobs and C J Milhaupt, 241.

of shareholders of target companies, from intimidating bids of acquiring investors and the defensive mechanisms of the managements of target companies. The responses at both federal and state levels are essentially limited to the interest of shareholders of target companies. The interest of acquiring company shareholders has not been considered. Effectively, acquiring managers are at liberty to make acquisition decisions as they deem fit, just like other usual investment decisions.

While it may appear that the focus on the interest of target shareholders was informed by the challenges that affected target shareholders, it is not clear why protection was not offered to shareholders of acquiring companies. Perhaps the problems affecting target shareholders were prevalent at the time the *Williams Act* and the Delaware Supreme Court sought to address the issues and acquiring shareholders' problems were non-existent or at least not prevalent at that time. Developments in recent times indicate otherwise. The scope of the problems of target company shareholders may have been enhanced by the increase in development in commercial activities and challenges to shareholders of acquiring companies have not only emerged, but have also become prominent and need attention just like target shareholders. Although the efforts that have been made to address the problems that are experienced by target shareholders are commendable, it is not clear whether the existing regulatory framework is totally fit for its purpose. Hence, an examination of the regulatory framework for shareholder protection is imperative.

5.3 Shareholders of target companies

As indicated, the regulatory framework for takeovers in the United States has been developed mainly as a response to the challenges encountered by shareholders of target companies. The responses at both federal and state levels attempted to address the problems caused by acquiring investors and managements of target companies.

5.3.1 The Williams Act *of 1968*

In 1968, the *Williams Act*[11] was enacted as an amendment to the *Securities Exchange Act of 1932.* The Act introduced new mandatory disclosure requirements and procedures that acquirers should observe. Any person who, after acquiring directly or indirectly beneficial ownership of more than 5% of the shares of the target company, shall within ten days of the acquisition or a shorter time be required to file a statement with the *Securities and Exchange Commission*, to disclose as follows: '*if the purpose of the purchases or prospective purchases is to acquire control of the business of the issuer of the securities, any plans or proposals which such persons may have to liquidate such issuer, to sell its assets to or merge it with any other persons, or to make any other major change in its business or corporate structure*'.[12]

11 Codified as 15 U.S.C. § 78m(d)-€.

12 *Securities and Exchange Act 1934*, s 13(d).

This disclosure requirement ensures that target shareholders are informed of the intentions of the acquirer when they are approached to sell their shares. The declaration of intention ensures that shareholders that are willing to tender their shares are informed that the acquirer is purchasing shares in order to obtain control over the company. It provides the opportunity for the shareholders to negotiate the sale of potential 'control', not just the usual or ordinary sale of shares and it seeks to prevent acquirers from adopting all manner of tactics that conceal their acquisition intention to acquire shares for the ultimate purpose of gaining control. The information relating to the plans or proposals of the acquirer after obtaining control over the target company may not be relevant to the shareholders, since they would have sold their shares and exited the company at the time such plans are implemented. The relevance of the disclosure is only limited to the need for target shareholders to be informed of the reasons that the acquirer needs to purchase the shares. This would ensure that the shareholders are not short-changed in the negotiation process, and also to ensure that the shareholders that are willing to sell their shares can demand to be treated equally by the purchaser.

Further protection available to shareholders in target companies is contained in section 14(d) of the Act. Securities deposited pursuant to tender offers may be withdrawn by target shareholders at any time within seven days when the offer or request are first published or sent to the shareholders or at any time after 60 days from the date of the original tender offer or request or invitation.[13] This ensures that shareholders in target companies are given a reasonable time to make an informed decision about the sale of their shares to the acquirer. This provision directly addresses one of the prevalent challenges of shareholders in target companies before the Act was passed. Shareholders were previously required to either tender their shares for sale as quickly as possible to be bought by the acquirer or risk the sale of the shares at lower prices, leading to panic sale on a 'first come, first served' basis. The ability to withdraw their shares afterwards is an indication that shareholders are allowed a reasonable time to make informed investment decisions,[14] including the opportunity to seek advice where necessary before the sale is concluded. This can prevent panic sale or sale at undervalue.

The equal treatment of all shareholders that have tendered their shares is another important provision of the *Williams Act*. Where any person makes a tender offer, or requests an invitation for tenders, for less than all the outstanding equity securities of a class, and where a greater number of securities are deposited, the securities taken up shall be taken up as nearly as may be *pro rata*, disregarding fractions, according to the number of securities deposited by each depositor.[15] Effectively, every shareholder that tenders their shares must be considered, and the acquirer would be required to purchase the required number of shares pro-

13 Ibid., s 14(d) (5).

14 Guhan Subramanian, Steven Herscovici and Brian Barbetta, 'Is Delaware's Antitakeover Statute Unconstitutional? Evidence from 1988–2008' (2010) 65 *The Business Lawyer* 685, 689.

15 S 14(d) (6).

portionately from every shareholder that has tendered their shares. This ensures that target shareholders are treated equally and it addresses the problem of panic sale where acquirers dictate the prices of shares by offering to pay a higher sum to the shareholders that tendered their shares on a 'first come, first served' basis. It ultimately has the capacity to ensure that shareholders in target companies avoid making hasty decisions in tendering their shares, since the acquirers would be required to purchase an appropriate proportion of shares from all shareholders that have tendered their shares if the number of shares tendered exceeds the amount of shares that are required by the acquirers. The equal treatment of shareholders also applies where acquirers vary the terms of tender offers by increasing the cost of the shares.[16] The acquirer would be required to pay the additional value of the consideration to all the shareholders whose shares were taken up, whether or not their shares had been taken up before the variation.

From the analyses detailed, it can be observed that the provisions under sections 13(d) and 14(d) of the *Williams Act* have made substantial changes to the procedure required for acquisition through tender offers. While the tactics of acquirers have been restricted and are now strictly regulated, shareholders in target companies now enjoy a certain level of protection. However, the scope of application of the relevant sections of the Act is limited. The provisions under section 14(d) examined earlier may not apply if the acquisition of such security, together with all other acquisitions by the same person of securities of the same class, would not exceed 2%. The provision would also not apply if the Commission, by rules or regulations, exempt the provisions of the subsection as not entered into for the purpose of changing or influencing the control of the issuer.[17] This means that the provisions apply only where at least 5% of the shares of a particular class in the target company are being tendered for the purpose of transferring control of the company to the acquirer. Furthermore, the provision relating to the equal treatment of shareholders only applies to those shareholders that have tendered their shares as indicated under s 14(d) (6). What is required is that a proportionate number of shares should be acquired from every shareholder that tenders their shares, irrespective of whether the shareholders that tendered their shares are only 50% or 99% of the total number of shareholders. The subsection applies to exclude other minority shareholders that have not tendered their shares within the required time. Hence, the opportunity for every shareholder in the target company to receive a value of the acquisition premium may not arise, since a mandatory bid does not apply. Acquirers are not required to make a mandatory bid to the remaining minority shareholders in the target company, even if 99% of the shares in the target company have been tendered and acquired by the acquirer. However, Maine, Pennsylvania and South Dakota have adopted the 'control share cash-out' provisions in their corporation laws. These states require that, unless the organisational documents of a corporation provide otherwise, if a

16 S 14(d) (7).
17 S 14 (d) (8).

shareholder obtains a certain level of voting power (20% in Pennsylvania, 25% in Maine and 50% in South Dakota), the remaining shareholders can demand that the acquirer purchase their shares at a fair price.[18] These state regulations apply generally to the acquisition of voting power, irrespective of the intentions of the shareholders that have acquired the relevant percentage of shares, unlike the relevant provisions of the *Williams Act* which applies nationwide and only in relation to the acquisition of shares for the purpose of acquisition of the target company. This implies that the combined effects of the *Williams Act* and the regulations in the states of Pennsylvania, Maine and South Dakota can potentially provide a comprehensive protection of the interests of shareholders in target companies, including minority shareholders who can demand that their shares should be purchased at a fair price. It further implies that the protection offered by the *Williams Act* does not extend to minority shareholders in the other states in the absence of the mandatory bid requirement. Even though a mandatory bid may not apply in relation to tender offers under the *Williams Act*, the procedure under the Act would nevertheless be complied with if the shares of the minority shareholders are to be acquired in the future. However, if the shares are acquired after an extensive period of time of concluding the acquisition, it is doubtful whether the acquirers and majority shareholder(s) would be required to pay the same amount of consideration that they used to obtain control from other shareholders, especially where the value of the shares has diminished. The protection of target shareholders by the regulatory mechanism in the state of Delaware is examined next.

5.3.2. Target shareholder protection in Delaware

The protective mechanisms that have been provided for target shareholders by the *Williams Act* are a partial response to the challenges that were prevalent in the early periods. As examined, the challenges to shareholders in target companies emerged from the acquiring tactics of acquirers and the defensive strategies of managements of target companies.[19] The *Williams Act* only addresses the challenges that were caused by the acquiring investors. The role of the management of target companies was not challenged. The state of Delaware has attempted to address this problem through case law and statutory provisions.

The influential role of the Delaware judiciary has been further exhibited by two streams of landmark cases that specifically challenged the role of managements of target companies.

a) Unocal Corp v Mesa Petroleum Company

To ensure that the interests of shareholders of target companies are protected from the defensive mechanisms adopted by management boards, the Delaware

18 See the In-House Lawyer Online, 'Are There Circumstances Where a Buyer May Have to Make a Mandatory or Compulsory Offer for a Target Company?' 18 April 2017 www.inhouselawyer.co.uk/wgd_question/are-there-circumstances-where-a-buyer-may-have-to-make-a-mandatory-or-compulsory-offer-for-a-target-company/ accessed 20 April 2018.

19 See 5.2.

Supreme Court in *Unocal Corp v Mesa Petroleum Company*[20] established a two-part test that should determine whether defensive tactics are valid.

In the first part, the Supreme Court recognises the fact that directors are confronted with the prospect of conflict of interests; hence it is difficult for directors to make an objective decision.[21] The court stated that 'in the face of this inherent conflict, directors must show that they had reasonable grounds for believing that a danger to corporate policy and effectiveness existed because of another person's stock ownership'.[22] The board satisfies this burden by showing good faith and reasonable investigation. Further, the court observed that:

> In the board's exercise of corporate power to forestall a takeover bid our analysis begins with the basic principle that corporate directors have a fiduciary duty to act in the best interests of the corporation's stockholders. . . . As we have noted, their duty of care extends to protecting the corporation and its owners from perceived harm whether a threat originates from third parties or other shareholders.[10] But such powers are not absolute. A corporation does not have unbridled discretion to defeat any perceived threat by any Draconian means available.[23]

The second part of the test was described by the court as the element of balance. The Supreme Court stated that if a defensive measure is to come within the ambit of the business judgement rule,[24] it must be reasonable in relation to the threat posed.[25]

From the response of the Delaware Supreme Court to target shareholder challenges caused by target managements, certain implications can be deduced. First, it confirms the likelihood of conflicts of interests in the agency relationship between managements and shareholders,[26] as evidenced in the early periods. Hence the need to protect shareholders as explained by the court. Second, while the court recognises the business judgment rule and seeks to avoid undermining the purpose of the rule, the test indicates that business judgment must be exercised reasonably. It further implies that shareholders can challenge the decisions of management that can successfully be argued to be in conflict with the decision of the court. Also, although managements are expected to act strictly in the interests of their shareholders, defensive tactics of managements have not been

20 493 A.2d 946 (Del.Supr. 1985).
21 Ibid. 955.
22 Ibid.
23 Ibid.
24 The business judgment rule is a 'presumption that in making a business decision the directors of a corporation acted on an informed basis, in good faith and in the honest belief that the action taken was in the best interests of the company' *Unitrin, Inc. v Am. Gen. Corp.*, 651 A.2d at 1373 (quoting *Aronson v Lewis*, 473 A.2d 805, 812 (Del. 1984).
25 Ibid. 955.
26 Eugene F. Fama and Michael C. Jensen, 'Agency Problems and Residual Claims' (1983) 26 *Journal of Law and Economics* 327–349.

outlawed. Managements can engage in takeover defences as long as the defensive mechanism satisfies the scope of the test.

Furthermore, shareholders are not required to approve defensive measures. Even if shareholders do not sanction a defensive tactic, managements can nevertheless exercise the defence, if the tests can be satisfied. As indicated earlier, defensive tactics would be valid if it can be shown that a danger to corporate policy and effectiveness existed because of another person's stock ownership and that in opposing the bid, management has acted reasonably and in good faith in relation to their business judgment. Hence, the application of the tests to managerial defensive tactics would be subject to judicial review where any shareholder is not convinced that managerial defensive acts have been exercised reasonably in the interests of the shareholders and the corporate entity. For example, in *Moran v Household Int'l Inc.*,[27] the Supreme Court of Delaware demonstrated that managements of target companies are not barred from engaging in defensive measures if in light of the test it is reasonable to do so. The court held that a poison pill defence, adopted by the management of the target company, leading to the exercise of 'right plans' was validly within the business judgment rule. The court stated that the business judgment rule is a 'presumption that in making a business decision the directors of a corporation acted on an informed basis, in good faith and in the honest belief that the action taken was in the best interests of the company'.[28] Further, the court observed that:

> The record reflects a concern on the part of the Directors over the increasing frequency in the financial services industry of 'boot-strap' and 'bust-up' takeovers. The Directors were also concerned that such takeovers may take the form of two-tier offers. . . . In sum, the Directors reasonably believed *Household* was vulnerable to coercive acquisition techniques and adopted a reasonable defensive mechanism to protect itself.[29]

Despite the judicial review that managements decisions may be subjected to, the decision of the court in *Moran v Household Int'l Inc.* indicates that the court is not keen on reversing the defensive decisions of managements at the slightest opportunity when shareholders challenge the defensive measures, except when there is a very good reason to do so. This view was further demonstrated by the court in *Paramount Communications Inc. v Times Inc.*,[30] where the court appeared to expand the scope for acceptable defensive measures that can be undertaken by target managements. The court held that the propriety of a defensive measure adopted by management boards may be valid by reference to the selected time frame that managements have adopted to promote corporate value. The court observed as follows:

27 500 A.2d 1346 (Del. 1985).
28 Ibid. 1356; *Bennett v Propp*, 41 Del.Supr. 14, 187 A.2d 405, 409 (1962).
29 Ibid. 1357.
30 571 A.2d 1140 (Del. 1989).

> Once again, the contention stems, we believe, from a fundamental misunderstanding of where the power of corporate governance lies. Delaware law confers the management of the corporate enterprise to the stockholders' duly elected board representatives. 8 Del.C. § 141(a). The fiduciary duty to manage a corporate enterprise includes the selection of a time frame for achievement of corporate goals. That duty may not be delegated to the stockholders. . . . Directors are not obliged to abandon a deliberately conceived corporate plan for a short-term shareholder profit unless there is clearly no basis to sustain the corporate strategy.[31]

This indicates that the role of management in making investment decisions for corporate entities has been confirmed by the court to extend to defensive measures that management deem to be appropriate in the circumstances, as long as reasonableness is satisfied.

However, to prevent target managements from having unrestricted powers that could be dubiously linked to the scope of the test established in *Unocal Corp v Mesa Petroleum Company*, the court sought to clarify and restrict the role of target managements to apparently meet the expectations of their shareholders. This restriction is examined next in *Revlon Inc. v MacAndrews & Forbes Holdings Inc.*[32]

b) Revlon Inc. v MacAndrews & Forbes Holdings Inc.

In *Revlon Inc. v MacAndrews & Forbes Holdings Inc.*, the Delaware Supreme Court appears to depart from its earlier decision in *Unocal Corp v Mesa Petroleum Company* wherein directors were held to be entitled to engage in a range of defensive mechanisms that were consistent with reasonability and the exercise of business judgement. The court effectively limited the extent to which managements can engage in defensive mechanism. The board of Revlon entered into a lock-up agreement with Forstmann Little & Co. to thwart the efforts of Pantry Pride, Inc. (Pantry Pride) in acquiring Revlon. Revlon promised to deal exclusively with Forstmann in the face of a takeover (the no-shop provision), and agreed to pay $25 million cancellation fee to Forstmann if the transaction was aborted. The Court of Chancery found that the Revlon directors had breached their duty of care by entering into the foregoing transactions and effectively ending an active auction for the company. The Delaware Supreme Court affirmed the decision of the lower court; it held that once a sale of a company is inevitable, the role of the management is transformed from preserving the corporate entity to maximising the entity's value at a sale for the benefit of the shareholders.

> when Pantry Pride increased its offer to $50 per share, and then to $53, it became apparent to all that the break-up of the company was inevitable. The

31 Ibid. 1154.
32 506 A.2d 173 (Del. 1986).

> Revlon board's authorization permitting management to negotiate a merger or buyout with a third party was a recognition that the company was for sale. The duty of the board had thus changed from the preservation of Revlon as a corporate entity to the maximization of the company's value at a sale for the stockholders' benefit. This significantly altered the board's responsibilities under the Unocal standards. It no longer faced threats to corporate policy and effectiveness, or to the stockholders' interests, from a grossly inadequate bid. The whole question of defensive measures became moot. The directors' role changed from defenders of the corporate bastion to auctioneers charged with getting the best price for the stockholders at a sale of the company.[33]

Revlon Inc. v MacAndrews & Forbes Holdings Inc. was decided after *Unocal Corp v Mesa Petroleum Company*. The restriction that was applied to the role of the target management's board in *Revlon* when a sale became inevitable is an indication that the test established by the court in *Unocal* is of secondary importance. The paramount role of target managements would simply be to promote the sale at the highest possible price for the interests of the shareholders when a sale is inevitable, rather than jeopardising the sale through defensive tactics. Since the decision in *Revlon* was reached after *Unocal*, it can be observed that the Delaware Supreme Court sought to further restrict the role of target managements beyond the scope of the test established in *Unocal*. This was further explained by the court in *Paramount Communications Inc. v Time Inc.*,[34] where the court distinguished the Revlon decision. Time Inc. needed to expand their enterprise. It decided to merge with Warner. Time Inc. wanted to merge with a company that would ensure that it would be able to continue its journalism integrity after the merger. Time Inc. was concerned that other parties may consider this merger as a sale of the company, therefore Time Inc.'s board enacted several defensive tactics. This includes a no-shop clause that would make them unattractive to a third-party investor. In view of the merger talks, Paramount made a competing offer of $175 per share which was raised at one point to $200. Time Inc. was concerned that its journalism integrity would not be promoted under Paramount's ownership. They thought that shareholders may not understand why merging with Warner was a better option. Paramount then brought this action to prevent the Time Warner merger. It argued that Time Inc. has put itself up for sale and invoked the Revlon principle requiring directors to act solely to maximise the shareholders' profit. It further argued that the merger was invalid under the Unocal test because Time's directors did not act in a reasonable manner. It argued that the use of a lock-up agreement, a no-shop clause, and so-called 'dry-up' agreements prevented shareholders from obtaining a control premium in the immediate future and thus violated Revlon. The court stated that the Revlon principle was not triggered.

33 Ibid. 182D.
34 571 A.2d 1140 (Del. 1989).

> In our view, the pivotal question presented by this case is: 'Did Time, by entering into the proposed merger with Warner, put itself up for sale?' . . . Under Delaware law there are, generally speaking and without excluding other possibilities, two circumstances which may implicate Revlon duties. The first, and clearer one, is when a corporation initiates an active bidding process seeking to sell itself or to effect a business reorganization involving a clear break-up of the company. See, e.g., *Mills Acquisition Co. v. Macmillan*, Inc, Del.Supr., 559 A.2d 1261 (1988). However, Revlon duties may also be triggered where, in response to a bidder's offer, a target abandons its long-term strategy and seeks an alternative transaction involving the breakup of the company. . . . If, however, the board's reaction to a hostile tender offer is found to constitute only a defensive response and not an abandonment of the corporation's continued existence, Revlon duties are not triggered, though Unocal.[35]

The decision of the Court in *Paramount* indicates that the limitation imposed in Revlon is retained and that where the Revlon principle is not triggered, the Unocal principles would be applicable. The court went on to hold that directors are not obliged to abandon a deliberately conceived corporate plan for a short-term shareholder profit unless there is clearly no basis to sustain the corporate strategy.[36] Applying the Unocal principle, the court held that board of directors, while always required to act in an informed manner, is not under any *per se* duty to maximise shareholder value in the short term, even in the context of a takeover.[37]

Also, in *Unitrin Inc. v American General Corporation*,[38] American General (which had publicly announced a proposal to merge with Unitrin for $ 2.6 billion at $ 50–3/8 per share) and certain Unitrin shareholder plaintiffs filed suit in the Court of Chancery to restrain Unitrin from repurchasing up to 10 million shares of its own stock (the 'Repurchase Program'). On 26 August 1994, the Court of Chancery temporarily restrained Unitrin from making any further repurchases on the ground that the Repurchase Program was a disproportionate response to the threat posed by American General's inadequate 'all cash for all shares' offer. Despite the proposed merger, the Revlon principle was not triggered; the Unocal principles were applicable. On appeal, the Supreme Court of Delaware held that the chancery court incorrectly determined that the Repurchase Program was a disproportionate defensive response; the Supreme Court remanded the case to the chancery court, to apply the appropriate standard. The court held that;

> The Unitrin Board had the power and the duty, upon reasonable investigation, to protect Unitrin's shareholders from what it perceived to be the

35 Ibid. 1150.
36 Ibid. 1154.
37 Ibid. 1150.
38 651 A.2d 1361 (Del. 1995).

> threat from American General's inadequate all-cash for all-shares Offer. . . . The adoption of the poison pill and the limited Repurchase Program was not coercive and the Repurchase Program may not be preclusive. Although each made a takeover more difficult, individually and collectively, if they were not coercive or preclusive the Court of Chancery must determine whether they were within the range of reasonable defensive measures available to the Board.[39]

Despite the impending acquisition arrangement between American General and Unitrin, wherein some Unitrin shareholders were opposed to the defensive measures adopted by Unitrin board, the Revlon principle was not triggered, and the Unocal principles were held to be applicable. This further indicates that the Unocal principle would always be applicable to determine the scope of the powers of target managements, except the Revlon principle has been clearly triggered. It was suggested that the court in *Unitrin Inc. v American General Corporation* expanded the discretion of directors to resist takeovers, since the court held that defensive measures approved by an independent board were permissible as long as they were not draconian and were within a range of reasonableness.[40] Although the independent board's approval appears to expand the scope of directors discretion in resisting takeovers, the requirement of reasonableness indicates that directors' discretion has not actually been expanded. The validity of the discretion that directors seek to exhibit must nevertheless be determined by reference to the tests of reasonableness developed in *Unocal Corp v Mesa Petroleum Company*, provided that the principles established in *Revlon Inc. v MacAndrews & Forbes Holdings Inc.* have not been triggered. For example, in *Mills Acquisition Co. v Macmillan, Inc.*,[41] when the management of the company started taking bids for the sale of the company, the Revlon principle was triggered since the sale of the company became inevitable. The management preferred one of the bidders and acted contrary to the Revlon principle which required that once the sale of a company became inevitable, the role of target managements was to ensure that the best price is achieved for the shareholders. The Supreme Court of Delaware held that the decision of the board to engage in defensive measures was induced by breaches of fiduciary duties.[42] The defensive measures had not been used to improve the bids or induce more bids for the interests of the shareholders.

The principles established by the Supreme Court of Delaware in *Unocal Corp v Mesa Petroleum Company* and *Revlon Inc. v MacAndrews & Forbes Holdings Inc.* have substantially challenged managements of target companies. The court has ensured that the role of target managements is put in the spotlight for judicial

39 Ibid. 1389–1390.
40 William Magnuson, 'Takeover Regulation in the United States and Europe: An Institutional Approach' (2009) 21 *Pace International Law Review* 205, 216.
41 559 A.2d 1261 (1988).
42 Ibid. 1248.

scrutiny. This represents a marked difference from what applied in the early periods. Nevertheless, defensive tactics are still permitted, as long as they are within the permitted scope of the principles set out in Unocal and Revlon. Also, the principles introduced by the Supreme Court of Delaware do not require shareholder approval. Hence, the main difference between the role of target managements in the early period and the current dispensation is that managements are now aware that their defensive measures may potentially be declared invalid.[43] Thus, even though defensive measures that can potentially be influenced by conflict of interests cannot be totally prevented, the actions of managements will be judged by the standard of their fiduciary duty.[44] The potential for review of managerial defensive tactics can largely mitigate the incidence of conflict of interests, since managements would consider the prospect of judicial review before embarking on any defensive measures.

The responses to the challenges of takeovers in the early period were mainly aimed at protecting the interests of shareholders in target companies. This became necessary as a result of the acquisition tactics of acquirers and the defensive tactics of management of target companies. The combined effects of the provisions of the *Williams Act* and the principles established by the Delaware Supreme Court have been examined to show the extent to which this problem has been addressed. It can be observed that the responses that were directed towards addressing the challenges that were experienced by shareholders in target companies are the cornerstone of the regulatory mechanism of corporate acquisition in the United States, including Delaware. Although the Delaware antitakeover regulation under the *Delaware General Corporation Law* §.203 is not specifically linked to the challenges from the early periods, nevertheless, it provides minimum protection to target shareholders. The three-year period for delayed acquisition from an interested stockholder can arguably prevent shareholders in the company from being intimidated to sell their shares. The opportunity for target shareholders to approve the acquisition before the three-year period[45] nevertheless ensures that they can determine when an acquisition should be concluded. Thus, the focus of the regulatory mechanisms is to promote the interests of target shareholders.

Although, it is justifiable for the regulatory mechanism of corporate acquisitions to address the challenges experienced by target shareholders, the challenges are not limited to target shareholders. The interests of acquiring shareholders have also been progressively undermined by the dominant role of managements when they engage in costly and overambitious acquisitions leading to negative gains or losses to acquiring companies. Despite this problem, it is doubtful whether

43 For example, see *Mills Acquisition Co. v Macmillan, Inc, Del.Supr.* (559 A.2d 1261 1988) examined.

44 *Cede v Co. v Technicolor Inc.*, 634 A.2d 345, 368 (Del. 1993); *Smith v Van Gorkom*, 488 A.2d 858 872–873 (Del. 1985).

45 The Delaware General Corporation Law, § 203 (a) (3).

sufficient responses have been attempted to protect the interests of shareholders of acquiring companies in the United States.

5.4 Shareholders of acquiring companies

In the United States, the development of the framework for takeover regulation has mainly been directed towards addressing the challenges that undermined the interests of shareholders of target companies in the early periods. While the *Williams Act*[46] addressed the challenges of target shareholders that were caused by acquiring investors, managerial defences that undermined the interests of target shareholders have largely been addressed by the Supreme Court of Delaware.[47] Although these efforts are commendable, they do not completely address the scope of challenges that undermine shareholder interests in takeovers. The interests of shareholders in acquiring companies can be disregarded by company managements when they make acquisitions. It is apparently because conflict of interests has the propensity to manifest when managements have an extensive level of discretion. This is demonstrated by managements in acquiring companies when they make acquisitions. It is comparable to the scope of discretion that management of target companies had in the early periods before the regulatory review by the *Williams Act* and the Delaware Supreme Court. For example, acquiring managements can engage in acquisitions that would lead to an increase in the size of the company without a corresponding increase in the economic value of the corporate entity,[48] and ultimately fail to increase shareholder value.

5.4.1 Managerial conflict of interests

Although, the challenges to shareholders in target and acquiring companies are caused by conflicts between the interests of managers and shareholders, the conflicts manifest differently. In acquiring companies, shareholders can potentially derive zero or negative gains post-takeover. The influence of conflict of interests on the role of acquiring managements can be manifested in one or more of the following ways.

a) Market power

The dominant reason for engaging in corporate acquisition is to promote synergistic gains to the combined company.[49] Arguably, it ensures that the combined

46 *The Williams Act 1968* ss 13d and 14d of the *Securities Exchange Act 1934.*

47 See the examination of Unocal and Revlon principles.

48 Gary Gorton, Matthias Kahl, and Richard J. Rosen 'Eat or Be Eaten: A Theory of Mergers and Firm Size' (2009) 64 *The Journal of Finance* 1291; David Offenberg, 'Firm Size and the Effectiveness of the Market for Corporte Control' (2009) 15 *Journal of Corporate Finance* 66.

49 Roberta Romano, 'A Guide to Takeovers: Theory, Evidence and Regulation' (1992) 19 *Yale Journal on Regulation* 119, 125–128.

value of the target and acquiring companies is greater than the sum of the individual entities for companies in the same line of business.[50] Hence acquiring managers often moot the idea that an increase in market power can achieve synergistic gains. Since an increase in market power through corporate acquisition can only be achieved by acquiring or merging with a firm in the same line of business, the overambitious quest to acquire competitors to increase market power can undermine corporate value. For example, Time Warner was acquired by America Online (AOL) in the year 2000 for about $160 billion, in addition to about $17 billion liability of Time Warner. The acquisition of Time Warner by AOL is currently the largest corporate acquisition in the United States. The acquisition was driven by the need to enhance the market power of AOL. The deal was completed with a premium of about 70% over the market price of $64.75 of Time Warner shares, at the rate of $110 *per* share.[51] This acquisition was subsequently described as a misguided idea by the Chairman/Chief Executive of Time Warner, after synergies between the combined companies failed to materialise, leading to a loss of about $99 billion.[52] This led to the separation of AOL from Time Warner in December 2009 with plans to disengage about one-tenth of AOL's 7,000 workforce.[53] The premium value of 70% and the post-acquisition challenges clearly indicate that the acquisition was completed to enhance the market power of AOL in the media industry, without particular regard to the need for scrutiny and caution. Similarly, the largest corporate acquisition in the telecommunications industry was motivated by market power. In February 2000 Mannesmann was acquired by Vodafone. The acquisition was completed for about

50 See generally H. Igor Ansoff, *Corporate Strategy: An Analytic Approach to Business Policy for Growth and Expansion* (New York, McGraw-Hill, 1965); Lynn Hodgkinson and Graham H. Partington, 'The Motivation for Takeovers in the UK' (2008) 35 *Journal of Business Finance & Accounting* 102.

51 Ianthe Jeanne Dugan and Ariana Eunjung Cha, 'AOL to Acquire Time Warner for 183 Billion Merger' *The Washington Post* 11 January 2000 www.washingtonpost.com/archive/politics/2000/01/11/aol-to-acquire-time-warner-in-record-183-billion-merger/f3bf2f07-c32b-4052-b5a6-8489bb9d7013/?noredirect=on&utm_term=.69ae04545d2d accessed 30 April 2018; 'AOL Buyout of Time Warner: Merger Frenzy Sweeping Corporate America' *World Socialist Web* 14 January 2000 www.wsws.org/en/articles/2000/01/merg-j14.html accessed 2 May 2018; Seth Sutel, 'AOL Buys Time Warner for $162 billion' *ABC News* 10 January 2000 http://abcnews.go.com/Business/Decade/aol-buys-time-warner-162-billion/story?id=9279138 accessed 30 April 2018.

52 Emma Barnett and Amanda Andrews, 'AOL Merger Was "The Biggest Mistake in Corporate History", Believes Time Warner Chief Jeff Bewkes' *The Telegraph* 28 September 2010 www.telegraph.co.uk/finance/newsbysector/mediatechnologyandtelecoms/media/8031227/AOL-merger-was-the-biggest-mistake-in-corporate-history-believes-Time-Warner-chief-Jeff-Bewkes.html accessed 30 April 2018.

53 James Quinn, 'AOL Officially Splits from Time Warner after 10 Years' *The Telegraph* 9 December 2009 www.telegraph.co.uk/finance/newsbysector/mediatechnologyandtelecoms/6774324/AOL-officially-splits-from-Time-warner-after-10-years.html accessed 30 April 2018; Emily Steel, 'AOL-Time Warner Divorce Is Official' *The Wall Street Journal* 10 December 2009 www.wsj.com/articles/SB10001424052748704825504574586393655471238 accessed 30 April 2018.

$183/€204 billion (including liabilities of about $17b)[54] at €353/share against the market value of about –143. This deal was completed for a premium of about 160% – previously intended offers included 76% premium of €253 valuation of Mannesmann..[55] The high cost of the acquisition led to a write-down of £28 billion after a period of five years of completing the acquisition;[56] *Vodafone* had paid too much for the acquisition.[57]

Also, in October 2007, the Royal Bank of Scotland Group (UK) led a consortium of banks – RBS, Fortis (Belgian) and Banco Santander (Spanish), known as RFS Holdings B.V. – in what was considered to be the largest acquisition in the banking sector, acquired the Dutch bank ABN AMRO Bank N.V. for about –71 billion, almost $100B. The deal was concluded for (79% cash) a premium of about 70% at –38.40/share of *ABN AMRO*.[58] Just about one year after the acquisition, the consortium of banks suffered severed financial setbacks. The banks had to be rescued to avoid impending national economic woes. The UK government bailed RBS. RBS's vulnerability to failure was largely as a result of capital challenges from the acquisition.[59] The ABN AMRON bank was nationalised by

54 *CNN Money* 4 February 2000 https://money.cnn.com/2000/02/04/europe/vodafone/ accessed 11 July 2018. Edmund L. Andrews and Andrew Ross Sorkin, 'Europe's Megadeal: The Overview; $183 Billion Deal in Europe to Join Two Wireless Giants' *New York Times* 4 February 2000 www.nytimes.com/2000/02/04/business/europe-s-megadeal-overview-183-billion-deal-europe-join-2-wireless-giants.html accessed 11 July 2018.

55 Carol J. Williams, 'As in Mannesmann Deal, Globalization Forcing Germany Inc. Out of Business' *Los Angeles Times* 14 February 2000 http://articles.latimes.com/2000/feb/14/business/fi-64162 accessed 11 May 2018; Terry Barwick et al., Director of Corporate Affairs 'Intended Offer to Mannesmann Shareholders' *Press Release* 29 December 1999 www.vodafone.com/content/index/media/vodafone-group-releases/1999/press_release29_11.html accessed 11 May 2018; Santiago Simon, 'Mergers and Acquisition: Vodafone – Mannesmann' (2013) *Esade Business School* Working paper www.academia.edu/22609752/MAcase_Vodafone-Mannesmann accessed 1 June 2018, 19–20.

56 Kevin Reed, 'Vodafone's Goodwill Write Down Sends Shock Waves through City' *Accountancy Age* 9 March 2006 www.accountancyage.com/aa/analysis/1751470/vodafones-goodwill-write-sends-shock-waves-city accessed 11 May 2018; 'Vodafone Books $40.9 Billion Loss' *CNN International* Tuesday 30 May 2006 http://edition.cnn.com/2006/BUSINESS/05/30/vodafone.earns/ accessed 11 May 2018.

57 Lina Saigol, 'Vodafone Hope to Banish Ghost of Acquisition Past' *Financial Times* 12 June 2013 www.ft.com/content/7ead3928-d342-11e2-b3ff-00144feab7de accessed 14 May 2018.

58 Lina Saigol, 'The Real Deal: The Sobering Message of RBS's Sky-High ABN Bid' *Financial Times* 1 October 2007 https://ftalphaville.ft.com/2007/10/01/7720/the-real-deal-the-sobering-message-of-rbss-sky-high-abn-bid/ accessed 12 November 2018; FSA Board Report, 'The Failure of the Royal Bank of Scotland' *Financial Services Authority* 2011, 415. www.fca.org.uk/publication/corporate/fsa-rbs.pdf accessed 31 May 2018.

59 FSA Board Report, 'The Failure of the Royal Bank of Scotland' *Financial Services Authority* 2011, 407 www.fca.org.uk/publication/corporate/fsa-rbs.pdf accessed 12 November 2018; Harry Wilson, Philip Aldrick, and Kamal Ahmed, 'The Royal Bank of Scotland Investigation: The Full Story of How the Biggest Bank in the World Went Burst' *The Telegraph* 05 March 2011 www.telegraph.co.uk/finance/newsbysector/banksandfinance/8363417/Royal-Bank-of-Scotland-investigation-the-full-story-of-how-the-worlds-biggest-bank-went-bust.html accessed 31 May 2018.

the Dutch Government in 2009 and the government took control of the Fortis operation of the bank in Netherlands as part of the bailout plan after the bank came under serious solvency problems post-acquisition.[60] Also, the Belgian government announced a bailout plan for Fortis under certain agreed terms with Netherlands and Luxembourg.[61] The ambitious attempt to create the biggest market in the banking sector influenced the desire to pay the 70% premium over the market value of ABN AMRO shares. Also, about $3.5 billion financial losses were recorded when Pfizer acquired Pharmacia in 2002[62] for 36% premium.[63] Qwest Communications also wrote off $30 billion from its goodwill after acquiring US West in 2000.[64]

Although, enhanced market power can promote synergistic gains in takeovers, the extensive scope of discretion exercised by acquiring managers indicate that the quest to enhanced market power can be either a blessing or a curse for acquiring companies. Thus, the deciding factor is an objective and prudent ambition of acquiring managers in the absence of legal restraint.

b) Competition among bidders

Competitive bids can potentially enhance the cost of acquisition,[65] since bidders seek to outbid competitors. As long as investors have a strong opinion about the prospective economic value of the stock of a target company, they would be incentivised to make improved bids to win the contest. It has been suggested

60 'Nationalisation of ABN AMRO' www.government.nl/topics/state-owned-enterprises/nationalisation-of-financial-institutions-abn-amro-asr-and-sns-reaal/nationalisation-of-abn-amro accessed 12 November 2018; ABN AMRO Bank Press Release 'Completion of ABN AMRO Bank and Fortis Bank Nederland Legal Merger' 30 June 2010 www.abnamro.com/en/newsroom/press-releases/2010/completion_of_legal_merger.html accessed 31 May 2018; Yvette Essen 'Financial Crisis: Fortis' Dutch Assets are Nationalised' *The Telegraph* 03 October 2008 www.telegraph.co.uk/finance/financialcrisis/3131247/Financial-Crisis-Fortis-Dutch-assets-are-nationalised.html accessed 12 November 2018.

61 Tina Wang 'Fortis Pulled Back from the Brink' *Forbes* www.forbes.com/topstories/2008/09/28/fortis-bailout-pingan-markets-equity-cx_tw_0928markets01.html accessed 31 May 2018; Ian Traynor Brussels, 'Fortis: Belgium Acts to Prevent Financial Group's Collapse' *The Guardian* 29 September 2008 www.theguardian.com/money/2008/sep/29/insurance.europeanbanks accessed 12 November 2018.

62 Scott Hensley, 'Pfizer Posts $3.59 Billion Loss Due to Pharmacia Acquisition' *The Wall Street Journal* 27 July 2003 www.wsj.com/articles/SB105880674230792000 accessed 11 December 2018.

63 Robert Frank and Scott Hensley, 'Pfizer to Buy Pharmacia for $60 Billion in Stock' *The Wall Street Journal* 15 July 2002 www.wsj.com/articles/SB1026684057282753560 accessed 18 December 2018.

64 Jonathan Lambeth, 'Qwest Faces Write Off Up to $30B' *The Telegraph* 03 April 2002, www.telegraph.co.uk/finance/2758662/Qwest-faces-writing-off-up-to-30bn.html accessed 18 December 2018.

65 Michael Bradley, Anand Desai, and Han E. Kim, 'Synergistic Gains from Corporate Acquisitions and Their Division between the Stockholders of Target and Acquiring Firms' (1988) 21 *Journal of Financial Economics* 3.

that the incentive to make higher bids is based on the view that certain stocks that are underpriced should be acquired and those that are overpriced should not be acquired.[66] This may not largely reflect the reality of costly acquisitions that are based on premiums paid to acquire the shares of target shareholders. When several investors are engaged in a competitive bid, the tendency for the successful bid to be significantly higher than the market value of the shares is highly likely. The desire to obtain control is determined by the preference of acquiring managements who have extensive discretion. Each bidder seeks to outbid other competitors and rather than establish a price ceiling that must not be exceeded by bidders to avoid triggering losses post-takeovers, the measure of success shifts to the ability to acquire the company in the acquisition battle.

Apart from the hope of synergistic gains, it is not clear why acquiring managers engage in very costly acquisitions, since the expected gains may be undermined by the effects of the overwhelming costs post-takeover. Most likely, there are alternative incentives that encourage acquirers to make enhanced bids. The availability of free cash flow has been suggested to be one of the incentives that could promote high bid prices.[67] While it is not suggested that acquiring managers deliberately engage in costly acquisitions, the effect of costly acquisition on the value of the combined company is difficult to justify. High costs of acquisitions can almost certainly increase the wealth of shareholders of acquired companies with immediate effect, while acquiring shareholders may not derive similar benefits. Acquiring shareholders would have to wait for synergistic gains to materialise on the basis of net gains post-acquisition.

Competition is a market characteristic and it is not expected to be applied differently in relation to takeovers. The efficiency argument in takeovers applies mainly in favour of target shareholders. This has been demonstrated in the regulatory framework for takeovers in the United States and the United Kingdom. For example, as examined, the challenges in corporate acquisitions that have been undisputedly known to have been caused by corporate managers undermined the interests of target company shareholders. Hence, the *Williams Act*[68] and the Supreme Court of Delaware[69] have responded to restrict the role of target managements in order to protect the interests of target shareholders. Also, the UK[70]

66 Lynn A. Stout, 'Are Takeover Premiums Really Premiums? Market Price, Fair Value and Corporate Law' (1990) 99 *Yale Law Journal* 1235, 1246; Irwin Friend, Randolph Westerfield, and Michael Granito, 'New Evidence on the Capital Asset Pricing Model' (1978) 33 *The Journal of Finance* 903.

67 Larry H. P. Lang, René M. Stulz, and Ralph A. Walkling, 'A Test of Free Cash Flow Hypothesis: The Case of Bidder Returns' (1991) 29 *Journal of Financial Economics* 315; Larry H. P. Lang, Ralph Walkling, and René Stulz, 'Managerial Performance, Tobin's Q and the Gains from Successful Tender Offers' (1989) 24 *Journal of Financial Economics* 137–154; Vijay B. Gondhalekar, R. Raymond Sant, and Stephen P. Ferris, 'The Price of Corporate Acquisition: Determinants of Cash Takeover Premia' (2004) 11 *Applied Economics Letters*, 735.

68 *The Williams Act 1968.*

69 *Unocal Corp v Mesa Petroleum Company* 493 A.2d 946 (Del.Supr. 1985) and *Revlon Inc. v MacAndrews & Forbes Holdings Inc.* 506 A.2d 173 (Del. 1986).

70 *UK Takeover Code 2016.*

and EU[71] framework for takeover regulation have mainly been designed to promote target shareholder interests. These developments were occasioned by the need to protect target shareholder interests because it is believed that protecting target shareholder interests would promote competitive bids, since it would remove the barriers created by defensive bids. Importantly, the ways that competitive bids affect the interests of acquiring shareholders have not been given sufficient thought. A competitive bid does not necessarily promote the interests of acquiring shareholders. Rather it provides the opportunity for the market to determine the value of shares when corporate acquisitions are made. However, the dominant role of managers can undermine this market function where the prices of shares are determined by managerial preferences rather than by market forces. The extensive discretion of acquiring managers in the determination of the costs of shares is subtly encouraged by regulations that restrict managers in target companies from defending bids. The restriction on target managers in defending takeovers has the effect of removing the barriers that prevent or limit acquisition attempts. Thus, acquiring managers are encouraged to freely engage in acquisitions and this can lead to competitiveness since the barrier to successful acquisitions is no longer defensive bids, but rather enhanced bid prices. The enhanced bid prices have the effect of not only defeating other competitive bidders, but it can also incentivise target shareholders to sell their shares at irresistible premium rates. Thus, while competitive bids may be a feature of the market, the prices attached to the shares may not actually be determined by market forces. Rather, they may be decided by alternative managerial objectives. This is demonstrated in costly acquisitions that lead to losses for acquiring shareholders. Hence, a competitive bid can almost certainly promote target shareholder value through takeover premiums, but the extent to which it enhances the interests of acquiring shareholders is largely dependent on managerial preferences. In light of the agency problems of conflict of interests, it is imperative to establish mechanisms towards ensuring that acquiring managers engage in productive acquisitions.

c) Managerial hubris – corporate size

While the need to increase market power and the effects of competitive bids can potentially lead to costly acquisitions, other factors leading to costly acquisitions can broadly be classified under the effects of managerial hubris. Managerial hubris leads to the loss of corporate value and, ultimately, the loss of shareholder wealth since the economic gains to the combined companies post-acquisition is non-positive.[72] An increase in the size of a corporation without a corresponding increase in the economic value of the corporation is undesirable, since the objective of acquisition is synergistic gain.

71 *EU Takeover Directive* 2004.

72 Richard Roll, 'The Hubris Hypothesis of Takeovers' (1986) 59 *The Journal of Business* 197, 201–203.

When acquiring managers engage in acquisitions without sufficient or reasonable economic grounds for believing that synergistic gains are highly likely to occur, certain assumptions may be implied. First, managers may be genuinely interested in enhancing the economic value of their companies, but they may have failed to exercise the required level of prudence in relation to the costs of the acquisition. Second, it was suggested that managers may be influenced by arrogance as a result of past success and may fail to objectively assess the likelihood of the success of the acquisition.[73] Third, managerial motives may be influenced by their personal interests stirred by agency conflicts; this may include the office perquisites that are attached to the larger sized corporation. Fourth, the volume of business that newly enlarged enterprise will generate. rather than the business potential in terms of returns to shareholders,[74] may also incentivise managers to expand corporate size. Further, managers could be incentivised to make acquisitions if there are large financial resources without any net present value projects to invest in, irrespective of the indefinite potential for success. This is consistent with the acquisition failures or losses involving large companies.[75] Also, since managers of smaller firms have a higher level of firm ownership than their counterparts in larger firms, the economic interests of the shareholders and managers of smaller firms are better aligned.[76] Thus, the incidence of managerial hubris is present mainly in larger firms, because of the higher potential for agency conflict leading to a mere increase in the size of a corporation, without a corresponding increase in economic value.[77]

It has been suggested that CEOs can ultimately assess expected value from their experience of successive acquisitions, leading to their ability to integrate the combined companies, despite paying a higher price for acquisitions.[78] Even though learning is substituted for hubris,[79] the positive effects of learning may not successfully mitigate the effects of costly acquisitions. First, it does not specifically address the losses suffered by acquiring shareholders. Second, it is unclear as to how to ascertain the total number of acquisitions that would be required before managements fully learn to make productive acquisitions, bearing in mind that each acquisition would likely be very costly. Also, it is unlikely that every member of the management team would retain their position for an indefinite time. When new managers are appointed, the process would likely recommence,

73 M. Raj and M. Forsyth, 'Hubris amongst UK Bidders and Losses to Shareholders' (2003) 8/1 *International Journal of Business* 2–16 at 8–15.

74 Robert B. Reich, *The Next American Frontier* (New York, Times Books, 1983) 166.

75 See (a) Market power above.

76 Harold Demsetz and Kenneth Lehn, 'The Structure of Corporate Ownership: Causes and Consequences' (1985) 96 *Journal of Political Economy* 1155, 1158.

77 Cyrus A. Ramezani, Luc Soenen, and Alan Jung, 'Growth, Corporate Profitability and Value Creation' (2002) 58 *Financial Analysts Journal* 56, 65.

78 Kevin J. Davis and John A. Martin, 'Learning or Hubris? Why CEOs Create Less Value in Successive Acquisitions' (2010) 24 *Academy of Management Perspectives* 79.

79 Nihat Aktas, Ericde Bodt, and Richard Roll, 'Serial Acquirer Bidding: An Empirical Test of the Learning Hypothesis' (2011) 17 *Journal of Corporate Finance* 18.

except managers with previous acquisition experience are hired. These challenges and limitations indicate that it is imperative to challenge acquiring managers and address the problem of CEO dominance and overconfidence[80] towards ameliorating agency problems,[81] to ensure that they engage in productive acquisitions.

The challenges of shareholders in target and acquiring companies are largely linked to the ways that managements in both companies exercise their roles. This is evident from the response of the *Williams Act* and the Supreme Court of Delaware which challenge management functions, to protect the interests of shareholders in target companies. While the interests of shareholders in acquiring companies are also undermined by managements, sufficient attention has not been given to acquiring shareholders. Acquiring managements remain dominantly in control of the acquisition objectives of corporate entities, without any significant role for acquiring shareholders,[82] or mechanism for accountability. This has the capacity to encourage costly acquisition and indirectly undermine the interests of other corporate constituents, such as employees. The implication of these on employment is examined next.

5.5 Costly acquisitions and employee dismissal

There is abundant evidence in the literature to show that corporate acquisitions can have negative consequences on employment. It was indicated that employee dismissal may be carried out within three years of an acquisition.[83] Employment reduction, rather than mass dismissal was suggested to accompany changes in corporate ownership in an earlier research.[84] Also, while it is indicated that there was no significant change in employment generally, it was shown that there was over 17% decrease in completed hostile tender offers within a period of acquisition.[85] Another study which examined the effects of ownership changes on employment, wages and plant closing indicate that mere ownership changes do not affect jobs; rather, ownership changes with bigger plants are associated with job losses.[86] Using annual time series data from 1978 to 2008, it was suggested

80 Rayna Brown and Neal Sarma, 'CEO Overconfidence, CEO Dominance and Corporate Acquisitions' (2007) 59 *Journal of Economics and Business* 358.

81 Jay Dahya, Andrey Golubov, Dimitris Petmezas, and Nickolaos G. Travlos, 'Governance Mandates, Outside Directors, and Acquirer Performance' (2016) *Journal of Corporate Finance* 1.

82 Afra Afsharipour, 'Reevaluating Shareholder Voting Rights in M&A Transactions' (2017) 70 *Oklahoma Law Review* 127.

83 Vojislav Maksimovic, Gordon Phillips, and N. R. Prabhala, 'Post Merger Restructuring and the Boundaries of the Firm' (2011) 102 *Journal of Financial Economics* 317.

84 Frank R. Lichtenberg and Donald Siegel, 'Productivity and Changes in Ownership of Manufacturing Plants' in Frank R. Lichtenberg (ed.), *Corporate Takeovers and Productivity* (Cambridge, MIT Press, 1992) 665.

85 Diane K. Denis, 'Evidence on the Effects of Hostile and Friendly Tender Offers on Employment' (1994) 15 *Managerial and Decision Economics* 341.

86 Robert H. McGuckin and Sang V. Nguyen, 'The Impact of Ownership Changes: A View from Labor Markets' (2001) 19 *International Journal of Industrial Organization* 739.

that acquisitions did not negatively affect jobs in certain sectors of the economy.[87] Despite the differences in the results of these studies, they mostly indicate that job losses are associated with acquisitions. For example, it was suggested that acquisitions involving related companies dismiss employees to achieve economies of scale, synergy and to discipline inefficient managers.[88] Also, it was argued that costly acquisitions where large premiums are paid to acquire shares in target companies lead to employee dismissal in the combined company.[89]

Arguably, economies of scale, synergy and managerial discipline identified as reasons for dismissing employees are mainly cost-saving measures. They are cost-saving measures because the need to dismiss an employee is aimed at saving corporate costs, by reducing recurrent expenditure, especially where the role of the dismissed employee(s) can be carried out by another employee or shared by other employees. Since the need to dismiss employees in related businesses is necessary for synergy and economies of scale, it implies that employees would almost certainly be dismissed where corporate acquisitions are concluded at great cost. The combined effects of the need to achieve cost-saving synergy and the effects of costly acquisition on the firm would have the dual effects of enhancing the need for employees to be dismissed and increase the numbers of employees to be dismissed.

The effects of corporate acquisition on employment in the United States have been widely demonstrated. Even though a study failed to find an adverse effect of acquisitions on labour demand in the United States, it nevertheless found that takeovers through tender offers reduce labour demand.[90] This is consistent with the analyses that costly acquisitions can have a negative effect on employment,[91] since tender offers are often concluded after premiums have been paid. Despite the effects of acquisitions on employment, there is no general employment protection regulation in the United States, in relation to takeovers. However, corporate regulation in certain states, excluding Delaware, requires the interests of employees to be considered. For example, in Pennsylvania, the board is required to consider the interests of stakeholders such as employees:[92]

> a) In discharging the duties of their respective positions, the board of directors, committees of the board and individual directors of a business corporation may, in considering the best interests of the corporation, consider to the extent they deem appropriate

87 Nadia Doytch, Franklin G. Mixon, and Kamal P. Upadhyaya, 'Employment Effects of Mergers and Acquisitions in the United States by Sector' (2011) 18 *Applied Economics Letters* 925.

88 K. C. O'Shaughnessy and David J. Flanagan, 'Determinants of Layoff Announcements Following M&As: An Empirical Investigation' (1998) 19 *Strategic Management Journal* 989.

89 Hema A. Krishnan, Michael A. Hitt, and Daewoo Park, 'Acquisition Premiums, Subsequent Workforce Reductions and Post-Acquisition Performance' (2007) 44 *Journal of Management Studies* 709.

90 Klaus Gugler and B. Burcin Yurtoglu, 'The Effects of Mergers on Company Employment in the USA and Europe' (2004) 22 *International Journal of Industrial Organization* 481, 498.

91 Ibid.

92 Pennsylvania Statutes Title 15 Pa. C.S.A.

1) The effects of any action upon any or all groups affected by such action, including shareholders, employees, suppliers, customers and creditors of the corporation, and upon communities in which offices or other establishments of the corporation are located.

and (c) and (3) as follows:

c) In exercising the powers vested in the corporation, including, without limitation, those powers pursuant to section 1502 (relating to general powers), and in no way limiting the discretion of the board of directors, committees of the board and individual directors pursuant to subsections (a) and (b), the fiduciary duty of directors shall not be deemed to require them:
3) to act as the board of directors, a committee of the board or an individual director solely because of the effect such action might have on an acquisition or potential or proposed acquisition of control of the corporation or the consideration that might be offered or paid to shareholders in such an acquisition.

Also, the New York *Business Corporation Law* requires interested shareholder(s) to obtain approval from target company board before obtaining 20% or more of the outstanding voting stock ownership in target companies, otherwise they would be prevented from engaging in business combination with the company for a period of five years.[93] The approval process is required to include employment considerations, to ensure that employees are protected from the effects of acquisitions.[94] The requirement for employee interests to be considered is an indication of the vulnerability of employees. However, the extent to which the interests of employees can actually be protected is limited, since the board is merely required to consider the interests of employees; they are not mandated to positively protect employee interests. Also, it is doubtful whether employees would successfully challenge managements in an attempt to enforce the provisions, since managements do not owe their fiduciary duties to employees.

The Delaware General Corporation Law does not contain similar provisions that require company management to consider the interests of employees when a takeover is imminent. However, the Supreme Court observed in *Unocal Corp. v Mesa Petroleum Co.*[95] that it may be reasonable to consider the impact that an acquisition could have on other stakeholders, such as employees.

> If a defensive measure is to come within the ambit of the business judgment rule, it must be reasonable in relation to the threat posed. This entails an

93 New York Business Corporation Law BSC, s 912 (b). See 912 (10) (A) i & ii.

94 See Alan E. Garfield, 'State Competence to Regulate Corporate Takeovers: Lessons from State Takeover Statutes' (1989) 17 *Hofstra Law Review* 535, 552.

95 493 A.2d 946 (1985); *Time v Paramount*, 571 A.2d 1140, 1153 (Del. 1990).

> analysis by the directors of the nature of the takeover bid and its effect on the corporate enterprise. Examples of such concerns may include: inadequacy of the price offered, nature and timing of the offer, questions of illegality, the impact on 'constituencies' other than shareholders (i.e., creditors, customers, employees, and perhaps even the community generally), the risk of non-consummation, and the quality of securities being offered in the exchange.[96]

This requires target managements to consider the extent to which an acquisition would affect the interests of employees and other constituents when they defend bids. Acquiring managements make decisions that affect the interests of these stakeholders after the acquisition has been concluded; target managements are not saddled with such responsibility. Hence, the extent to which target managements can successfully consider and protect the interests of these stakeholders, including employees, is dependent on the extent to which they can extract enforceable assurances from the acquiring management. Decisions affecting the combined entity and its stakeholder are only made after the acquisition and the target management may not be available to ensure that these decisions would not undermine the interest of the stakeholders, such as employees.

Meanwhile, even though target managements may validly consider the interests of employees and other corporate constituents when a takeover bid is made, the scope of discretion that they can exercise is limited to the extent that the interests of their shareholders would be enhanced. In *Revlon Inc. v MacAndrews & Forbes Holdings Inc.*[97] the court observed that 'A board may have regard for various constituencies in discharging its responsibilities, provided there are rationally related benefits accruing to the stockholders'.[98] While the court effectively reaffirms shareholder primacy, it also recognises the potential for shareholder interests to be enhanced concurrently with the interests of other stakeholders, as long as managements can reasonably justify their actions.

It can be observed that the protection available to employees is largely dependent on the views and objectives of managements. For example, the provisions in the Pennsylvania and New York statutes are required to be acted upon by managements, since managements are responsible for considering the interests of employees based on their own judgment. Managerial dominance is also reflected in the decision of the Supreme Court of Delaware already identified. This implies that the role of managements is central in the determination of whether employees can be protected when a takeover is made. In acquiring companies, the role of management in the decisions relating to employment protection post-acquisition is also quite prominent. Since costly acquisition has been identified as a prominent reason for employee dismissal, the decision of acquiring managements to engage in costly acquisitions can significantly enhance the prospect of employee dismissal. The next section concludes the chapter.

96 Ibid. 955.
97 506 A.2d 173 (Del. 1986).
98 Ibid. 182D III.

5.6 Conclusion

This chapter examined the extent to which shareholder interests are protected when a corporate acquisition is made in the United States, with particular focus on Delaware. Also, the impact of acquisitions on employee interests was evaluated to ascertain the role of managements.

It was shown that the regulatory framework for takeovers was developed mainly as a response to the dominant role of company managements.[99] The challenges that characterised takeovers in the early periods were addressed by restricting the role of managements in target companies,[100] and shareholders were shown to be provided with the opportunity to make informed decisions about the sale of their shares.[101] Since the challenges that characterised takeovers in the United States in the early period mainly affected target shareholder interests, the responses to the problems were directed at addressing the problems that affected target shareholders. While this is justifiable, the scope of the problems that currently affect shareholders was shown to extend to the shareholders of acquiring companies. The central role of managements in promoting market power and the implications of competitive bids and managerial hubris were shown to be partly responsible for the challenges of acquiring shareholders.[102] Hence it was suggested that regulatory mechanisms that can address the challenges of acquiring shareholders are desirable; to restrict managerial discretions in making acquisitions that have limited prospects for value creation.

The effect of costly acquisitions was further shown to affect employees. Although economies of scale and synergy may require a reduction in the numbers of employees, large-scale employee dismissal is often associated with costly acquisitions; it enhances the need to dismiss employees and it increases the number of employees to be dismissed. Hence, costly acquisitions can potentially undermine the interests of acquiring shareholders and employees.

There is no substantive regulatory mechanism for employment protection in the United States and Delaware when a corporate acquisition is made. Although the negative impact of acquisitions on employment is recognised by the Supreme Court of Delaware, managements are merely required to consider employee interests and to ultimately promote shareholder interests.[103] Thus, the extent to which employees can actually be protected is dependent on the acquisition objectives of managements. When managements engage in costly acquisitions, the potential for losses to shareholders in target companies is almost certainly absent, in light of the premiums paid to the shareholders. However, negligible gains or losses to acquiring shareholders are highly likely when a costly acquisition is made, and employee dismissal is often considered by managements to

99 See 5.3.
100 See 5.3.2.
101 See 5.3.1.
102 See 5.4.
103 See note 95.

mitigate the effects of costly acquisitions. This clearly indicates that as long as managerial discretion is unrestricted and unchallenged, gains to acquiring shareholders would be determined by the prerogative of managements. Also, large-scale employee dismissal post-takeover may not be considered an unavoidable consequence of takeovers, they are within the control of managements. The next chapter evaluates the role of managements in the market for corporate control as an extension of the dominant role of managements in corporate governance administration.

The challenges in takeovers are now dominated by the role of managers. Costly acquisition, takeover premiums, managerial hubris and conflict of interest now dominate challenges that arise from managerial defences, since managerial defences are restricted especially in Delaware.

References

Afsharipour, A., 'Reevaluating Shareholder Voting Rights in M&A Transactions' (2017) 70 *Oklahoma Law Review* 127.

Aktas, N., Ericde Bodt, and Richard Roll, 'Serial Acquirer Bidding: An Empirical Test of the Learning Hypothesis' (2011) 17 *Journal of Corporate Finance* 18.

Alcock, A., 'The Regulation of Takeovers' (2001) 5 *Journal of International Financial Markets* 163.

Ansoff, H. I., *Corporate Strategy: An Analytic Approach to Business Policy for Growth and Expansion* (New York, McGraw-Hill, 1965).

Armour, J., Jack B. Jacobs, and Curtis J. Milhaupt, 'The Evolution of Hostile Takeover Regimes in Developed and Emerging Markets: An Analytical Framework' (2011) 52 *Harvard International Law Journal* 219.

Bradley, M., Anand Desai, and Han E. Kim, 'Synergistic Gains from Corporate Acquisitions and Their Division between the Stockholders of Target and Acquiring Firms' (1988) 21 *Journal of Financial Economics* 3.

Brown, R. and Neal Sarma, 'CEO Overconfidence, CEO Dominance and Corporate Acquisitions' (2007) 59 *Journal of Economics and Business* 358.

Chandler, III, W. B., 'Hostile M&A and the Poison Pill in Japan: A Judicial Perspective' (2004) *Columbia Business Law Review* 45.

Dahya, J., Andrey Golubov, Dimitris Petmezas, and Nickolaos G. Travlos, 'Governance Mandates, Outside Directors, and Acquirer Performance' (2016) *Journal of Corporate Finance* 1.

Davis, K. J. and John A. Martin, 'Learning or Hubris? Why CEOs Create Less Value in Successive Acquisitions' (2010) 24 *Academy of Management Perspectives* 79.

Demsetz, H. and Kenneth Lehn, 'The Structure of Corporate Ownership: Causes and Consequences' (1985) 96 *Journal of Political Economy* 1155.

Denis, D. K., 'Evidence on the Effects of Hostile and Friendly Tender Offers on Employment' (1994) 15 *Managerial and Decision Economics* 341.

Doytch, Nadia, Franklin G. Mixon, and Kamal P. Upadhyaya, 'Employment Effects of Mergers and Acquisitions in the United States by Sector' (2011) 18 *Applied Economics Letters* 925.

Fama, E. F. and Michael C. Jensen, 'Agency Problems and Residual Claims' (1983) 26 *Journal of Law and Economics* 327.

Friend, I., Randolph Westerfield, and Michael Granito, 'New Evidence on the Capital Asset Pricing Model' (1978) 33 *The Journal of Finance* 903.

Garfield, A. E., 'State Competence to Regulate Corporate Takeovers: Lessons from State Takeover Statutes' (1989) 17 *Hofstra Law Review* 535.

Gondhalekar, V. B. R., Raymond Sant, and Stephen P. Ferris, 'The Price of Corporate Acquisition: Determinants of Cash Takeover Premia' (2004) 11 *Applied Economics Letters* 735.

Gorton, G., Matthias Kahl, and Richard J. Rosen, 'Eat or Be Eaten: A Theory of Mergers and Firm Size' (2009) 64 *The Journal of Finance* 1291.

Gugler, K. and B. Burcin Yurtoglu, 'The Effects of Mergers on Company Employment in the USA and Europe' (2004) 22 *International Journal of Industrial Organization* 481.

Hayes, III, S. L. and Russell A. Taussig, 'Tactics of Cash Takeover Bids' (1967) 45 *Harvard Business Review* 135.

Hodgkinson, L. and Graham H. Partington, 'The Motivation for Takeovers in the UK' (2008) 35 *Journal of Business Finance & Accounting* 102.

Kenyon-Slade, S., *Mergers and Takeovers in the US and UK* (Oxford, Oxford University Press, 2004) 333.

Krishnan, H. A., Michael A. Hitt, and Daewoo Park, 'Acquisition Premiums, Subsequent Workforce Reductions and Post-Acquisition Performance' (2007) 44 *Journal of Management Studies* 709.

Lang, L. H. P., René M. Stulz, and Ralph A. Walkling, 'A Test of Free Cash Flow Hypothesis: The Case of Bidder Returns' (1991) 29 *Journal of Financial Economics* 315.

Larry, H. P. Lang, Ralph Walkling, and René Stulz, 'Managerial Performance, Tobin's Q and the Gains from Successful Tender Offers' (1989) 24 *Journal of Financial Economics* 137.

Lichtenberg, F. R. and Donld Siegel, 'Productivity and Changes in Ownership of Manufacturing Plants' in Frank R. Lichtenberg (ed.), *Corporate Takeovers and Productivity* (Cambridge, MIT Press, 1992).

Magnuson, W., 'Takeover Regulation in the United States and Europe: An Institutional Approach' (2009) 21 *Pace International Law Review* 205.

Maksimovic, V., Gordon Phillips, and N. R. Prabhala, 'Post Merger Restructuring and the Boundaries of the Firm' (2011) 102 *Journal of Financial Economics* 317.

McGuckin, R. H. and Sang V. Nguyen, 'The Impact of Ownership Changes: A View from Labor Markets' (2001) 19 *International Journal of Industrial Organization* 739.

Offenberg, D., 'Firm Size and the Effectiveness of the Market for Corporte Control' (2009) 15 *Journal of Corporate Finance* 66.

O'Shaughnessy, K. C. and David J. Flanagan, 'Determinants of Layoff Announcements Following M&As: An Empirical Investigation' (1998) 19 *Strategic Management Journal* 989.

Raj, M. and M. Forsyth, 'Hubris amongst UK Bidders and Losses to Shareholders' (2003) 8/1 *International Journal of Business* 2.

Ramezani, Cyrus, A. Luc Soenen, and Alan Jung, 'Growth, Corporate Profitability and Value Creation' (2002) 58 *Financial Analysts Journal* 56, 65.

Reich, R. B., *The Next American Frontier* (New York, Times Books, 1983) 166.

Roll, R., 'The Hubris Hypothesis of Takeovers' (1986) 59 *The Journal of Business* 197.

Romano, R., 'A Guide to Takeovers: Theory, Evidence and Regulation' (1992) 19 *Yale Journal on Regulation* 119.

Stout, L. A., 'Are Takeover Premiums Really Premiums? Market Price, Fair Value and Corporate Law' (1990) 99 *Yale Law Journal* 1235.

Subramanian, G., Steven Herscovici, and Brian Barbetta, 'Is Delaware's Antitakeover Statute Unconstitutional? Evidence from 1988–2008' (2010) 65 *The Business Lawyer* 685.

Online sources

ABN AMRO Bank Press Release, 'Completion of ABN AMRO Bank and Fortis Bank Nederland Legal Merger' 30 June 2010 www.abnamro.com/en/newsroom/press-releases/2010/completion_of_legal_merger.html accessed 31 May 2018.

Aldrick and Kamal Ahmed, 'The Royal Bank of Scotland Investigation: The Full Story of How the Biggest Bank in the World Went Burst' *The Telegraph* 05 March 2011 www.telegraph.co.uk/finance/newsbysector/banksandfinance/8363417/Royal-Bank-of-Scotland-investigation-the-full-story-of-how-the-worlds-biggest-bank-went-bust.html accessed 31 May 2018.

Andrews, Edmund L. and Andrew Ross Sorkin, 'Europe's Megadeal: The Overview: $183 Billion Deal in Europe to Join Two Wireless Giants' *New York Times* 4 February 2000 www.nytimes.com/2000/02/04/business/europe-s-megadeal-overview-183-billion-deal-europe-join-2-wireless-giants.html accessed 11 July 2018.

Barnett, Emma and Amanda Andrews, 'AOL Merger Was "the Biggest Mistake in Corporate History", Believes Time Warner Chief Jeff Bewkes' *The Telegraph* 28 September 2010 www.telegraph.co.uk/finance/newsbysector/mediatechnologyandtelecoms/media/8031227/AOL-merger-was-the-biggest-mistake-in-corporate-history-believes-TimeWarner-chief-Jeff-Bewkes.html accessed 30 April 2018.

Barwick, Terry et al., Director of Corporate Affairs 'Intended Offer to Mannesmann Shareholders' *Press Release* 29 December 1999 www.vodafone.com/content/index/media/vodafone-group-releases/1999/press_release29_11.html accessed 11 May 2018.

Brussels, Ian Traynor, 'Fortis: Belgium Acts to Prevent Financial Group's Collapse' *The Guardian* 29 September 2008 www.theguardian.com/money/2008/sep/29/insurance.europeanbanks accessed 12 November 2018.

CNN Money 4 February 2000 https://money.cnn.com/2000/02/04/europe/vodafone/ accessed 11 July 2018.

Edmund, L. Andrews and Andrew Ross Sorkin, 'Europe's Megadeal: The Overview; $183 Billion Deal in Europe to Join Two Wireless Giants' *New York Times* 4 February 2000 www.nytimes.com/2000/02/04/business/europe-s-megadeal-overview-183-billion-deal-europe-join-2-wireless-giants.html accessed 11 July 2018.

Essen, Yvette, 'Financial Crisis: Fortis' Dutch Assets Are Nationalised' *The Telegraph* 03 October 2008 www.telegraph.co.uk/finance/financialcrisis/3131247/Financial-Crisis-Fortis-Dutch-assets-are-nationalised.html accessed 12 November 2018.

Frank, Robert and Scott Hensley, 'Pfizer to Buy Pharmacia for $60 Billion in Stock' *The Wall Street Journal* 15 July 2002 www.wsj.com/articles/SB1026684057282753560 accessed 18 December 2018.

FSA Board Report, 'The Failure of the Royal Bank of Scotland' *Financial Services Authority* 2011, 407 www.fca.org.uk/publication/corporate/fsa-rbs.pdf accessed 12 November 2018; Harry Wilson, Philip.

FSA Board Report, 'The Failure of the Royal Bank of Scotland' *Financial Services Authority* 2011, 415. www.fca.org.uk/publication/corporate/fsa-rbs.pdf accessed 31 May 2018.

Hensley, Scott, 'Pfizer Posts $3.59 Billion Loss Due to Pharmacia Acquisition' *The Wall Street Journal* 27 July 2003 www.wsj.com/articles/SB105880674230792000 accessed 11 December 2018.

Lambeth, J., 'Qwest Faces Write Off Up to $30B' *The Telegraph* 03 April 2002, www.telegraph.co.uk/finance/2758662/Qwest-faces-writing-off-up-to-30bn.html accessed 18 December 2018.

'Nationalisation of ABN AMRO' www.government.nl/topics/state-owned-enterprises/nationalisation-of-financial-institutions-abn-amro-asr-and-sns-reaal/nationalisation-of-abn-amro accessed 12 November 2018.

Quinn, James, 'AOL Officially Splits from Time Warner after 10 Years' *The Telegraph* 9 December 2009 www.telegraph.co.uk/finance/newsbysector/mediatechnologyandtelecoms/6774324/AOL-officially-splits-from-Time-warner-after-10-years.html accessed 30 April 2018.

Reed, Kevin, 'Vodafone's Goodwill Write Down Sends Shock Waves through City' *Accountancy Age* 9 March 2006 www.accountancyage.com/aa/analysis/1751470/vodafones-goodwill-write-sends-shock-waves-city accessed 11 May 2018.

Saigol, Lina, 'The Real Deal: The Sobering Message of RBS's Sky-High ABN Bid' *Financial Times* October 2007 https://ftalphaville.ft.com/2007/10/01/7720/the-real-deal-the-sobering-message-of-rbss-sky-high-abn-bid/ accessed 12 November 2018.

Saigol, Lina, 'Vodafone Hope to Banish Ghost of Acquisition Past' *Financial Times* 12 June 2013 www.ft.com/content/7ead3928-d342-11e2-b3ff-00144feab7de accessed 14 May 2018.

Simon, Santiago, 'Mergers and Acquisition: Vodafone – Mannesmann' (2013) *Esade Business School* Working paper www.academia.edu/22609752/MAcase_Vodafone-Mannesmann accessed 1 June 2018, 19–20.

Steel, Emily, 'AOL-Time Warner Divorce Is Official' *The Wall Street Journal* 10 December 2009 www.wsj.com/articles/SB10001424052748704825504574586393655471238 accessed 30 April 2018.

'Vodafone Books $40.9 Billion Loss' *CNN International* Tuesday 30 May 2006 http://edition.cnn.com/2006/BUSINESS/05/30/vodafone.earns/ accessed 11 May 2018.

Wang, Tina, 'Fortis Pulled Back from the Brink' *Forbes* www.forbes.com/topstories/2008/09/28/fortis-bailout-pingan-markets-equity-cx_tw_0928markets01.html accessed 31 May 2018.

Williams, Carol J., 'As in Mannesmann Deal, Globalization Forcing Germany Inc. Out of Business' *Los Angeles Times* 14 February 2000 http://articles.latimes.com/2000/feb/14/business/fi-64162 accessed 11 May 2018.

6 Management board

Corporate governance and the market for corporate control MCC

6.1 Introduction

The role of the board is central to the administration of a corporate entity as a going concern. Particularly, the extent to which corporate governance rules can be effectively implemented and observed is largely dependent on the role of the management board. For example, the effectiveness of the UK corporate governance administration is dependent on the extent to which the board complies with corporate governance codes or provides suitable explanations to their shareholders for failing to comply with certain governance codes.[1] In the United States, the effectiveness of corporate governance administration is dependent on the extent to which governance rules are complied with or whether liability for failing to comply with the provisions of the rules can be enforced against erring board members.[2]

These approaches have peculiar challenges. In the UK, there is a question about the capacity of shareholders to effectively perform monitoring roles.[3] While it is expected that institutional shareholders should assume the responsibility of monitoring the board, it has been suggested that they do not perform sufficiently effective monitoring roles on the board to be able to mitigate the problems of agency conflict.[4] Also, heterogeneous shareholding can undermine the ability of shareholders to have a common agenda and free-riding by minority shareholders is difficult to address.[5] In the United States, the enforcement of the rules is effectively a response to managerial failure to comply with certain provisions of the rules. Managerial liability may not necessarily enhance corporate

1 The 'comply or explain' approach allows flexibility. It prevents the challenges of 'one size fits all'; it can also encourage non-compliance.

2 For example, see the *Sarbanes-Oxley Act 2002*, s 302.

3 Sridhar Arcot, Valentina Bruno, and Antoine Faure-Grimaud, 'Corporate Governance in the UK: Is the Comply or Explain Approach Working?' (2010) 30 *International Review of Law and Economics* 193.

4 Marc Goergen, Luc Renneboog, and Chendi Zhang, 'Do UK Institutional Shareholders Monitor their Investee Firms?' (2008) 8 *Journal of Corporate Law Studies* 39.

5 Sanford J. Grossman and Oliver D. Hart, 'Takeover Bids, the Free-Rider Problem, and the Theory of the Corporation' (1980) 11 *The Bell Journal of Economics* 42.

value or shareholder value; rather, it may be detrimental to the corporate value as a result of negative publicity. In view of these challenges, the market for corporate control which can be exhibited through corporate takeovers has been argued to be a suitable alternative disciplinary mechanism for management boards.[6] However, in light of the dominant role of managements in takeovers, it is doubtful whether the disciplinary role of the market for corporate control can perform this alternative function.

This chapter briefly examines the role of managements in relation to corporate governance and the market for corporate control. It identifies the limit of corporate governance and the role of the market for corporate control as an alternative mechanism for managerial discipline. It further illustrates how the scope of management functions in takeovers can undermine the managerial disciplinary role of the market for corporate control. It argues that the challenges that restrict the capacity of corporate governance to effectively discipline managements can also be present in the market for corporate control to undermine its capacity to limit and direct managerial functions towards the specific objective of enhancing corporate entities values. First, the role of managements in corporate governance administration is examined. The 'comply or explain' approach of the UK and the strict liability approach of the US are examined in light of management board's functions. Next, the role of managements in takeovers is examined from the perspective of target and acquiring managements. Then, the effects of managerial dominance on synergistic gains and the disciplinary role of takeovers are examined before the conclusion.

6.2 Managements boards and corporate governance administration

6.2.1 Corporate governance in the United Kingdom

The definition of corporate governance as the system by which companies are directed and controlled[7] is a reference to the role of the board as administrators of corporate governance in their respective entities. This role is emphasised in the introduction to the *UK Corporate Governance Code*:

> The Code does not set out a rigid set of rules; instead it offers flexibility through the application of Principles and through 'comply or explain' Provisions and supporting guidance. It is the responsibility of boards to use this flexibility wisely and of investors and their advisors to assess differing company approaches thoughtfully.[8]

6 Randal Morck, Andrei Shleifer, and Robert Vishny, 'Alternative Mechanisms for Corporate Control' (1989) 79 *The American Economic Review* 842.

7 The Committee on the Financial Aspects of Corporate Governance (The Cadbury Report) 1992, 2.5.

8 The *UK Corporate Governance Code 2018*, Introduction, 1.

The important role of the board in the implementation of corporate governance rules is further highlighted by the 'comply or explain' approach which requires the board to determine whether compliance with any of the provisions of the code is necessary. The corporate governance codes that are expected to promote good governance and accountability in corporate entities when implemented by the board are also required to be reviewed by the board to determine whether there is a need for compliance. This provides boards with the flexibility to determine the specific needs of their entities and it directly addresses the challenge of 'one size fit all' approach.

However, the challenges of corporate governance do not appear to have been substantially addressed by this approach. The challenges are particularly linked to corporate governance administration rather than the 'comply or explain' approach because the successful administration of corporate governance is dependent on the role of the board. For example, despite the development of corporate governance regulation in the UK with expectations for accountability, there has been a recurrence of corporate governance failures. On 15 January 2018, a compulsory liquidation order was made against Carillion Plc., a former multinational facilities management and construction services company with a debt burden of over £1.5bn.[9] The failure of corporate governance was one of the prominent reasons that led to the collapse of the company. It was reported that the company experienced lack of accountability, professionalisation and expertise and lack of financial information for managements to do their job, among others.[10] Describing the role of the *Carillion* board in corporate governance failure, it was stated that:

> Corporate culture does not emerge overnight. The chronic lack of accountability and professionalism now evident in Carillion's governance were failures years in the making. The board was either negligently ignorant of the rotten culture at Carillion or complicit in it.[11]

This emphasises the culpability of the board, since the complacent attitude of the board was the remote cause of the collapse of Carillion. The particular position of the company as being a major handler of government contracts is worrisome because it was expected to be a prominent proponent of effective corporate governance.

Also, on 10 April 2017, Tesco Plc. entered into a Deferred Prosecution Agreement with the UK Serious Fraud Office and agreed to pay £129m fine and £3m

9 National Audit Office, 'Investigation into the Government's Handling of the Collapse of Carillion' 7 June 2018, 4, 35 www.nao.org.uk/wp-content/uploads/2018/06/Investigation-into-the-governments-handling-of-the-collapse-of-Carillion.pdf accessed 11 November 2018.

10 House of Commons, 'Business Energy and Industrial Strategy and Work and Pensions Committees on Carillion' – Second Joint report from the Business, Energy and Industrial Strategy and Work and Pensions Committees of Session 2017–19 16 May 2018, 27 https://publications.parliament.uk/pa/cm201719/cmselect/cmworpen/769/769.pdf accessed 11 January 2019.

11 Ibid.

investigation fee.[12] The agreement was in respect of an accounting fraud that was committed by Tesco in 2014. The company had overstated its profits by £250m.[13] The Managing Director and the Food Commercial Director were later acquitted for personal involvement on charges of fraud and false accounting.[14] The corporate governance issues in Tesco are similar to the challenges that occurred in Carillion with respect to the role of the board. The role of the board of directors can be broadly classified into fiduciary duties[15] and duty to exercise reasonable care, skill and diligence.[16] While fiduciary duties require directors to act with honesty and to avoid opportunistic behaviour and conflicts of interests, the duty of care relates to competence.[17] Although, the court has held that the board in Tesco was not personally liable for the fraudulent accounting practice, nevertheless, the board was negligent in failing to ensure that the financial statements reflected the true and fair view of the financial position of the company.

6.2.2 Corporate governance in the United States

The approach to corporate governance administration in the US differs from what applies in the UK. The use of strict legal rules reflects the regulatory approach to corporate administration in the US. The corporate governance failure in Enron was a defining moment for the review of corporate regulation in the US. The introduction of the *Sarbanes-Oxley Act* in 2002 was a clear indication of the significant level of corporate governance challenges in the United States. The personal responsibility of the CEO and CFOs in the accuracy, documentation and submission of financial reports[18] ensures that senior board officers take personal responsibility in ensuring that accurate financial information is regularly published by the company. This seeks to avoid the type of financial reporting scandal that occurred in Tesco. Other corporate governance regulatory mechanisms include the *Securities Exchange Act of 1932*, which requires certain mandatory reporting and disclosure. Also, the *Dodd-Frank Wall Street Reform and Consumer Protection Act 2010* seeks to strengthen corporate governance administration in firms, by requiring certain

12 Tesco PLC Deferred Prosecution Agreement www.sfo.gov.uk/cases/tesco-plc/ accessed 11 January 2019.

13 Josie Cox, 'Tesco Fined £129m by Serious Fraud Office for Overstating Profits' 28 March 2017 *The Independent* London www.independent.co.uk/news/business/news/tesco-fined-129-million-by-serious-fraud-office-overstating-profits-a7653166.html#comments accessed 11 January 2019.

14 James Davey, 'Former Tesco Directors Cleared of Fraud Over 2014 Accounting Scandal' *Reuters* 6 December 2018 https://uk.reuters.com/article/us-britain-tesco/former-tesco-directors-cleared-of-fraud-over-2014-accounting-scandal-idUKKBN1O516I accessed 11 January 2019.

15 UK Companies Act 2006, ss 171, 172, 173, 175, 176 and 177; see *General Corporation Law of the State of Delaware*, s 144. *McMullin v. Beran*, 765 A.2d 910, 917 (Del. 2000); *Malone v. Brincat*, 722 A.2d 5, 10 (Del. 1998).

16 UK Companies Act 2006, s 174.

17 *Estrasure Travel Insurances Ltd v Scattergood [2003] 1 BCLC* 598. See Andrew Keay, *Directors Duties* (3rd edn, Lexis, Nexis, 2016) 71–72.

18 *Sarbanes-Oxley Act 2002*, s 302.

disclosure relating to Chairman and CEO structures in a company.[19] Despite the strict regulatory approach to corporate governance regulation, corporate scandals still occur in the US. Recently on 2 February 2018, the US Federal Reserve, in an unprecedented move, announced an enforcement action against Wells Fargo. The growth of the firm was restricted until it sufficiently improves its governance and controls.[20] The bank was allegedly involved in certain corporate governance failures, such as making unsuitable mortgage modifications, selling unwanted auto insurance, improperly charging fees for locking in mortgage rates and adding chargeable add-ons to accounts without the customers' permission.[21] These corporate governance failures were described by the Federal Reserve System as

> pursue[ing] a business strategy that emphasized sales and growth without ensuring that senior management had established and maintained an adequate risk management framework commensurate with the size and complexity of the Firm, which resulted in weak compliance practices.[22]

The failure of the board of Wells Fargo to effectively supervise management to ensure that an effective risk management mechanism was in place to avoid weak compliance practice may not be a deliberate omission of the board. Rather, it was likely an act of overconfidence of the board on the integrity and honesty of the management.

Other examples of corporate governance failure in the US include the Equifax hack scandal announced in September 2017 which involved allegations of misleading or incomplete information about the extent of the hack.[23] Also, series of governance scandals including the money-laundering scandal have led to HSBC being fined several hundred millions of dollars.[24] Despite the strict regulatory

19 *Dodd-Frank Wall Street Reform and Consumer Protection Act 2010*, s 972.

20 Press Release of the Board of Governors of the Federal Reserve System, 2 February 2018 www.federalreserve.gov/newsevents/pressreleases/enforcement20180202a.htm accessed 29 January 2019.

21 Trefis Team, 'How Will Wells Fargo Be Affected If Fed's Growth Restrictions Remain in Place for All of 2019?' *Forbes* 11 December 2018 www.forbes.com/sites/greatspeculations/2018/12/11/how-will-wells-fargo-be-affected-if-feds-growth-restrictions-remain-in-place-for-all-of-2019/#106b2b6c168c accessed 28 January 2019.

22 See Docket No. 18–007-B-HC in the matter of Wells Fargo & Company San Francisco, California para 6. www.federalreserve.gov/newsevents/pressreleases/files/enf20180202a1.pdf accessed 29 January 2019.

23 Donna Borak and Kathryn Vasel, 'The Equifax Hack Could Be Worse Than We Thought' *CNN Money* 10 February 2018 https://money.cnn.com/2018/02/09/pf/equifax-hack-senate-disclosure/index.html accessed 11 February 2019.

24 James Moore, 'HSBC: Who Cares about Money Laundering When the City's Thrilled' *The Independent* Monday 30 October 2017 www.independent.co.uk/news/business/comment/hsbc-who-cares-about-money-laundering-when-the-citys-thrilled-a8027146.html accessed 11 February 2019; Tom Teodorczuk, 'Netflix Documentary Re-Examines HSBC'S $881 Million Money-Laundering Scandal' 24 February 2018 *Market Watch* www.marketwatch.com/story/netflix-documentary-re-examines-hsbcs-881-million-money-laundering-scandal-2018-02–21 accessed 29 December 2018.

approach to corporate governance in the United States, corporate governance failures still occur.

Different approaches to corporate governance regulation have been adopted by the United Kingdom and the United States; however, corporate governance challenges still occur in both jurisdictions. These governance challenges occur because of the limited capacity of boards to carry out effective supervision of the management team of the company. There are several conflicting arguments as to whether effective boards are dependent on the composition and size of the board,[25] leadership style and the structure of the board[26] and coordination and behavioural attitudes.[27] In light of the recurrent corporate scandals, these characteristics may not sufficiently address the challenges of ineffective boards. Hence it was suggested that evaluation of the boards, the professionalisation of the selection process of outside directors and the availability of information to outside directors can enhance board effectiveness.[28]

25 Kose John and Lemm A. W. Senbet, 'Corporate Governance and Board Effectiveness' (1998) 22 *Journal of Banking and Finance* 371, 380, 385; C. Thomas, 'The Contribution of Non-Executive Directors to the Effectiveness of Corporate Governance' (1998) 3 *Career Development International Bradford* 118; William Q. Judge and Carl P. Zeithaml, 'Institutional and Strategic Choice Perspectives on Board Involvement in the Strategic Decision Process' (1992) 35 *Academy of Management Journal*, 766; Brian R. Golden and Edward J. Zajac, 'When Will Boards Influence Strategy? Inclination x Power = Strategic Change' (2001) 22 *Strategic Management Journal*, 1087; Daniel P. Forbes and Frances Milliken, 'Cognition and Corporate Governance: Understanding Board of Directors as Strategic Decision-Making Groups' (1999) 3 *Academy of Management Review* 489; Jerry Goodstein, Kanak Gautam, and Warren Boeker, 'The Effects of Board Size and Diversity on Strategic Change' (1994) 15 *Strategic Management Journal* 241; Theodore Eisenberg, Stefan Sundgren, and Martin T. Wells, 'Larger Board Size and Decreasing Firm Value in Small Firms' (1998) 48 *Journal of Financial Economics* 35; Anup Agrawal and Charles R. Knoeber, 'Firm Performance and Mechanisms to Control Agency Problems between Managers and Shareholders' (1996) 31 *Journal of Financial and Quantitative Analysis* 377; Jerilyn W. Coles, Victoria B. McWilliams, and Nilanjan Sen, 'An Examination of the Relationship of Governance Mechanisms to Performance' (2001) 27 *Journal of Management* 23; Stuart Rosenstein and Jeffrey G. Wyatt, 'Outside Directors, Board Independence, and Shareholder Wealth' (1990) 26 *Journal of Financial Economics* 175; John A. Wagner, III, J. L. Stimpert, and Edward I. Fubara, 'Board Composition and Organizational Performance: Two Studies of Insider/Outsider Effects' (1998) 35 *Journal of Management Studies* 655.

26 Catherine M. Daily and Dan R. Dalton, 'Corporate Governance and the Bankrupt Firm: An Empirical Assessment' (1994) 15 *Strategic Management Journal* 643; Dan R. Dalton, Catherine M. Daily, Alan E. Ellstrand, and Jonathan L. Johnson, 'Meta-Analytic Reviews of Board Composition, Leadership Structure and Financial Performance' (1998) 19 *Strategic Management Journal* 269; Melinda Muth and Lex Donaldson, 'Stewardship Theory and Board Structure: A Contingency Approach' (1998) 6 *Corporate Governance – An International Review*, 5.

27 Hans van Ees, Jonas Gabrielsson, and Morten Huse, 'Toward a Behavioral Theory of Boards and Corporate Governance' (2009) 17 *Corporate Governance: An International Review* 307; J. Roberts, T. McNulty, and P. Stiles, 'Beyond Agency Conceptions of the Work of the Non-Executive Director: Creating Accountability in the Boardroom' (2005) 16 *British Journal of Management* S5–S26.

28 L. A. A. Van den Berghe and Abigail Levrau, 'Evaluating Boards of Directors: What Constitutes a Good Corporate Board?' (2004) 12 *Corporate Governance* 461, 470–471.

The foregoing characteristics and suggestions for enhancing the effectiveness of boards are a reflection of the multiple challenges that undermine board effectiveness. Although these characteristics have largely been reflected in corporate governance regulations, nevertheless, corporate scandals still occur. This is an indication of the limited capacity of the board to effectively perform monitoring and supervisory role over company managements.

The historical development of corporate governance regulatory mechanisms in the United Kingdom and United States show that regulatory mechanisms are often developed as a reaction to high-profile governance failures and scandals. Also, most of the control mechanisms address issues relating to the role of the board. For example, the *Sarbanes-Oxley Act* of the United States and the *UK Corporate Governance Code* mainly seek to promote effective boards. This is mainly because boards need to be complicit for corporate entities to experience corporate scandals. Conversely, to prevent corporate scandals, boards need to be active and effective. This implies that effective corporate governance practices can largely be determined by the extent to which boards can effectively challenge and support managements. However, in light of the inherent challenges of agency problems, the ability of the board to effectively perform their monitoring roles is limited. Also, as indicated earlier, shareholders lack the capacity to effectively monitor managers,[29] except large shareholders who would not likely promote the interests of minority shareholders.[30] Thus, a suitable alternative mechanism for managerial discipline is desirable to promote accountability and align managerial interests with corporate interests. The market for corporate control has been suggested to perform this alternative disciplinary function.[31] When a firm is poorly governed and managed, the diminished value of the firm can attract outside investors to seek to gain control of the firm to enhance its value, often resulting in the dismissal of the top management team of the acquired company. However, the role of the board in takeovers can undermine this disciplinary function. For example, while managements in target companies may device means towards defending bids, their counterparts in acquiring companies have extensive discretion in the decision to engage in takeovers. This is examined next.

6.3 The role of managers in corporate acquisitions

Company managements have performed dominant roles in corporate acquisitions since the earliest period of acquisitions. This is indicated in the analyses of

29 See notes 3, 4 and 5.

30 Michael J. Barclay and Clifford G. Holderness, 'Private Benefits from Control of Public Corporations' (1989) 25 *Journal of Financial Economics* 371; Michael J. Barclay, Clifford G. Holderness, and Jeffrey Pontiff, 'Private Benefits from Block Ownership and Discounts on Closed-End Funds' (1993) 33 *Journal of Financial Economics* 293.

31 Note 6; Henry G. Manne, 'Mergers and Market for Corporate Control' (1965) 73 *Journal of Political Economy* 110; Michael C. Jensen and Richard S. Ruback, 'The Market for Corporate Control: The Scientific Evidence' (1983) 11 *Journal of Financial Economics* 5, 6; Alvaro Cuervo, 'Corporate Governance Mechanisms: A Plea for Less Code of Good Governance and More Market Control' (2002) 10 *Corporate Governance* 84.

the early periods of corporate takeovers in the United Kingdom and the United States in Chapters 4 and 5.[32] From the analyses in these chapters, it was observed that the regulatory frameworks for takeover were developed in both jurisdictions as a response to the challenges caused by managerial dominant roles in takeovers.[33] These regulations were aimed at addressing the challenges caused by conflict of interests to ensure that managements are either restricted from taking certain decisions or to ensure that their decisions promote corporate value. However, in light of the dominant role that managements can still exert in acquisitions, the extent to which this objective has been achieved is doubtful.

6.3.1 Managements of target companies

The role of managements of target companies is mainly determined by their involvement in the negotiation process leading to acquisitions and the extent to which they can reject and defend takeover bids.

In the United Kingdom, the regulatory framework for takeovers is mainly designed to restrict the role of managements of target companies.[34] The board neutrality rule excludes managements from interfering with a bid; managers are prevented from making any decision that would indicate that a bid has either been accepted or rejected without the authority of their shareholders.[35] This restriction ensures that shareholders can make independent decisions on a bid. It supports the analyses that the market for corporate control is an alternative disciplinary mechanism for managers because it operates to prevent managers from defending bids to protect their positions in the company. However, board neutrality rule only applies when a takeover bid is made, it does not restrict pre-bid defences. It does not totally restrict target managements from defending bids. For example, target managements may contact 'white knights' to prevent the success of the bid; they may also adopt lucrative compensation packages that provide for compensation to be paid to managements if there is a change of control leading to the termination of their employment. They may also adopt staggered board appointment procedures.[36] While target shareholders are required to determine whether a takeover bid should be accepted or rejected, managements may devise means to defend and frustrate takeovers. This include advising shareholders, as part of their roles when a bid is made,[37] not to accept bids, except certain level of premiums is paid in addition to the market value of the shares, without shareholder clarity whether the premiums are realistic targets.

32 See Chapter 4, 4.2 and Chapter 5, 5.2.
33 Chapter 4, 4.3 and Chapter 5, 5.3.
34 Chapter 4, 4.3.1.
35 Directive 2004/25/EC of the European Parliament and of the Council of 21 April 2004 on takeover bids (The *EU Takeover Directive*) para 2, and art. 9(2) *UK Takeover Code* B1 General Principles 3.
36 See Chapter 4, 4.3.1 on further discussion and the restrictions relating to the use of these defensive measures.
37 *UK Takeover Code*, Rule 3.1.

In the United States, managerial defences are not exclusively prohibited. As explained in *Chapter 5*, target managements can defend bids in certain permitted circumstances. The Delaware Supreme Court established the *Unocal Corp v Mesa Petroleum Company*[38] principle and the *Revlon Inc. v MacAndrews & Forbes Holdings Inc.*[39] principle. These principles determine whether a defensive tactic may be considered valid.

First, in relation to the tests for determining the validity of a defensive tactic under the *Unocal* principle, directors must show that they had reasonable grounds for believing that a danger to corporate policy and effectiveness existed because of another person's stock ownership. Alternatively, if the defensive tactic that is adopted by the board is brought under the business judgment rule, it must be reasonable in relation to the danger that is posed to the corporation.[40]

Second, under, the Revlon principle, once it becomes clear that the sale of a company is inevitable, the role of management is to ensure that they maximise the value of the company for the interests of the shareholders. The duty to preserve the policy of the corporate entity is displaced by this duty.[41] This suggests that managements of target companies are not exclusively restricted from defending takeover bids. They can defend bids as long as they act within the scope of the Unocal and Revlon principles.

While it may appear that the effect of the Revlon principle is to prevent managements from defending bids, since they are required to maximise the value of the company for the interests of the shareholders, they are not actually prevented from defending bids. They are only prevented from defending bids when it becomes evident that the company would be sold. This may be determined by the prevailing circumstances such as the financial condition of the target company relative to its competitors, the offer from the acquiring companies and the views of the target shareholders.

Hence, managements can adopt defensive tactics to frustrate a takeover bid, until any of these or other prevailing circumstances are present and until it becomes clear that the bidder(s) are relentless in their bid to acquire the company. At this point the target management would be required to commence negotiations towards getting the best value for their shareholders.

Thus, generally, the Unocal principle determines the validity of managerial defensive tactics until the Revlon principle is activated. Unlike the applicable rules in the UK, target boards in the US are not restricted to providing advice to their shareholders about the merit of a bid; they can defend bids as long as a sale is not imminent. Also, unlike the rules in the UK which do not require managements to take positive actions towards ensuring that they maximise value for their

38 493 A.2d 946 (Del.Supr. 1985).
39 506 A.2d 173 (Del. 1986).
40 See Chapter 5, 5.3.2(a) for analyses.
41 See analyses in Chapter 5, 5.3.2(b).

shareholders when a sale is imminent,[42] in Delaware, managements are required to ensure that they obtained maximum value for their shareholders.

The Unocal and Revlon principles indicate that there is scope for target managements to defend bids and subtly determine whether a takeover bid would be successful or not, unlike the applicable rule in the UK which expressly restrains managements from defending bids. Since target managements are only prevented from defending bids when a sale is imminent, they can adopt defensive measures that would prevent the sale of the company to become imminent as long as they can justify the reasonableness of the defensive measure to comply with the Unocal principle. Thus, generally, managements of target companies can influence takeover decisions and undermine the disciplinary function of the market for corporate control which is expected to be an alternative disciplinary mechanism to corporate governance regulation. The role of management of acquiring companies is examined next.

6.3.2 Managements of acquiring companies

Managements of acquiring companies perform significant roles in corporate acquisitions, especially in the decision to make acquisitions. They identify target companies and decide the costs of the acquisition and the mode of acquisition. Apparently, they engage in acquisitions as a usual investment decision that they are ordinarily contracted to make. In light of the high costs of acquisition and the loss or insignificant gains to acquiring shareholders,[43] the role of acquiring managements has continued to attract attention.[44] For example, managerial hubris[45] has been suggested to be a likely outcome of takeovers, even though managements usually suggest that their decision to engage in acquisition is influenced by synergistic gains. Despite the potential for company managements to engage in costly acquisitions that can potentially be low-value-yielding or lead to losses, managements of acquiring companies exercise considerable discretion and independence in decisions to engage in acquisition.

In the United Kingdom, decisions relating to takeovers are made with the discretion of acquiring boards and managements with limited scope for legal control or shareholder approval. In very limited circumstances, shareholder approval may be required. For example, if the acquisition is considered to be a class 1 transaction, shareholder approval would be required.[46] Shareholder approval is not generally required when a listed company is involved in a takeover. What is required

42 See Chapter 4, 4.3.1. The fiduciary duties and the duty of care and skill under the UK *Companies Act 2006*, may nevertheless require boards to act towards obtaining maximum value for their shareholders.

43 See Chapter 4, 4.3.2 ii.

44 Gary Gorton, Matthias Kahl, and Richard Rosen, 'Eat or Be Eaten: A Theory of Mergers and Firm Size' (2009) 64 *Journal of Finance* 1291.

45 Richard Roll, 'The Hubris Hypothesis of Takeovers' (1986) 59 *The Journal of Business* 197.

46 The *United Kingdom Listing Rules 10.5; Rules 10.2 (3), R 10 (annex 1.1) (1G).*

is that the acquiring company must be a listed company with a premium listing and the size of the acquirer should exceed the target company by at least 25% or more, or 100% in reverse takeovers.[47] Shareholder approval of class 1 transactions is limited in scope; it does not significantly challenge the acquisition decisions of company managements in light of agency conflict and the hubris hypothesis.[48] The limited scope for shareholder approval may have been influenced by the underlying objective of protecting the interests of target shareholders in the United Kingdom. The regulatory framework for takeovers is aimed at protecting target shareholder interests.

> The Code is designed principally to ensure that shareholders in an offeree company are treated fairly and are not denied an opportunity to decide on the merits of a takeover and that shareholders in the offeree company of the same class are afforded equivalent treatment by an offeror.[49]

Also, the *EU Takeover Directive* has a similar objective.

> It is necessary to protect the interests of holders of the securities of companies governed by the law of a Member State when those companies are the subject of takeover bids or the changes of control.[50]

Thus, the limited restrictions of the powers of the management board to engage in acquisitions and the limited scope for shareholder involvement implies that managements of acquiring companies can influence the activities of the market for corporate control and undermine the role of the market which is expected to perform alternative disciplinary functions to the corporate governance mechanisms.

Similarly, in the United States, the regulatory framework for takeovers has mainly been designed to further the interests of shareholders in target companies. The relevant provisions of the *Williams Act* and the principles established by the Delaware Supreme Court in *Unocal Corp v Mesa Petroleum Company*[51] and *Revlon Inc. v MacAndrews & Forbes Holdings Inc.*[52] responded to the challenges that undermined the interests of shareholders in target companies.[53] The Act and judicial principles do not challenge the discretion of directors in making acquisition decisions. This implies that acquiring managements have an extensive scope of discretion in engaging in acquisitions despite the scope for takeover hubris and agency conflict. The implications of managerial discretion in acquisitions have already been demonstrated in costly acquisitions with high takeover premiums.

47 *UK Listing Rules 5.6.3.*
48 See the analysis in Chapter 4, 4.3.2.
49 See *The City Code on Takeovers and Mergers 2016* 2(a) the Nature and Purpose of the Code.
50 *EU Takeover Directive* 2004, Introductory paragraph 2.
51 493 A.2d 946 (Del.Supr. 1985).
52 506 A.2d 173 (Del. 1986).
53 See the analysis in Chapter 4, 5.4.

Even though takeovers do not generally lead to losses to shareholders of the acquiring company, the extensive discretionary powers of acquiring company managements in the United Kingdom and the United States is a challenge to the market for corporate control. Managements can undermine synergistic objectives of takeovers by engaging in unproductive acquisitions deliberately or carelessly. Thus, in the absence of any effective mechanism that can challenge managerial acquisition objectives, managements can influence the role of the market for corporate control. This can undermine the disciplinary role of takeovers, since managerial preferences would determine when an acquisition is made, including the costs of the acquisition, rather than prices being determined by market forces.

Since managers can defend or reject bids in certain circumstances and can largely determine the extent to which an acquisition should be made, the role of the market for corporate control can be influenced by managerial objectives.

As examined earlier, the role of the board and top managements of corporate entities influence the administration of corporate governance, hence the need for an alternative control to regulate managerial discretion.[54] However, in light of the extensive scope of director and managerial powers in corporate acquisitions, it can be observed that managements' dominance over corporate governance administration extends to the market for corporate control. In light of the problems of the agency conflict of interests, the dominant role of managements in corporate acquisitions must be challenged or perhaps a suitable and further alternative to the market for corporate control is desirable.

6.4 Conclusion

The role of the board in public companies and large private companies is central to company regulation and corporate governance administration. This important role remains the subject of recurrent debates because, first, regulatory compliance and corporate governance administration are largely exhibited by the role of the board.[55] Second, the incidence of conflict of interests can potentially undermine the effective performance of the board.

This chapter briefly examined the role of the board in corporate governance administration and the extent to which the board can influence the market for corporate control. It examined the approaches to corporate governance regulation in the United Kingdom and the United States in relation to the role of the board. It was shown that the role of the board influences the administration of corporate governance irrespective of the approach to governance. For example, the 'comply or explain' approach to corporate governance was demonstrated to be largely linked to the role of the board.[56] Boards are at liberty to decide whether to comply with the provisions of the corporate governance code and explain instances of no compliance to their shareholders, even though shareholders may not have

54 See 6.2.1 and 6.2.2.
55 See 6.2.
56 See 6.2.1.

the capacity to monitor non-compliance. Also, a strict regulatory approach to corporate governance regulation in the United States, was also shown to be closely linked to the role of the board. It was argued that the strict regulation of corporate governance in the United States is directly related to the extent to which the board is responsible for ensuring that corporate entities act in a certain way or abstain from acting. Hence, the measure of success of corporate governance with strict regulation is dependent on the extent to which the board complies with the provisions of the rules. It was further demonstrated that corporate scandals still occur despite the strict rules that are expected to make boards more effective and ultimately accountable. These challenges in the UK and US corporate governance approaches demonstrate the weakness of corporate governance, hence the market for corporate control was shown to have been mooted in the literature to provide an alternative disciplinary mechanism to corporate governance.

Further, an exposition of the role of the board and senior managements in corporate acquisitions show that the role of the market for corporate control as an alternative disciplinary mechanism may be undermined. For example, managements in target companies can defend takeover bids in the UK and US in certain circumstances, despite the restrictions. It was shown that while the UK require managements to abstain from defending takeover bids, the US does not specifically prevent managements from defending bids, except they can justify their actions or except certain circumstances exist.[57] Also, acquiring managements in the UK and US have extensive discretion in the decision to acquire a target company. In light of the potential for conflict of interests and the challenges of costly acquisitions, it was argued that the role of acquiring managements is capable of influencing the function of the market. For example, the costs of acquisitions may be determined by managerial preferences, rather than the market. Thus, it is imperative to challenge the role of managements in corporate acquisitions to ensure that the role of the market as an alternative disciplinary mechanism to corporate governance is preserved. This would ensure that the dominant role of managements in corporate governance administration is not extended to the market for corporate control.

References

Agrawa, A. L. and Charles R. Knoeber, 'Firm Performance and Mechanisms to Control Agency Problems between Managers and Shareholders' (1996) 31 *Journal of Financial and Quantitative Analysis* 377.

Arcot, S., Valentina Bruno, and Antoine Faure-Grimaud, 'Corporate Governance in the UK: Is the Comply or Explain Approach Working?' (2010) 30 *International Review of Law and Economics* 193.

Barclay, M. J. and Clifford G. Holderness, 'Private Benefits from Control of Public Corporations' (1989) 25 *Journal of Financial Economics* 371.

57 See 6.3.1.

Barclay, M. J., Clifford G. Holderness, and Jeffrey Pontiff, 'Private Benefits from Block Ownership and Discounts on Closed-End Funds' (1993) 33 *Journal of Financial Economics* 293.

Coles, J. W., Victoria B. McWilliams, and Nilanjan Sen, 'An Examination of the Relationship of Governance Mechanisms to Performance' (2001) 27 *Journal of Management* 23.

Cuervo, A., 'Corporate Governance Mechanisms: A Plea for Less Code of Good Governance and More Market Control' (2002) 10 *Corporate Governance* 84.

Daily, C. M. and Dan R. Dalton, 'Corporate Governance and the Bankrupt Firm: An Empirical Assessment' (1994) 15 *Strategic Management Journal* 643.

Dalton, D. R., Catherine M. Daily, Alan E. Ellstrand, and Jonathan L. Johnson, 'Meta-Analytic Reviews of Board Composition, Leadership Structure and Financial Performance' (1998) 19 *Strategic Management Journal* 269.

Eisenberg, T., Stefan Sundgren, and Martin T. Wells, 'Larger Board Size and Decreasing Firm Value in Small Firms' (1998) 48 *Journal of Financial Economics* 35.

Forbes, D. P. and Frances Milliken, 'Cognition and Corporate Governance: Understanding Board of Directors as Strategic Decision-Making Groups' (1999) 3 *Academy of Management Review* 489.

Goergen, M., Luc Renneboog and Chendi Zhang, 'Do UK Institutional Shareholders Monitor their Investee Firms?' (2008) 8 *Journal of Corporate Law Studies* 39.

Golden, B. R. and Edward J. Zajac, 'When Will Boards Influence Strategy? Inclination x Power = Strategic Change' (2001) 22 *Strategic Management Journal* 1087.

Goodstein, J., Kanak Gautam, and Warren Boeker, 'The Effects of Board Size and Diversity on Strategic Change' (1994) 15 *Strategic Management Journal* 241.

Gorton, G., Matthias Kahl, and Richard Rosen, 'Eat or Be Eaten: A Theory of Mergers and Firm Size' (2009) 64 *The Journal of Finance* 1291.

Grossman, Sanford J. and Oliver D. Hart, 'Takeover Bids, the Free-Rider Problem, and the Theory of the Corporation' (1980) 11 *The Bell Journal of Economics* 42.

Jensen, M. C. and Richard S. Ruback, 'The Market for Corporate Control: The Scientific Evidence' (1983) 11 *Journal of Financial Economics* 5.

Judge, W. Q. and Carl P. Zeithaml, 'Institutional and Strategic Choice Perspectives on Board Involvement in the Strategic Decision Process' (1992) 35 *Academy of Management Journal* 766.

Keay, A., *Directors Duties* (3rd edn, Lexis, Nexis, 2016).

Kose, John and Lemm A. W. Senbet, 'Corporate Governance and Board Effectiveness' (1998) 22 *Journal of Banking and Finance* 371, 380, 385.

Manne, H. G., 'Mergers and Market for Corporate Control' (1965) 73 *Journal of Political Economy* 110.

Morck, R., Andrei Shleifer, and Robert Vishny, 'Alternative Mechanisms for Corporate Control' (1989) 79 *The American Economic Review* 842.

Muth, M. and Lex Donaldson, 'Stewardship Theory and Board Structure: A Contingency Approach' (1998) 6 *Corporate Governance – An International Review* 5.

Roberts, J., T. McNulty, and P. Stiles, 'Beyond Agency Conceptions of the Work of the Non-Executive Director: Creating Accountability in the Boardroom' (2005) 16 *British Journal of Management* S5–S26.

Roll, R., 'The Hubris Hypothesis of Takeovers' (1986) 59 *The Journal of Business* 197.

Rosenstein, S. and Jeffrey G. Wyatt, 'Outside Directors, Board Independence, and Shareholder Wealth' (1990) 26 *Journal of Financial Economics* 175.

Thomas, C., 'The Contribution of Non-Executive Directors to the Effectiveness of Corporate Governance' (1998) 3 *Career Development International Bradford* 118.

Van den Berghe, L. A. A. and Abigail Levrau, 'Evaluating Boards of Directors: What Constitutes A Good Corporate Board?' (2004) 12 *Corporate Governance* 461, 470–471.

Van Ees, H., Jonas Gabrielsson, and Morten Huse, 'Toward a Behavioral Theory of Boards and Corporate Governance' (2009) 17 *Corporate Governance: An International Review* 307.

Wagner, III, J. A., J. L. Stimpert, and Edward I. Fubara, 'Board Composition and Organizational Performance: Two Studies of Insider/Outsider Effects' (1998) 35 *Journal of Management Studies* 655.

Online reports

Borak, Donna and Kathryn Vasel, 'The Equifax Hack Could Be Worse Than We Thought' *CNN Money* 10 February 2018 https://money.cnn.com/2018/02/09/pf/equifax-hack-senate-disclosure/index.html accessed 11 February 2019.

Cox, J., 'Tesco Fined £129m by Serious Fraud Office for Overstating Profits' *The Independent* 28 March 2017 London www.independent.co.uk/news/business/news/tesco-fined-129-million-by-serious-fraud-office-overstating-profits-a7653166.html#comments accessed 11 January 2019.

Davey, J., 'Former Tesco Directors Cleared of Fraud Over 2014 Accounting Scandal' *Reuters* 6 December 2018 https://uk.reuters.com/article/us-britain-tesco/former-tesco-directors-cleared-of-fraud-over-2014-accounting-scandal-idUKKBN1O516I accessed 11 January 2019.

Moore James, 'HSBC: Who Cares about Money Laundering When the City's Thrilled' *The Independent* Monday 30 October 2017 www.independent.co.uk/news/business/comment/hsbc-who-cares-about-money-laundering-when-the-citys-thrilled-a8027146.html accessed 11 February 2019.

Teodorczuk, Tom, 'Netflix Documentary Re-Examines HSBC'S $881 Million Money-Laundering Scandal' *Market Watch* 24 February 2018 www.marketwatch.com/story/netflix-documentary-re-examines-hsbcs-881-million-money-laundering-scandal-2018-02–21 accessed December 29th 2018.

Trefis Team, 'How Will Wells Fargo Be Affected If Fed's Growth Restrictions Remain in Place for All of 2019?' *Forbes* 11 December 2018 www.forbes.com/sites/greatspeculations/2018/12/11/how-will-wells-fargo-be-affected-if-feds-growth-restrictions-remain-in-place-for-all-of-2019/#106b2b6c168c accessed 28 January 2019.

Part III

7 Complementary interests of shareholders and employees

7.1 Introduction

The effects of costly acquisition on employment were briefly examined in Chapters 4 and 5. The analysis of the effects of acquisitions on employment shows that employment reduction post-acquisitions are mainly aimed at reducing corporate costs.[1] Corporate managements have little challenges in dismissing employees after acquisitions because employees are non-financial stakeholders in companies and they do not participate in the negotiation process before acquisition deals are concluded. Much focus has been directed towards promoting shareholder value during takeovers without realising that the interests of other constituents such as employees' can indirectly be linked to the interests of shareholders, especially shareholders of acquiring companies.

This chapter examines the relationship between the role of managements, shareholder interests and employee interests in takeovers. It illustrates how the role of managements can be restricted towards ensuring that employee dismissal during takeovers is avoided or clearly justified to ultimately promote shareholder interests and corporate value. First, the limitations to employment protection in takeovers are identified and examined. Second, the default beneficiaries of corporate acquisitions are identified among the major corporate constituents. Next, the effect of transaction cost economics, its application to corporate acquisition and its effects on corporate value and shareholder interests, are examined. Then a new paradigm that challenges managerial expertise towards protecting shareholder and employee interests is presented before the conclusion.

7.2 Limitations to employment protection in takeovers

Employee dismissal has gradually become an integral part of corporate acquisition, primarily as a result of the need to save costs after engaging in costly acquisition. The negative effects of acquisition on employment have been acknowledged by regulations. For example, the *EU Takeover Directive* recognises the threat that

1 Chapter 4, 4.4 and Chapter 5, 5.5.

takeovers pose to employment, hence it requires that employee interests should be considered.[2] Similarly, the Delaware Supreme Court has observed that it may be reasonable to consider the impact of acquisition on employment.[3] Despite these acknowledgements and the threats that acquisitions pose to employment,[4] the interests of employees are not actually protected in takeovers, mainly because company employees are non-financial stakeholders and the framework for corporate regulation is designed to promote shareholder interests among other reasons.

7.2.1 Employees as non-financial stakeholders

Corporate stakeholders refer to all individuals or groups who can substantially affect or be affected by the welfare of the firm, including non- financial claimholders such as employees, customers, communities and government officials.[5] As financial stakeholders, shareholders are financial claimants. They dispose of or obtain financial interests when corporate acquisitions are made – either as target shareholders or acquiring shareholders respectively – hence, they participate in negotiations leading to acquisitions. Employees are non-financial stakeholders; they do not participate in negotiations leading to acquisitions; hence, their interests may not be protected.

7.2.2 Shareholder value approach to corporate regulation

Corporate regulation and corporate governance administration are dominated by shareholder value approach in several jurisdictions, including the United Kingdom and the United States. In the United Kingdom, although directors' duties are stated to be owed to the company,[6] they are to promote the success of the company for the benefit of the shareholders.[7] The interests of other financial and non-financial stakeholders in a company are only required to be considered to the extent that it would enhance the interests of shareholders.[8] Corporate governance administration is also expected to largely promote shareholder interests. The 'comply or explain' approach to corporate governance requires company boards to comply with the provisions of the code or explain their reasons for non-compliance to their shareholders.[9] Apparently as the residual claimants and dominant financial stakeholders in corporate entities, shareholders can decide

2 *EU Takeover Directive* art 9(5); the *Fair Trading Act 1973*, s 84.
3 *Unocal Corp. v Mesa Petroleum Co.*, 493 A.2d 946, 955 (1985); *Time v Paramount*, 571 A.2d 1140, 1153 (Del. 1990).
4 See Chapter 5, 5.5.
5 Michael C. Jensen, 'Value Maximization, Stakeholder Theory and the Corporate Objective Function' (2001) 14 *Journal of Applied Corporate Finance* 8, 9.
6 *Companies Act 2006*, s 170.
7 *Companies Act 2006*, s 172.
8 Ibid.
9 The *UK Corporate Governance Code 2018*.

whether they are satisfied with the level of the board's compliance with the corporate governance code to the exclusion of other stakeholders in the company.

In the United States, particularly in Delaware, directors' duties are owed to the corporation for the benefit of the shareholders. In *Harris v Carter*[10] it was observed that a person who occupies the position of director owes fiduciary duty to the shareholders of the company. This case relates to the acts of controlling shareholders who were also directors in the company. The court stated that the conducts of the defendants (who were the controlling shareholders and directors) should be considered on the basis of foreseeable harm to other shareholders in the company.

> It is established American legal doctrine that, unless privileged, each person owes a duty to those who may foreseeably be harmed by her action to take such steps as a reasonably prudent person would take in similar circumstances to avoid such harm to others.[11]

In distinguishing between the duties of directors and the protection provided to company creditors, the Delaware Supreme Court reiterated in *In North American Catholic Educational Programming Foundation, Inc. v Gheewalla*[12] that the duty of directors is owed to the corporation and its shareholders. It observed that

> It is well established that the directors owe their fiduciary obligations to the corporation and its shareholders. While shareholders rely on directors acting as fiduciaries to protect their interests, creditors are afforded protection through contractual agreements, fraud and fraudulent conveyance law, implied covenants of good faith and fair dealing, bankruptcy law, general commercial law and other sources of creditor rights.[13]

The responsibility of directors to promote the interests of shareholders above the interests of creditors, who are also financial stakeholders, is an indication that the dominant objective of corporate entities is to maximise shareholder value. This implies that the interests of non-financial stakeholders, such as employees, are not considered to be relevant to the corporate objective. These regulatory approaches that promote shareholder value in the United States and the United Kingdom are the frameworks upon which other acquisition-related regulations are based. For example, takeover regulation in the United Kingdom was developed to protect shareholder interests despite the threat of takeovers to employee interests. The *UK*

10 *Harris v Carter*, 582 A.2d 222, 234–236 (Del. Ch. 1990).

11 Ibid. 234–235. Note generally that a shareholder has a right to sell his or her stock and in the ordinary case owes no duty in that connection to other shareholders when acting in good faith. *Frantz Manufacturing Co. v EAC Industries*, Del.Supr., 501 A.2d 401, 408 (1985).

12 930 A.2d 92, (Del. 2007).

13 Ibid. 99.

Takeover Code is specifically aimed at protecting shareholders from unfair treatment.[14] The *EU Takeover Directive* is essentially aimed at protecting shareholder interests.[15] It merely acknowledges threats to employee interests;[16] directors are not required to protect employee interest. Attempts towards protecting employee interests in the UK led to the development of employment protection regulation when businesses are sold.[17] However, TUPE has failed to provide the required protection to employee interests.[18] The United States does not have a TUPE-styled regulation; hence, employees would have to rely on the mainstream employment law for protection. Despite the differences in the framework for corporate regulation in the United States and the United Kingdom, employees have similar challenges in both jurisdictions when a takeover is made. This problem persists because employees are non-financial stakeholders; corporate regulations promote shareholder value and managements have extensive scope of discretion. The next section briefly identifies the default beneficiaries of corporate acquisitions.

7.3 Default beneficiaries of corporate acquisitions

The main beneficiaries of corporate acquisitions can be identified from the effects of acquisition on the interests of the major corporate constituents: shareholders, employees, management board and creditors. The extent to which the interests of these constituents are affected by acquisition is dependent on regulation and the role of managements. It was earlier examined that shareholders are protected from takeover challenges mainly because they are financial stakeholders and corporate regulatory framework in the United States and the United Kingdom promote shareholder value.[19] However, the protection available to shareholders is largely limited to shareholders in target companies, as indicated in the regulatory framework for takeovers in both jurisdictions.[20] Thus, the status of shareholders as default beneficiaries of takeovers applies in relation to shareholders in target companies.

7.3.1 Shareholders in target companies

Shareholders of target companies are among the default beneficiaries of corporate acquisitions; they receive premium value from the sale of their shares. Since managements are largely restricted from interfering with takeover bids, shareholders have the opportunity to cash in on the offer from acquiring companies to acquire

14 *Takeover Code 2016*, see Nature and Purpose of the code.

15 Directive 2004/25/EC of the European Parliament and of the Council of 21 April 2004 on takeover bids (the *EU Takeover Directive*), Introductory paragraph 2.

16 *EU Takeover Directive* art. 9(5).

17 *The Transfer of Undertakings (Protection of Employment) Regulations 1981*. Amended in 2006 (TUPE).

18 See the analyses in Chapter 4, 4.4.1.

19 See 7.2.

20 See Chapter 4, 4.3.1 and Chapter 5, 5.3.

their shares. Different factors influence the premium value attached to shares. The desire of the acquiring investors to obtain control and the loss of control by the target shareholder can enhance the prices of shares beyond their ordinary market value. Control is considered to be an asset.[21] It is generally believed by acquirers that obtaining control over target companies has potential realisable value, especially underperforming companies. Hence, when shares are acquired with the objective of having control over the target company, the acquiring investor is incentivised to pay more than the market value of the shares.[22] Once the payments are made, the shareholders receive the financial value of their shares and they become beneficiaries of the concluded acquisition.

7.3.2 Management board

Managements of target and acquiring companies are among the default beneficiaries of takeovers. They are directly involved in the negotiation process leading to takeovers in their capacity in acquiring or target companies. Although the disciplinary effect of takeovers can lead to the dismissal of target managements, nevertheless managements receive certain financial benefits as compensation for the termination of their contract or as an appreciation award from the target board for negotiating a high premium. The compensation and award are so lucrative that they have been challenged by litigation.[23] Although challenging the level of award and compensation may appear to limit the benefit accruing to target managements, nevertheless they are compensated even at reduced rates.

Managements of acquiring companies have a broader scope of benefit than their counterparts in target companies for various reasons. First, there is limited regulatory control over the role of acquiring managers. In the United Kingdom, acquiring managers have extensive discretion in determining whether to engage in acquisition. They are not usually required to obtain shareholder approval, except in limited circumstances where the takeover transaction is considered to be a class 1 transaction.[24] This kind of transaction rarely occurs; thus managers retain extensive discretion. Similarly, in the United States, acquiring managers have extensive discretion in decisions relating to acquisitions. In light of the challenges of conflict of interests, acquiring managements in both jurisdictions may

21 Lucian A. Bebchuk, 'Efficient and Inefficient Sales of Corporate Control' (1994) 109 *Journal of Economics* 957, 962; Sanford J. Grossman and Oliver D. Hart, 'One Share One Vote and the Market for Corporate Control' (1988) 20 *Journal of Financial Economics* 175.

22 Donald M. DePamphilis, *Mergers, Acquisitions and other Restructuring Activities: An Integrated Approach to Process, Tools, Cases and Solutions* (9th edn, London, Academic Press United Kingdom, 2018) 22; Nikhil P. Varaiya and Kenneth R. Ferris, 'Overpaying in Corporate Takeovers: The Winner's Curse' (1987) 43 *Financial Analysts Journal* 64; Jeffrey N. Gordon and Lewis A. Kornhauser, 'Efficient Markets, Costly Information and Securities Research' (1985) 60 *New York University Law Review* 761, 825.

23 Reinier Kraakman et al., *Anatomy of Corporate Law: A Comparative and Functional Approach* (3rd edn, Oxford: Oxford University Press, 2017) 67.

24 See the analyses in Chapter 4, section 4.3.2.

engage in takeover hubris. Hubris is an acquisition behaviour that is exclusively linked to acquiring managers. It promotes larger corporate sizes without a corresponding increase in economic value. For example, the RBS-led *acquisition of ABN AMRO Bank N.V.* was concluded for about 70% premium over the market value of the shares of ABN AMRO. The acquisition significantly increased the size of the financial institution; however, significant losses were recorded, leading to governments bailouts.[25] Similarly, the acquisition of Time Warner by America Online (AOL) was meant to increase the size of the combined media companies. The botched acquisition that was concluded led to a loss of about $99 billion.[26] Irrespective of whether hubris is a deliberate act or genuine error,[27] the benefit that accrues to acquiring managers from hubris includes the prestige of presiding over a larger company and other economic perquisites.

7.3.3 Creditors

Debt financing has been demonstrated as an important aspect of the capital structure of corporate entities, with different determining factors and benefits.[28] Its importance is arguably evident from the continuous use of debt capital as a prolific source of capital by corporate entities. Corporate acquisition does not ordinarily undermine creditor interests, since acquiring companies obtain the benefits and detriments of target companies, including their debt obligations. Thus, regulations that protect secured creditors are not rendered ineffective by acquisitions; rather, they apply to ensure that the secured assets remain subject to the credit agreement and bind the acquiring company. This also applies to unsecured creditors. Thus, generally, creditors are unaffected by acquisitions. However, this does not take into account the most recent debt capital that is obtained for the purpose of completing acquisition transactions. Where such debt capital would alter the capital structure of the company in a way that would affect the rights of creditors, creditor control rights may be enforced to ensure that entities avoid deals that would earn negative abnormal returns on announcement.[29] Hence, as financial stakeholders, creditors with existing debt covenants may be actively involved in takeover negotiations. The extent to which cost of acquisition influences managerial roles is examined next.

25 See Chapter 5.

26 See the analyses in Chapter 5, 5.4.1(a).

27 Chapter 3, 3.4.3.

28 Milton Harris and Artur Raviv, 'The Theory of Capital Structure' (1991) 46 *The Journal of Finance* 297.

29 David Becher, Thomas Griffin, and Gregory Nini, 'Creditor Control of Corporate Acquisitions' (2018) https://ssrn.com/abstract=3046910 or http://dx.doi.org/10.2139/ssrn.3046910 accessed 5 March 2019. See also Nuri Ersahin, Rustom M. Irani, and Hanh Le, 'Creditor Control Rights and Resource Allocation Within Firms' (2019) ECGI – Finance Working Paper No. 484/2017; US Census Bureau Center for Economic Studies Paper No. CES-WP-15-39 https://ssrn.com/abstract=2689866 or http://dx.doi.org/10.2139/ssrn.2689866 accessed 11 July 2019.

7.4 Costs of acquisitions and the role of managements

Shareholders of target companies, managements and creditors have been identified as the default beneficiaries of corporate acquisitions. Since shareholders in acquiring companies are not protected from the challenges arising from loss or insignificant gains post-takeover and employees are likely to be dismissed post-takeover, acquiring shareholders and employees make up the list of corporate constituents whose interests are most likely to be undermined when acquisitions are concluded. In light of the effect of costly acquisitions on the interests of employees and acquiring shareholders' interests,[30] the extent to which their interests may be protected in takeovers is dependent on the role of managements. The challenges of conflict of interests and the incidence of managerial hubris limit the capacity of managements to protect shareholders and employees. Managerial hubris[31] and conflict of interests[32] in relation to acquiring managements can be linked to costly acquisitions. Hence, costly acquisitions are arguably the remote cause of losses to acquiring shareholders and employee dismissal and it is suggested that if managements are not empowered to dismiss employees as a result of acquisitions, it is likely that fewer acquisitions would be concluded.

It has been argued that employment protection has the capacity to reduce total synergy gains, since employee dismissal helps to reduce the costs associated with the takeovers to promote synergistic gains.[33] This ultimately suggests that employment reduction is an integral aspect of acquisitions and that it is required to promote economic gains in corporate acquisition. If acquisitions cannot yield synergistic gains without the need for employment reduction in a large scale, it implies that economic value in acquisitions are not created, but merely transferred from acquiring shareholders and employees to shareholders in target companies. If employees are dismissed as a result of acquisitions, it means that the company is trying to save costs. Impliedly, reduction in the costs of acquisitions can limit the need to dismiss employees in order to save costs. It is acknowledged that there may be genuine need to reduce employment numbers post-acquisitions, to avoid duplicity of positions and to ultimately promote synergies. This requirement for employee dismissal is not expected to lead to significant dismissals, since acquisitions lead to an increase in corporate size, value and volume of transactions, customers and demand and supply.

Costly acquisitions do not automatically lead to efficient outcomes, rather, the efficient allocation of capital does. While costly acquisition may nevertheless be inevitable, it is doubtful whether it is can be deemed a characteristic of acquisition since economic gains to acquiring shareholders are not as guaranteed as

30 Chapter 3, 3.4.3; Chapter 4, 4.3.2 (ii); Chapter 5, 5.4, 5.5.
31 Chapter 3, 3.4.3.
32 Chapter 3, 3.6.
33 Olivier Dessaint, Andrey Golubov, and Paolo Volpin, 'Employment Protection and Takeovers' (2017) 125 *Journal of Financial Economics* 369; Kose John, Anzhela Knyazev, and Diana Knyazeva, 'Employee Rights and Acquisitions' (2015) 118 *Journal of Financial Economics* 49.

the economic gains to their counterparts in target companies. The analysis that corporate regulation tends to promote shareholder value in the United Kingdom and the United States[34] is limited to shareholders in target companies, since managerial discretion and intervention in takeovers have only been significantly limited in target companies.[35] Less desperate and prudent managers would only engage in acquisitions with a high prospect of economic gains, where employee dismissal would not be a prerequisite to economic gains and synergy.

Arguments against the propriety of addressing employee issues in takeovers through corporate law may be misguided by a lack of understanding of the scope of issues covered and the ultimate result it seeks to achieve. For example, it was suggested that an understanding of the desirability of an 'end' is important when considering the 'means'.[36] The protection offered to employees is beyond employee interests, it extends to acquiring shareholder interests. It can specifically deter hubris and ensure that the opportunity for employee dismissal does not encourage managers to engage in costly acquisitions – for example, without adequate compensation. The cost of acquisitions is already undermining acquiring shareholder interests. The additional cost of compensating employees would significantly undermine corporate value. Hence managements would only engage in acquisitions that have high potential for economic gains. They would no longer be able to engage in costly acquisitions where they can dismiss employees to reduce further corporate costs in order to address shareholder concerns. Employee dismissal does not add economic value to acquiring shareholders, it only reduces further corporate costs and it provides an opportunity for management to merely engage in costly acquisition without considerable thought for its effects on acquiring shareholders. While it is not suggested that managers deliberately engage in costly acquisition because of the opportunity to dismiss employees to control further corporate costs, there is a potential opportunity to dismiss employees for this purpose. The basis for restricting this opportunity is illustrated next.

7.5 A new paradigm for employment protection and shareholder interests

The role of company managements during takeovers can determine the extent to which synergy, managerial discipline or hubris can be a feature of takeovers. Managements of target companies cannot protect the interests of their employees. They are already engaged in negotiating for the interests of their shareholders in the form of higher premiums. They may also be engaged in negotiations for their own interests, especially where they are less likely to be retained post-takeovers. The inclusion of employees' interests into the negotiations would mitigate their

34 See 7.2.(b).

35 Chapter 4, 4.3.1; Chapter 5, 5.3.

36 See the analysis in relation to corporate voluntarism in David L. Engel, 'An Approach to Corporate Social Responsibility' (1979) 32 *Stanford Law Review* 1, 4.

negotiating powers. The view that employment reduction can be used to achieve synergistic functions of acquisition to achieve efficiency[37] suggests that employee dismissal should be considered a necessary aspect of takeovers. In light of this, the extent to which employees should be compensated ought to be specially considered as well.

One of the ways of protecting the interests of shareholders of acquiring companies is to protect the interest of employees during takeovers. The new institutional economics support the view that the market where exchange occurs is not perfect because of scarcity which can lead to competition and opportunism.[38] It is at the level of the market that the agent and principal interact. Uncertainties which are envisaged by the new institutional economics can lead to an increase in the costs of takeovers. There is much consensus in the literature that shareholders of target companies record significant gains post-takeover from share premium, while their counterparts in acquiring companies experience insignificant or zero gains.[39] Opportunism and uncertainties through managerial hubris can influence employee disengagements post-takeover. When a takeover is concluded, shareholders of target companies receive economic gains through the premiums that are paid for their shares. Also, managements gain the prestige of a bigger-sized firm in addition to any extra economic perquisites that accompany a 'bigger' company. Thus, as rightly observed, the main beneficiaries of takeovers are managements and shareholders of target companies.[40]

However, shareholders of acquiring companies must retain their shares until any possible synergy materialises. In the absence of any immediate gain,[41] employees can be disengaged as a cost-saving measure. Since they do not have the capacity to negotiate for their interests, they become 'victims' of takeovers.[42] This implies that employee disengagements can be a direct consequence of managerial hubris.

37 Deepak K. Datta et al., 'Causes and Effects of Employee Downsizing: A Review and Synthesis' (2010) 36 *Journal of Management* 281, 291.

38 See Chapter 2.

39 See Peter Dodd and Richard Ruback, 'Tender Offers and Stockholder Returns' (1977) 5 *Journal of Financial Economics* 351; Paul Asquith and E. Han Kim, 'The Impact of Merger Bids on the Participating Forms' Security Holders' (1982) 37 *The Journal of Finance* 1209; Paul Asquith, Robert F. Bruner, and David W. Mullins Jr., 'The Gains to Bidding Firms from Merger' (1983) 11 *The Journal of Financial Economics* 121; Sara B. Moeller, Frederik P. Schlingemann, and René M. Stulz, 'Wealth Destruction on a Massive Scale' (2005) 60 *The Journal of Finance* (2005) 757–782.

40 See Aeron Davis et al., 'Takeovers and the Public Interest' (London Policy Network 2013) 1, 4 www.policy-network.net/publications/4435/Takeovers-and-the-public-interest accessed 19 June 2019 Managements of target companies that are apparently dismissed are likely to be compensated. Lucian A. Bebchuck, Jesse M. Fried, and David I. Walker, 'Managerial Power and Rent Extraction in the Design of Executive Compensation' (2002) 69 *The University of Chicago Law Review* 751,834.

41 Costs of acquisitions may indicate apparent losses to acquiring shareholders.

42 Anthony F. Buono and James L. Bowditch, *The Human Side of Mergers and Acquisitions* (San Francisco, Jossey-Bass Publishers, 1989).

Disengaging employees may prove to be beneficial only in the short term, as against the long-term corporate interests.[43] The short-term and immediate goal is for managements to gain the support of their shareholders. Hence employees can be dismissed to demonstrate to the shareholders that managements seek to promote their interests by mitigating the overall corporate costs, whereas the costs were actually caused by expensive acquisitions. The freedom to disengage employees to gain shareholder approval provides an opportunity for managements to undermine their agency responsibilities towards their shareholders. As long as managements are unrestricted in this regard, they can be indirectly encouraged to engage in costly acquisitions that can create uncertainty which is envisaged by the new institutional economics. The transaction cost economics of the new institutional economics seeks to ensure that transactions are conducted with the least possible costs. Costly acquisitions have the potential to create uncertainties, since higher premiums would lead to an increase in the costs to acquiring shareholders; the extent to which gains can materialise could be unclear. In view of the costs, managerial hubris and empire-building may be promoted directly or indirectly.

It is not clear whether losses are anticipated by managements of acquiring companies. However, disengaging employees after a takeover has occurred may suggest that the interests of the employees have been 'traded' for the interests of shareholders of acquiring companies. Continuous long-term employment can make employees so attached to a firm that they can hardly function effectively in a different firm. This can be caused by long-term commitment to the firm. Also, since employees shoulder more risks during takeovers than shareholders, they occupy the position of ultimate risk-bearers,[44] not in respect to the corporation generally, but with respect to a corporation during takeovers specifically. Employees who have put long years of service into a company would be faced with the reality of having the firm as their only means of livelihood, whereas shareholders can sell their shares and they can invest in different companies at the same time without regard to the long-term objective of the company.[45]

43 See Victor B. Wayhan and Steve Werner, 'The Impact of Workforce Reductions on Financial Performance: A Longitudinal Perspective' (2000) 26 *Journal of Management* 341–363; The Kay Review, 'Review of UK Equity Markets and Long-Term Decision Making' (London, July 2012) 1, 16–18 www.ecgi.org/conferences/eu_actionplan2013/documents/kay_review_final_report.pdf accessed 29 June 2018. D. R. King et al., 'Meta-Analyses of Post-Acquisition Performance: Indications of Unidentified Moderators' (2004) 25 *Strategic Management Journal* 187, 194; Daniel Attenborough, 'Giving Purpose to the Corporate Purpose Debate: An Equitable Maximisation and Viability Principle' (2012) 32 *Legal Studies* 4, 24; Adrian Payne, Sue Holt, and Pennie Frow, 'Integrating Employee, Customer and Shareholder Value through an Enterprise Performance Model: An Opportunity for Financial Services' (2000) 18 *International Journal of Bank Marketing* 258; Lynn A. Stout, 'New Thinking On Shareholder Primacy' (2011) *UCLA School of Law, Law-Econ Research Paper No. 11-04* 1–28.

44 Vincent Di Norcia, 'Mergers, Takeovers and a Property Ethic' (1988) 7 *Journal of Business Ethics* 109, 115.

45 Marleen A. O'Connor, 'Restructuring the Corporation's Nexus of Contracts: Recognizing a Fiduciary Duty to Protect Displaced Workers' (1990–1991) 69 *North Carolina Law Review*

The new institutional economics asserts that the existence of well-defined property rights can influence behaviours. Transactions between or among individuals occur at the agency theory level and these transactions are governed by transaction cost economics by reference to the established principles formulated under property rights. Employee dismissal during takeovers is mainly directly influenced by the existence of property rights in shares. A strict application of the property right doctrine is not practicable especially in relation to the interests of other stakeholders.[46] Since there could be negligible gains to shareholders of acquiring companies, managements are constrained to reduce further costs through employment reduction. Managers can assert rightly or wrongly that employee disengagement is influenced by the property rights resident in the shareholders.

Acts of managements in employment reduction undermine their important role of conducting transactions at the least possible costs. Employment reduction as an aftermath of a costly takeover does not effectively reduce the costs of takeovers; rather, it transfers value from both the shareholders and employees to managements.

Managements of acquiring companies benefit from takeovers, irrespective of whether it leads to gains. Reducing employment levels would reduce the operational costs of the company. While this can reduce further loss that the company may have incurred as a result of premiums paid during the takeover, the value of the acquiring shareholders may not be enhanced. This means that employment reduction serves the interests of the managements and this can undermine the objective of the market for corporate control as an alternative to the internal control mechanisms.

7.6 Conclusion

In light of the conceptualisation of the firm as being characterised by separation of ownership and control and the potential for conflict of interests, the role of managements in corporate entities has become central to corporate regulation. This has been demonstrated by developments in corporate takeovers. For example, some aspects of the regulatory framework for takeovers were largely influenced by the need to define and professionalise the role of managements when takeovers are made.[47] This chapter has examined and illustrated the need for further reforms. It examined the relationships amongst the role of management, acquiring shareholder and employee interests.

1189, 1242. See also Margaret M. Blair and Lynn A. Stout, 'Team Production Theory of Corporate Law' (1992) 85 *Virginia Law Review* (1999) 247; Luca Cerioni, 'The Success of the Company in s. 172(1) of The UK Companies Act 2006: Towards an "Enlightened Directors" Primacy' (2008) 4 *The Original Law Review* 1, 5; Janet Williamson, 'The Road to Stakeholding' (1996) 67 *The Political Quarterly* 209.

46 See Andrzej Rapaczynski, 'The Roles of the State and the Market in Establishing Property Rights' (1996) 10 *Journal of Economic Perspectives* 87, 88–90.

47 These were examined as part of the historical development of takeovers in the United Kingdom and the United States in Chapters 4 and 5 respectively.

It was shown that company managements, shareholders in target companies and creditors are the default beneficiaries of acquisitions.[48] Consequently, shareholders in acquiring companies and employees were identified as the corporate constituents whose interests are most likely to be undermined. The analyses show that employees are unlikely to be protected because they are non-financial stakeholders and corporate regulations are designed towards protecting shareholder value. Further, it was shown that the role of managements is central to these issues and a framework for addressing the problem was identified. The analysis does not seek to prevent managements from dismissing employees, rather, it seeks to ensure that employees are not merely dismissed by reasons of takeover; and in particular it addresses the existing gap in the limitation of TUPE to address this problem[49] and similar limitations in the United States. Specifically, it has the capacity to ultimately promote acquiring shareholders' interests, by ensuring that the issue of losses or negative gains caused by costly acquisitions are addressed. Despite the role of management being central to this problem, it is not suggested that the role of managements should be undermined. Rather, it seeks to enhance the effectiveness of managerial decisions in takeovers. Prudent and effective managerial investment decisions that can link acquisitions to enhanced economic values of entities are desirable, to ensure that the interests of acquiring shareholders and employees are not 'traded'. It is acknowledged that conflicting interests in corporate entities enhance the challenges of managements in effective decision-making; however, regulations, judicial intervention and reforms can provide clarity towards ensuring that an appropriate balance is struck amongst the conflicting interests. Regulations do not appear to have addressed this problem, as can be observed from the analyses detailed; hence, the need to examine judicial responses is justified. The next chapter examines the scope and effects of judicial intervention in corporate acquisitions.

References

Adrian, P., Sue Holt, and Pennie Frow, 'Integrating Employee, Customer and Shareholder Value through an Enterprise Performance Model: An Opportunity for Financial Services' (2000) 18 *International Journal of Bank Marketing* 258.

Asquith, P., Robert F. Bruner, and David W. Mullins, Jr., 'The Gains to Bidding Firms from Merger' (1983) 11 *The Journal of Financial Economics* 121.

Asquith, P. and E. Han Kim, 'The Impact of Merger Bids on the Participating Forms' Security Holders' (1982) 37 *The Journal of Finance* 1209.

Attenborough, D., 'Giving Purpose to the Corporate Purpose Debate: An Equitable Maximisation and Viability Principle' (2012) 32 *Legal Studies* 4.

Bebchuk, L. A., 'Efficient and Inefficient Sales of Corporate Control' (1994) 109 *Journal of Economics* 957, 962.

Bebchuck, L. A., Jesse M. Fried, and David I. Walker, 'Managerial Power and Rent Extraction in the Design of Executive Compensation' (2002) 69 *The University of Chicago Law Review* 751.

48 See 7.3.
49 See the analysis in Chapter 4, 4.4.1.

Becher, D., Thomas Griffin, and Gregory Nini, 'Creditor Control of Corporate Acquisitions' (2018) SSRN https://ssrn.com/abstract=3046910 or http://dx.doi.org/10.2139/ssrn.3046910 accessed 5 March 2019.

Blair, M. M. and Lynn A. Stout, 'Team Production Theory of Corporate Law' (1992) 85 *Virginia Law Review* 247.

Buono, A. F. and James L. Bowditch, *The Human Side of Mergers and Acquisitions* (San Francisco, Jossey-Bass Publishers, 1989).

Cerioni, L., 'The Success of the Company in s. 172(1) of the UK Companies Act 2006: Towards an "Enlightened Directors" Primacy' (2008) 4 *The Original Law Review* 1.

Datta, D. K. et al., 'Causes and Effects of Employee Downsizing: A Review and Synthesis' (2010) 36 *Journal of Management* 281.

Davis, A. et al., *Takeovers and the Public Interest* (London, Policy Network, 2013) 1, 4 www.policy-network.net/publications/4435/Takeovers-and-the-public-interest accessed 19 June 2019 Managements of target companies that are apparently dismissed are likely to be compensated.

DePamphilis, D. M., *Mergers, Acquisitions and Other Restructuring Activities: An Integrated Approach to Process, Tools, Cases and Solutions* (9th edn, London, UK, Academic Press, 2018).

Dessaint, O., Andrey Golubov, and Paolo Volpin, 'Employment Protection and Takeovers' (2017) 125 *Journal of Financial Economics* 369.

Dodd, P. and Richard Ruback, 'Tender Offers and Stockholder Returns' (1977) 5 *Journal of Financial Economics* 351.

Di Norcia, V., 'Mergers, Takeovers and a Property Ethic' (1988) 7 *Journal of Business Ethics* 109.

Engel, D. L., 'An Approach to Corporate Social Responsibility' (1979) 32 *Stanford Law Review* 1, 4.

Ersahin, N., Rustom M. Irani, and Hanh Le, 'Creditor Control Rights and Resource Allocation within Firms' (2019) *ECGI – Finance* Working Paper No. 484/2017; US Census Bureau Center for Economic Studies Paper No. CES-WP-15–39. Available at SSRN: https://ssrn.com/abstract=2689866 or http://dx.doi.org/10.2139/ssrn.2689866 accessed 11 July 2019.

Gordon, J. N. and Lewis A. Kornhauser, 'Efficient Markets, Costly Information and Securities Research' (1985) 60 *New York University Law Review* 761.

Grossman, S. J. and Oliver D. Hart, 'One Share One Vote and the Market for Corporate Control' (1988) 20 *Journal of Financial Economics* 175.

Harris, Milton and Artur Raviv, 'The Theory of Capital Structure' (1991) 46 *the Journal of Finance* 297.

Jensen, M. C., 'Value Maximization, Stakeholder Theory and the Corporate Objective Function' (2001) 14 *Journal of Applied Corporate Finance* 8.

John, K., Anzhela Knyazev, and Diana Knyazeva, 'Employee Rights and Acquisitions' (2015) 118 *Journal of Financial Economics* 49.

King, D. R. et al., 'Meta-Analyses of Post-Acquisition Performance: Indications of Unidentified Moderators' (2004) 25 *Strategic Management Journal* 187.

Kraakman, Reinier et al., *Anatomy of Corporate Law: A Comparative and Functional Approach* (3rd edn, Oxford, Oxford University Press, 2017) 67.

Moelle, S. B. R., Frederik P. Schlingemann, and René M. Stulz, 'Wealth Destruction on a Massive Scale' (2005) 60 *The Journal of Finance* 757.

O'Connor, Marleen, A., 'Restructuring the Corporation's Nexus of Contracts: Recognizing a Fiduciary Duty to Protect Displaced Workers' (1990–1991) 69 *North Carolina Law Review* 1189.

Rapaczynski, Andrzej, 'The Roles of the State and the Market in Establishing Property Rights' (1996) 10 *Journal of Economic Perspectives* 87.

Stout, L. A., 'New Thinking on Shareholder Primacy' (2011) *UCLA School of Law, Law-Econ Research Paper No. 11–04.*

Varaiya, N. P. and Kenneth R. Ferris, 'Overpaying in Corporate Takeovers: The Winner's Curse' (1987) 43 *Financial Analysts Journal* 64.

Wayhan, V. B. and Steve Werner, 'The Impact of Workforce Reductions on Financial Performance: A Longitudinal Perspective' (2000) 26 *Journal of Management* 341.

Williamson, J., 'The Road to Stakeholding' (1996) 67 *the Political Quarterly* 209.

8 Judicial intervention in corporate acquisitions

8.1 Introduction

The series of negotiations that characterise pre-acquisition decisions may suggest that acquisitions are usually concluded after the concerns of the relevant corporate constituents have been addressed. Also, regulatory controls that have been developed in response to takeover challenges may indicate that these concerns have been addressed. However, in light of the variety of interests involved in corporate acquisitions in target and acquiring companies, conflicts are often not completely addressed at different stages of the acquisition process. Thus, regards to the courts may be inevitable in certain circumstances. This chapter identifies these circumstances. It examines the scope of judicial intervention in corporate acquisitions by reference to the regulatory framework for takeovers in the UK and in Delaware. In light of the shareholder value approach of corporation law and corporate governance rules in the United Kingdom and the United States, there is insignificant scope for judicial intervention in takeovers in relation to employee interests. Hence, judicial intervention in relation to employees would not be examined.

A brief description of the case search methodology is presented next. Then, the relevant decisions of the courts in the UK and Delaware are examined. The analysis includes judicial decisions from shareholder actions in both jurisdictions, before the conclusion.

8.2 Case search methodology

The premiums paid by acquirers to obtain shares of target shareholders indicate that acquisitions are characterised by high costs. The most expensive corporate acquisition occurred in 2000 when Vodafone acquired Mannesmann. The acquisition was completed for about \$183/€204 billion (including liabilities of about \$17b).[1] In the same year, the most expensive acquisition in the United State occurred. Time Warner was acquired by America Online (AOL) for over \$160

1 CNN Money 4 February 2000 https://money.cnn.com/2000/02/04/europe/vodafone/ accessed 11 July 2018. Edmund L. Andrews and Andrew Ross Sorkin, 'Europe's Megadeal: The Overview; \$183 Billion Deal in Europe to Join Two Wireless Giants' *New York Times* 4 February 2000 www.nytimes.com/2000/02/04/business/europe-s-megadeal-overview-183-billion-deal-europe-join-2-wireless-giants.html accessed 11 July 2018.

billion, in addition to about $17 billion liability of Time Warner, with a takeover premium of about 70% over the market price of $64.75 of Time Warner shares, at the rate of $110 *per* share.[2] The year 2000 is a significant year for corporate acquisitions, having recorded the most expensive acquisitions that also led to significant losses. For example, the Time Warner acquisition led to a loss of about $99 billion.[3] Thus, it is imperative to ascertain the extent to which shareholder grievances arising from acquisitions are litigated, especially after the year 2000. The case search covers the period from 1 January 2001 to 31 July 2019. This is further explained in 8.3 below.

8.3 Shareholder litigations in the United Kingdom

Directors' duties are stated to be owed to the company, not to any particular shareholder,[4] except the acts of directors caused personal loss to shareholders.[5] There is also an exception if the company is unable to pursue its own cause of action precisely because of the acts of the wrongdoer(s) and personal losses arise from the same wrong that was done to the company.[6] In addition, personal action can arise, if it can be shown that a special relationship was created between directors and shareholders to make the directors personally accountable to the shareholders.[7] In light of these, shareholder litigations in the UK are mainly limited to matters relating to fraud on the minority, which is an exception to the rule in *Foss v Harbottle*.[8] Other causes of action on shareholder litigations include derivative action,[9] unfairly prejudicial conduct[10] and a petition on just and equitable grounds to wind up a company.[11]

2 Ianthe Jeanne Dugan and Ariana Eunjung Cha, 'AOL to Acquire Time Warner for 183 Billion Merger' *The Washington Post* 11 January 2000 www.washingtonpost.com/archive/politics/2000/01/11/aol-to-acquire-time-warner-in-record-183-billion-merger/f3bf2f07-c32b-4052-b5a6-8489bb9d7013/?noredirect=on&utm_term=.69ae04545d2d accessed 30 April 2018; 'AOL Buyout of Time Warner: Merger Frenzy Sweeping Corporate America' *World Socialist Web* 14 January 2000 www.wsws.org/en/articles/2000/01/merg-j14.html accessed 2 May 2018; Seth Sutel, 'AOL Buys Time Warner for $162 Billion' *ABC News* 10 January 2000 http://abcnews.go.com/Business/Decade/aol-buys-time-warner-162-billion/story?id=9279138 accessed 30 June 2019.

3 Emma Barnett and Amanda Andrews, 'AOL Merger Was "The Biggest Mistake in Corporate History", Believes Time Warner Chief Jeff Bewkes' *The Telegraph* 28 September 2010 www.telegraph.co.uk/finance/newsbysector/mediatechnologyandtelecoms/media/8031227/AOL-merger-was-the-biggest-mistake-in-corporate-history-believes-Time-Warner-chief-Jeff-Bewkes.html accessed 30 June 2019.

4 *Companies Act 2006*, s 170 (1).

5 *Heron International Ltd v Lord Grade [1983] BCLC* 244, 262 (Lawton LJ).

6 *Giles v Rhind* [2002] All ER (D) 233.

7 *Peskin v Anderson* [2001] 12 WLUK 421, [2001]BCC 874; *Briess v* Woolley [1954] A C 333, HL; *Allen v Hyatt* [1914] 30 T.L.R. 444, PC.

8 (1843) 2 Hare 461.

9 *Companies Act 2006*, ss 260–269.

10 *Companies Act 2006*, ss 994–996.

11 *Insolvency Act 1986*, s 122(1) (g).

The protection available to shareholders in relation to takeovers applies to protect the personal interests of shareholders. In *Heron International Ltd v Lord Grade*, it was observed that,

> Our conclusion on this aspect can be readily demonstrated. Suppose that the Bell takeover goes through as a result of the allegedly reckless decision of the Board of ACC and that, in consequence, the entire shareholding in ACC becomes vested in the Bell Group at a lower takeover price than that available from the Heron Group. The payment of damages by the directors of ACC to ACC would be no compensation whatever to the former shareholders of ACC for the loss which they would have suffered. Only an action by the former shareholders in their own right, and not in right of the company, could compensate them for that loss.[12]

The protection of the personal interests of shareholders in takeovers as explained in Heron International applies similarly in relation to the protection provided for target shareholders in the *UK City Code*[13] and the *EU Takeover Directive*.[14] The provisions of these regulations show that the personal interests of individual shareholders could be undermined when a takeover is made. This implies that the 'no reflective loss' principle may not necessarily apply, except it can be shown that losses to shareholders occurred despite the strict compliance with the provisions of the regulations.

In light of the application of the 'no reflective loss' principle and the requirements that shareholders can only institute actions arising from personal loss, the extent to which shareholders can succeed in actions against directors in matters relating to takeovers is unclear. Case search based on section 8.2 indicate that judicial review is not a prominent way for shareholders to address challenges that arise from takeovers. Only a negligible number of cases were filed within the period under review. A case search was conducted on WESTLAW of the term(s) 'mergers OR acquisitions OR takeovers' and 'merger OR acquisition OR takeover' within the period of 01/01/2001 to 31/07/2019.[15] A few cases where shareholders instituted actions to challenge the role of directors in takeovers emerged from the search. They are examined next.

8.3.1 Charterhouse Capital Ltd

In *Charterhouse Capital Ltd*,[16] the appellant was a founder shareholder who joined others to acquire the LLP 'C' on a management buyout from the previous owner. Charterhouse Capital 'C' carried on a private equity business through various subsidiaries and limited partnerships. The appellant had become a founder

12 [1983] BCLC 244, 262.
13 *The City Code on Takeovers and Mergers* section A1, B1, (2) and (3).
14 *EU Takeover Directive* art. 9.
15 See 8.2 for case search criteria.
16 [2015] EWCA Civ 536.

shareholder in C on a management buyout from its then owner. The basis of participation of those involved in the management buyout was set out in a shareholders' agreement. The agreement provided that if a founder majority, (excluding any founder who was a proposed purchaser) agreed to pursue an exit, the shareholder would agree to sell his shares on the same terms as those offered to the other shareholders i.e., non-founder shareholders. By the end of 2011, the appellant and a number of other members of the buyout team had either retired or indicated an intention to retire from the business. The retired and retiring members held over 50% of the shares in C. The remaining shareholders proposed a new structure for those remaining in the business which involved purchasing the shares in C. All other retiring shareholders accepted offers for their shares from the remaining shareholders. The appellant did not accept the offer for his shares; he thought that the offer for the shares was too low. The articles of the LLP were then amended to permit the appellant to be bought out without his consent. He presented an unfair prejudice petition that C had repudiated an oral agreement for an independent valuation and purchase of his shares, that irregularities within C had not been properly investigated, and that the takeover offer and amendment of the articles had been carried out improperly in order to expropriate his shares at a gross undervalue rather than for any genuine corporate purpose.

It was held that the amendment of a company's articles of association to permit the shares of a minority shareholder to be compulsorily acquired under a takeover offer was consistent with the terms of a shareholder's agreement and did not involve any unfairly prejudicial conduct under the *Companies Act 2006* s.994.

The petition by the minority shareholder was aimed at preventing his shares from being acquired by the management of the LLP who were also the remaining shareholders. He sought to prevent the management of the company from acting on an offer to acquire his shares in a takeover involving the existing management of the LLP. As a target shareholder, the petitioner was generally protected by the *Takeover Code*;[17] however, the protection was limited by the combined effects of the squeeze out provision[18] and the company's article of association which was amended to permit the shares of minority shareholders to be compulsorily acquired in a takeover. Arguably, a remedy would have been available under the *Takeover Code*. In addition, a remedy would have been available under unfairly prejudicial conduct, since the acquiring shareholders were also in control of the company. However, the remedies were contingent on the inapplicability of the squeeze out provisions. This indicates that the court would not interfere with managerial decisions, especially where it is satisfied that the decision was made in good faith and in furtherance of the commercial objectives of a corporate entity as a going concern.

17 Shareholder should be allowed to make independent decisions on an offer to acquire their shares. See *The City Code on Takeovers and Mergers* section A1, B1, (2) and (3).

18 An offeror who acquires or contract to acquire more that 90% of the voting shares in a company, may give notice to the holders of other shares which has not been acquired, that he desires to acquire those shares. See *Companies Act 2006*, s 979. In the instant case, the minority shareholders held 8.91% of the shares. This indicates that the offeror had acquired or already agreed to acquire more than 90% of the shares of the company.

8.3.2 Expro International Group Plc

The support for managerial commercial decision was also demonstrated in *Expro International Group Plc.*,[19] where a group of shareholders challenged the decision of the board to reject a takeover bid from a bidder in a scheme of arrangement. The scheme was a takeover whereby Expro's entire issued share capital would be acquired by a consortium of investors, acting through a company Umbrellastream formed for that purpose. Initially, Umbrellastream offered £14.35 per share, but when another company Halliburton indicated to offer £15.25, Umbrellastream raised its bid to £15.50. The City Panel on Takeovers and Mergers set a date by which Halliburton had to announce either an offer or its withdrawal. A shareholders meeting was held and the scheme was approved by a large majority of the shareholders present. Subsequently, Umbrellastream further raised its offer to £16.15. Just before its deadline, Halliburton stated that its proposed price was £16.25. Expro's board rejected Halliburton's proposal. Halliburton announced its withdrawal but reserved the right to make an offer for Expro if the court declined to sanction, or there was a delay of 14 days or more in sanctioning, the scheme involving Umbrellastream. Then a group of minority shareholders applied for a 14-day adjournment to see if Halliburton made an offer. They challenged the decision of Expro's board to reject Halliburton's proposal.

The application of the shareholders was refused. The court observed that the proposed adjournment would lead to uncertainty to the potential disadvantage of shareholders; this was the main reason that the board rejected Halliburton's offer. Explaining further, the court observed.

> In my judgment, no criticism can be made of the Board's assessment of the relative benefits and risks associated with accepting or rejecting Halliburton's proposal made late on 23 June . . . , the certainty of Umbrellastream's offer which could become fully effective in a short time outweighed commercially either a firm offer from Halliburton of £16.25 or the uncertainty of a higher offer in due course from either Halliburton or Umbrellastream.[20]

The board of Expro decided to weigh the interests of the vast majority of shareholders in the company against the group of shareholders who were hopeful that Halliburton might make a higher bid to acquire their shares. The commercial decision of facilitating a bid that was certain to promote shareholder interests was made by the board against a potentially higher bid that may provide a better deal to their shareholders. The reasoning of the court in supporting the decision of the board of Expro was further influenced by the failure of Halliburton to make a definite offer, or at least signalling its intention to do so. Hence, shareholders voted in support of the scheme to transfer their shares, despite knowing of Halliburton's interests which they had apparently considered uncertain. This was rightly suggested to indicate that a change in circumstances which occurs after a

19 [2008] EWHC 1543 (Ch).
20 [2008] EWHC 1543 (Ch), para 45, David Richards J.

vote had been held by shareholders will be considered by the court in the exercise of its discretion. However, if shareholders were aware of a potential bid at the time they approved a scheme with another bidder, any proposed bid by the potential bidder would not constitute a material change in circumstance[21] to warrant the court's intervention. The decision of the court confirms the restricted protection available to minority shareholders when a takeover is concluded by a scheme of arrangement.[22] The individual capacity of shareholders to negotiate with bidders in tender offer is not available in a scheme of arrangement.

8.3.3 Diamix Plc

In circumstances where the court considers that the interests of shareholders may be potentially undermined in a takeover attempt, appropriate relief may be granted to protect shareholder interests.

In *Diamix Plc*,[23] minority shareholders challenged the validity of a squeeze out offer in an attempted takeover of the company. The claimant shareholders acquired 10% of the shares in Diamix, a company registered in the UK, on the basis that it would obtain a listing on the Alternative Investment Market. Prior to the acquisition, they had established that *The City Code on Takeovers and Mergers* did not apply, as the company's other shareholders were resident in South Africa, where the company conducted its business. Another company, Dwyka Diamond, listed on the Australian Stock Exchange, acquired 51% of the shares in Diamix and subsequently made a takeover offer for the shares held by the claimant shareholders. They rejected the offer. The offer was however accepted by 90% of Diamix's other shareholders and Dwyka Diamond served a compulsory acquisition notice on the claimant shareholders. The claimant shareholders contended that the offer was unfair, that no independent valuation had been given for the shares in Diamix and that Diamix would, in effect, be providing all Dwyka Diamond's assets, which had no real asset value of its own, and that Diamix's other shareholders were closely connected with Dwyka Diamond. The court upheld the contention of the claimant minority shareholders.

It was held that the offer did not contain sufficient information to enable the minority shareholders to reach an informed decision. Further, the close connection between the other shareholders in Diamix and Dwyka Diamond meant that acceptance of the offer by 90% of the other shareholders was not accorded much weight; the shares making up the 90% were held in family trusts and by close associates of Dwyka Diamond. Thus, the court declared that Dwyka Diamond was neither entitled nor bound to purchase the shares of the minority shareholders in Diamix, that Dwyka Diamond can only purchase the shares on the basis of a valuation to be carried out by an independent valuer.[24]

21 Leon Ferera and Hannah Mehta, 'Scheming to Get Around the Takeover Code: Does It Work?' (2008) 23 *Butterworths Journal of International Banking & Financial Law* 476, 478.

22 See generally Jennifer Payne, 'Schemes of Arrangement, Takeovers and Minority Shareholder Protection' (2011) 11 *Journal of Corporate Law Studies* 67.

23 [2002] EWHC 770 CH.

24 Ibid. 29–39.

Although a majority shareholder with 90% of voting shares can compulsorily acquire the remaining shares of the minority shareholders through the squeeze out mechanism,[25] the court refused to sanction the squeeze out because of the flawed process leading to the acquisition of the 90% shareholding. Also, the takeover offer was not fair, not having being valued by an independent valuer. This indicates that while the court may not be keen to intervene in the private arrangements of corporate entities as indicated in *Expro International Group Plc*,[26] an intervention may be necessary to ensure a fair and equal treatment of all shareholders when a takeover bid is made.

8.3.4 Sharp v Blank

The intervention of the court may also be necessary where there has been a breach of directors' duty; however, the duty must be owed to the shareholders in special circumstances. This was observed in *Sharp v Blank*,[27] where shareholders sought the intervention of the court to address what was considered to be alleged misrepresentations and breach of duty by directors.

The claimant shareholders in Lloyds Banking Group alleged that misrepresentations were made by the bank's directors in relation to the acquisition of Halifax Bank of Scotland. The shareholders contend that the directors had known that Halifax Bank of Scotland had manipulated its LIBOR submissions. An extraordinary general meeting of Lloyds shareholders had been called to approve, and did approve the proposed acquisition. Before the meeting, the directors of Lloyds had sent a circular to shareholders. The shareholders alleged that the circular and other communications contained material misrepresentations and omissions and that the directors were in breach of tortious and fiduciary duties owed to them. Among the issues was that the defendants knew, but did not disclose to the shareholders, that HBOS was manipulating its LIBOR submissions.

The directors accepted that they owed a 'sufficient information duty', namely a duty to provide shareholders with sufficient information to enable them to make an informed decision about how to vote in relation to the acquisition. They also accepted that they owed duties not to mislead or conceal material information and to advise and inform the shareholders in clear and comprehensible terms, but they did not owe fiduciary duties to the company's shareholders.

The court held that directors owed fiduciary duties to the company. They did not, solely by virtue of their office of director, owe fiduciary duties to the shareholders, collectively or individually, except a 'special factual relationship' exists between the directors and the shareholders. There was no special relationship in the instant case. The relationship between the directors and shareholders was one of giving advice and information for a particular purpose but the directors had

25 *Companies Act 2006*, s 979.
26 [2008] EWHC 1543 (Ch).
27 [2015] EWHC 3220 (Ch).

not undertaken to act for or on behalf of the shareholders in any more extended sense.[28]

The reasoning of the court in *Sharp v Blank* suggests that shareholders are personally responsible for obtaining all relevant information that would be aid them in making an informed decision whether to approve a takeover bid. This is notwithstanding that directors fail to disclose some relevant information that may be helpful to shareholders in reaching an informed decision. Where shareholders vote on a matter in the absence of proper guidance, the essence of the vote is undermined, since the shareholders lacked the capacity to make any informed decision. If directors are aware that shareholders are making a decision without access to relevant information which the directors are privy to, especially where the takeover was proposed by the directors, the essence of the vote is undermined. This is a manifestation of the challenges experienced by acquiring shareholders; it suggests the need for a review of the role of acquiring boards.

8.3.5 Rock Nominees Ltd v RCO (Holdings) Plc

The interests of shareholders in target companies may also be undermined in circumstances where their minority status may limit their ability to address the problem. For example, in *Rock Nominees Ltd v RCO (Holdings) Plc*,[29] a petition was filed by the minority shareholders alleging that the sale of the company had been completed at an undervalue, that the directors should have insisted on a higher price. They alleged that directors had breached their fiduciary duties. The court held that although the directors had concluded the sale in a clumsy manner, the best price was obtained and no harm was caused to the shareholders.

> As to the judge's finding of breach of fiduciary duty on the part of the Respondent Directors, it is plain that, as the judge found, the Respondent Directors were in a position of hopeless conflict. Further, they would undoubtedly have been well-advised to obtain an independent valuation. However, no harm was in fact done and no damage or prejudice caused. . . . The clumsy manner in which the sale was carried through is not in itself sufficient, as it seems to me, to found a finding of breach of fiduciary duty in circumstances where no relief or remedy is required from the court.[30]

The harm which the shareholders allegedly suffered was the loss of added economic value that would have accrued to them had the directors negotiated for a higher price. The court reasoned that there was no guarantee that the use of an independent value would have led to an increase in the price of the company. Also, the majority shareholder was in a position to place the company

28 Ibid. para 12, 23.
29 [2004] EWCA Civ 118.
30 Ibid. para 79.

in members' voluntary liquidation and put the company in a position where it had no alternative but to realise its assets on the open market. Hence the court reasoned that the company was sold for the best price at the material time. This demonstrates the odds against minority shareholder interests. The decisions in *Rock Nominees Ltd*[31] *and Sharp v Blank*[32] merely reaffirm the view that the court would not allow itself to be dragged into private corporate dispute in the absence of manifest breach of duty or procedure; neither would it allow its jurisdiction to be used as a weapon in the tactical battle between or amongst corporate constituents.

8.3.6 Vald Nielsen Holding A/S v Baldorino

Similarly, in *Vald Nielsen Holding A/S v Baldorino*,[33] shareholders alleged that the management board of the company had been fraudulent and had breached their fiduciary duties by selling the company below the valued price. They further allege that the business being sold was far more successful than the sellers had been led by the management to believe, and that the sellers were misled into selling at the time when they did, and for the price which they received. The court held that there was no special relationship between the directors and shareholders to create a fiduciary relationship, hence the claim based on breach of fiduciary duty failed. However, the claim for fraud or conspiracy against the directors succeeded and the shareholders were awarded damages for the loss suffered, less the amount that they actually received.

Even though the shareholders failed in their claim for breach of fiduciary duty, they were awarded damages against the directors for fraudulent conduct. The sufficiency of the damages is dependent on whether they would have wanted the sale to be set aside and actually have pleaded such. While it appears that shareholders succeeded in the action against the directors, it can also be argued that the remedy they received was a partial one because they might as well never have intended to sell the company. Practically, setting aside a sale would lead to severe inconveniences for the purchasers of value and it would also undermine the integrity of commercial transactions and create uncertainty; such remedy is unrealistic and undesirable. Hence, it is more reasonable to prevent managements from fraudulent practices that undermine shareholder interests when a takeover is made. One of the biggest challenges of shareholders is information asymmetry. Shareholders are expected to make an informed decision about a takeover, yet directors are not obliged to provide all relevant information that would enable the shareholders to make a considered and informed decision. As observed by the court in *Sharp v Blank*,[34] directors are not bound to provide more information to the shareholders even though directors are privy to much more information

31 [2004] EWCA Civ 118.
32 [2015] EWHC 3220 (Ch).
33 [2019] EWHC 1926 (Comm).
34 [2015] EWHC 3220 (Ch), 12, 23.

about the company than the shareholder. This indicates that there is scope for additional protection for shareholder interests, especially in relation to the scope of advice that is provided by the board when a takeover is made.[35] This can ensure that the advisory role of directors is not a mere 'box-ticking' exercise. Judicial intervention in takeovers in Delaware in examined next.

8.4 Judicial intervention in Delaware

The role of the board of directors when a takeover is imminent has been clearly outlined by the courts in Delaware. Directors must not frustrate a takeover attempt by an acquiring company, except where they had reasonable grounds for believing that a danger to corporate policy and effectiveness existed because of another person's stock ownership. This burden is satisfied by showing good faith and reasonable investigation.[36] To ensure that the defensive measure is within the scope of the business judgement rule, it must be reasonable in relation to the threat posed.[37] However, once a sale of a company becomes inevitable, rather than preserving the corporate entity, the directors' role is transformed to maximising the entity's value at a sale for the benefit of the shareholders.[38]

These rules clarifying directors' duties became necessary to address the challenges that occurred in the early periods of takeovers in the United States.[39] Ultimately, the clarification is aimed at ensuring that directors do not act beyond the scope of their duties and breach their fiduciary duties.

The limitation of directors' duties when a takeover is made implies that their conducts are liable to be challenged, if there is a reasonable ground to believe that they are acting outside the scope of their duties. Thus, several shareholder actions have been instituted to challenge the role of directors in relation to acquisitions.

Further to the case search methodology,[40] 39 shareholder actions were instituted between 01 January 2001 and 31 July 2019 to challenge the role of directors in acquisitions in Delaware.[41] The cases were typically shareholder actions challenging directors' decisions as a breach of fiduciary duties and often seeking to enjoin the process leading to the consummation of the acquisition. Some of the

35 Georgina Tsagas, 'A Long-Term Vision for UK Firms? Revisiting the Target Director's Advisory Role since the Takeover of Cadbury's PLC' (2014) 14 *Journal of Corporate Law Studies* 241.

36 *Unocal Corp v Mesa Petroleum Company* 493 A.2d 946 (Del.Supr. 1985), 955.

37 Ibid.

38 *Revlon Inc. v MacAndrews & Forbes Holdings Inc.* 506 A.2d 173 (Del. 1986) 182D.

39 Chapter 5, 5.2.

40 See 8.2.

41 The cases are particularly shareholder actions that allege a breach of fiduciary duties by the directors or seeking injunction to restrain directors from acting in breach of fiduciary duty. Actions are against directors of acquiring or target companies, other shareholder actions were not considered. For example, derivative actions were excluded because they are usually instituted on behalf of the company as against shareholder personal interests.

reasons for shareholder actions include allegations of a flawed sale process, unreasonable provisions in the sale agreement or inadequate disclosures.

Most of the cases were based on application for preliminary injunction. Out of the 39 cases, 14 were decided in favour of shareholder plaintiffs and 25 cases were either dismissed or had shareholder applications denied. The plaintiffs were predominantly target shareholders; only two of the cases had acquiring shareholders as plaintiffs or applicants as illustrated in Table 8.1.

Table 8.1

Delaware shareholder action

S/N	*Name*	*Plaintiff*	*Decision*
1.	*Air Products and Chemicals, Inc. v Airgas, Inc.* 16 A.3d 4 (Del Ch. 2011)	Target shareholder	Denied
2.	*In re Cogent, Inc. Shareholder Litigation* 7 A.3d 487 (Del Ch. 2010)	Target shareholder	Denied
3.	*Mercier v Inter-Tel (Delaware), Inc.* 929 A.2d 786 (Del Ch. 2007)	Target shareholder	Denied
4.	*Yucaipa American Alliance Fund II, L.P. v Riggio* 1 A.3d 310 (Del Ch. 2010)	Target shareholder	Denied
5.	*In re Toys 'R' Us, Inc. Shareholder Litigation* 877 A.2d 975 (Del Ch. 2005)	Target shareholder	Denied
6.	*In re MONY Group Inc. Shareholder Litigation* 852 A.2d 9 (Del Ch. 2004)	Target shareholder	Denied
7.	*Versata Enterprises, Inc. v Selectica, Inc.* 5 A.3d 586 (Del. 2010)	Target shareholder	Denied
8.	*In re El Paso Corp. Shareholder Litigation* 41 A.3d 432 (Del Ch.2012)	Target shareholder	Denied
9.	*Louisiana Municipal Police Employees' Retirement System v Crawford* 918 A.2d 1172 (Del Ch. 2007)	Target shareholder	Denied
10.	*In re MFW Shareholders Litigation* 67 A.3d 496 (Del Ch.2013)	Target shareholder	Denied
11.	*In re Family Dollar Stores, Inc. Stockholder Litigation* *Unreported. Del Ch.* C.A. No. 9985 – CB Bouchard, C. December 19, 2014	Target shareholder	Denied

(*Continued*)

Table 8.1 (Continued)

S/N	*Name*	*Plaintiff*	*Decision*
12.	*In re Pennaco Energy, Inc.* 787 A.2d 69 (Del Ch. 2001)	Target shareholder	Denied
13.	*In re Cysive, Inc. Shareholders Litigation* 836 A.2d 531 (Del Ch. 2003)	Target shareholder	Denied
14.	*C & J Energy Services, Inc. v City of Miami General Employees* 107 A.3d 1049 (Del. 2014)	**Acquiring shareholder	Denied
15.	*Gaines v Narachi Unreported Del Ch* C.A. No. 6784 – VCN. John W Noble Sept. 30, 2011.	**Acquiring shareholder	Denied
16.	*Emerald Partners v Berlin Unreported* No. Civ.A. 9700. Jack B. Jacobs 28 April 003.	Target shareholder	Denied
17.	*In re Trados Inc. Shareholder Litigation* 73 A.3d 17 (Del Ch. 2013)	Target shareholder	Denied
18.	*In re KKR Financial Holdings LLC* 101 A.3d 980 (Del Ch. 2014)	Target shareholder	Denied
19.	*LC Capital Master Fund, Ltd v James* 990 A.2d 435 (Del Ch. 2010)	Target shareholder	Denied
20.	*David P. Simonetti Rollover IRA v Margolis* *Unreported* C.A. No. 3694 – VCN. John W. Noble 27 June 2008.	Target shareholder	Denied
21.	*In re Aquila Inc.* *(Del Ch.* 2002) 805 A.2d 184	Target shareholder	Denied
22.	*In re Smurfit-Stone Container Corp.* *Unreported* C.A. No. 6164 – VCP. Donald F. Parsons Jr. 20 May 2011. Revised 24 May 20011	Target shareholder	Denied
23.	*In re Sirius XM Shareholder Litigation* *Unreported* C.A. No. 7800 – CS Leo E. Strine Jr. 27 September 2013	Target shareholder	Denied
24.	*In re Synthes, Inc. Shareholder Litigation* 50 A.3d 1022 (Del Ch. 2012)	Target shareholder	Denied
25.	*Koehler v NetSpend Holdings Inc.* *Unreported C. A.* No. 8373 – VCG. Sam Glasscock III. 21 May 2013.	Target shareholder	Denied

S/N	Name	Plaintiff	Decision
26.	*In re Lear Corp. Shareholder Litigation* 926 A.2d 94 (Del Ch. 2007)	Target shareholder	Ordered in part
27.	*In re Netsmart Technologies, Inc.* 924 A.2d 171 (Del Ch. 2007)	Target shareholder	Ordered
28.	*Omnicare, Inc. v NCS Healthcare, Inc.* 818 A.2d 914 (Del. 2003)	Target shareholder	Ordered
29.	*In re Rural Metro Corp.* 88 A.3d 54 (Del Ch. 2014)	Target shareholder	Ordered
30.	*In re Del Monte Foods Co. Shareholders Litigation* 25 A.3d 813 (Del Ch. 2011)	Target shareholder	Ordered
31.	*Gantler v Stephens . . .* 965 A.2d 695 (Del. 2009)	Target shareholder	Ordered
32.	*Police & Fire Ret. Sys. of City of Detroit v Bernal* *Unreported C.A.* No. 4663 – CC. William b. Chandler III, 26 June 2009	Target shareholder	Ordered
33.	*In re Comverge, Inc.* *Unreported* C.A. No. 7368-VCP Donald F. Parsons Jr. 25 November 2014	Target shareholder	Ordered in part
34.	*In re Atheros Communications, Inc.* *Unreported* C.A. No. 6124 – VCN. John W. Noble 4 March 2011.	Target shareholder	Ordered
35.	*Arkansas Teacher Retirement System v Alon USA Energy, Inc.* *Unreported* C.A. No. 2017-0453-KSJM McCormick, V.C.28 June 2019	Target shareholder	Ordered in part
36.	*In re Primedia, Inc. Shareholders Litigation* 67 A.3d 455 (Del Ch. 2013)	Target shareholder	Ordered
37.	*In re Topps Co. Shareholders Litigation* 926 A.2d 58 (Del Ch. 2007)	Target shareholder	Ordered
38.	*Chen v Howard-Anderson* 87 A.3d 648 (Del Ch. 2014)	Target shareholder	Ordered in part
39.	*In re Orchard Enterprises, Inc. Stockholder Litigation* 88 A.3d 1 (Del Ch. 2014)	Target shareholder	Ordered in part

8.4.1 Shareholder application denied

While it may appear that the strict illustration of the scope of directors' duties in *Unocal Corp v Mesa Petroleum Company*[42] and *Revlon Inc. v MacAndrews & Forbes Holdings Inc.*[43] exposes directors' conduct to shareholder litigation, the courts must be clearly and evidently persuaded before shareholder applications can be granted. For example, in *Air Products and Chemicals, Inc. v Airgas, Inc.*,[44] in a hostile takeover, shareholders of the target company brought action against the board of directors of the company for declaratory and injunctive relief. They applied to the court to require the board to fulfil their fiduciary obligations and to stop the board's takeover defences, including having the 'poison pill' removed or deemed inapplicable to offeror's tender. The application was denied.

The defendant company (Airgas) has a staggered board of directors, divided into three equal classes with one class (three directors) up for election each year. As a result of Airgas's classified board structure, it would take two annual meetings to obtain control of the board. Also, the company has three main takeover defences, namely: (1) a shareholder rights plan ('poison pill') with a 15% triggering threshold, (2) Airgas has not opted out of Delaware General Corporation Law ('DGCL') § 203, which prohibits business combinations with any interested stockholder for a period of three years following the time that such a stockholder became an interested stockholder, unless certain conditions are met, and (3) Airgas's Certificate of Incorporation includes a supermajority merger approval provision for certain business combinations. Namely, any merger with an 'interested stockholder' (defined as a stockholder who beneficially owns 20% or more of the voting power of Airgas's outstanding voting stock) requires the approval of 67% or more of the voting power of the then-outstanding stock entitled to vote, unless approved by a majority of the disinterested directors or certain fair price and procedural requirements are met.

Airgas's board, composed mainly of independent directors, concluded that the offeror company Air Product's offer clearly undervalues Airgas in a sale transaction. The board believes that the offer price is inadequate by no small margin.

In pursuit of its takeover plan, Air Product through proxy contest replaced a minority of the Airbag board with three independent directors. The independent directors looked at the numbers themselves. They requested outside legal counsel. They requested a third outside financial advisor and they supported the board's view that Air Product's offer was inadequate.

The court observed that the directors conducted good faith and reasonable investigation with respect to the threat posed by the tender offer. It held that the target board met its burden to articulate a legally cognisable threat, such that the board could employ 'poison pill' and other defensive measures which were proportionate. The court was persuaded to deny the application because of the

42 493 A.2d 946 (Del. 1985).
43 506 A.2d 173 (Del. 1986).
44 16 A.3d 48 (Del Ch. 2011).

overwhelming support of the defendant board to the defensive measures. Particularly, the directors that were appointed by the claimant shareholders as part of the proxy context supported the defensive measures. Hence the court observed that the defensive measures of the board were aimed at protecting the overall shareholder interests, since the offeror's bid was clearly below the value of the shares of the company.

Similarly, in *Yucaipa American Alliance Fund II, L.P. v Riggio*,[45] in response to a takeover threat where the corporation's stockholders could relinquish control without the benefit of receiving a control premium, the board adopted a poison pill that protected the company's shareholders. The claimant shareholder-controlled company had doubled its stake in the defendant company to almost 18% over a four-day period. The pill is triggered when a shareholder acquires over 20% of outstanding stock, or when two or more shareholders with over 20% enter into an agreement, arrangement or understanding. The plaintiff shareholder brought an action against the board of the target company, challenging the adoption of the poison pill as a breach of directors' fiduciary duties. The court dismissed the action. It was held that the board in good faith made a reasonable judgment that the corporation faced a legitimate threat and that the takeover defence was a reasonable and proportional response to the threat. The court observed that:

> Indeed, the record indicates that even with the pill in place, Yucaipa not only has a reasonable chance to, but is in fact likely to, prevail in a proxy contest if it runs a credible slate of candidates and articulates a sound business platform justifying the slate's election. Thus, the board's decision to use the pill to ensure that Yucaipa could not acquire control while bypassing negotiations with the board was reasonable because it addressed that threat while leaving Yucaipa with a fair chance to prevail in a proxy contest. Moreover, the pill is subject to a stockholder vote this year, a feature that further limits its inhibiting potency.[46]

The decision to acquire control of the company by acquiring shares in the open market without paying for 'control' may not necessary imply that the shareholders who sold their shares did not receive value for their shares. The shareholders may not necessarily be interested in powers of control. However, the court appears to have been mainly persuaded by the fact that despite the poison pill, the claimant shareholder still has the opportunity to obtain control of the company through a fairly contested proxy contest. Hence, the poison pill was not an absolute measure to prevent a change of control.

Further, in *Family Dollar Stores, Inc.*[47] shareholders challenged the process leading to the acquisition of the company. They applied for an injunction to restrain a shareholder vote on the proposed acquisition between the company

45 1A.3d 310 (Del Ch. 2010).
46 Ibid. 313.
47 Unreported Del Ch. C.A. No. 9985–CB, 19 December 2014.

and prospective buyer, in light of the tender offer from a competing bidder which was awaiting antitrust approval. They argue that the directors breached their fiduciary duties to maximise the value of the firm by declining to negotiate with an alternative buyer for a higher sum.

Dismissing the application, the court held that the directors acted reasonably when they decided not to engage in negotiations with the competing bidder, because of the antitrust risks associated with that proposal. The board had also been advised that the higher offer had only an approximately 40% chance of obtaining antitrust approval. Furthermore, the competing bidder still has a chance to improve its offer by addressing the antitrust risks associated with its bid. Meanwhile, the preliminary injunction would deprive Family's stockholders of the opportunity to decide for themselves whether to approve a transaction that offers them a significant premium for their shares in an apparently certain deal. The court was not willing to grant shareholder application to restrain the vote because it may deny the general shareholders the opportunity to obtain premiums for their shares if the competing bidder is unable to obtain antitrust approval even with a higher bid. Similar to *Air Products and Chemicals, Inc. v Airgas, Inc.*,[48] and *Yucaipa American Alliance Fund II, L.P. v Riggio*,[49] the court was concerned about the effect of directors' conduct on shareholder interests generally.

It can be observed from the cases that the court is not willing to review the decisions of directors in the absence of a clear threat to the interests of general shareholders. The court must be persuaded with material facts that either clearly show or are likely to indicate that directors are acting in breach of their fiduciary duty. For example, in *Pennaco Energy, Inc.*[50] the plaintiff shareholders argue that the directors of Pennaco failed to actively engage with other bidders to possibly secure the best value for the sale of the company. They further contend that Pennaco's two top-ranking directors were more concerned with severance benefits and options in furtherance of a sale; hence, they were motivated to secure less than the best price and diverted an unfair portion of the sale price to themselves. They also stated that the directors failed to disclose material information regarding the value of the company. The court denied the application for injunction and held that there was nothing to indicate that the directors failed to obtain the best value in negotiating the sale of the company. Particularly, the court explained that the directors were best equipped to make business decisions for the company.

> There are many business and financial considerations implicated in investigating and selecting the best value reasonably available. The board of directors is the corporate decision-making body best equipped to make these judgments. Accordingly, a court applying enhanced judicial scrutiny should

48 16 A.3d 48 (Del Ch. 2011).
49 1A.3d 310 (Del Ch. 2010).
50 787 A.2d 691 (Del Ch. 2001).

> be deciding whether the directors made a reasonable decision, not a perfect decision. If a board selected one of several reasonable alternatives, a court should not second-guess that choice even though it might have decided otherwise or subsequent events may have cast doubt on the board's determination.[51]

The mere fact that the board decided to focus on negotiating a favourable price with the bidder without seeking out other bidders is not conclusive proof that there had been a breach of fiduciary duty. The plaintiff shareholders also failed to show that a better acquisition deal from an alternative bidder was guaranteed, especially as none of the prospective bidders had made any bid.

A similar decision was reached in *Cysive, Inc.*[52] Shareholders brought breach of fiduciary duty action challenging a management buyout proposal made by Chief Executive Officer (CEO) of the corporation, who was also the company's dominant shareholder. Dismissing shareholder application, the court held that the transaction was fair in light of the diligent efforts of the special committee, which acted as an effective proxy for arm's-length bargaining; the absence of any bad faith conduct by the dominant shareholder and Chairman/CEO and his willingness to permit the special committee to do its job without pressure from him. Other reasons for holding that the acquisition transaction was fair include: the extensive market check that preceded and followed the signing of the merger agreement, which is material evidence of the fairness of the deal price, and the premium that the deal price represents to the pre-affected market trading price of the company's shares.

Similar to *Pennaco Energy*,[53] the inference that the company could not negotiate a better deal merely because the acquirer was the dominant shareholder and the CEO could not persuade the court to grant shareholder application. The court needed to be convinced that the interests of shareholders would be or have likely been undermined by the deal as a result of an act or an omission of the directors. The court was particularly satisfied that the negotiations leading to the deal was concluded by a special committee without any evidence of the dominant shareholder's influence.

The attitude of the court in the abovementioned cases and in the majority of the other cases where shareholder applications were denied in Table 8.1 is an indication that the courts are unwilling to challenge directors' conducts, in relation to acquisitions.

8.4.2 Successful shareholder application

Even though the court is unwilling to grant shareholder applications towards reviewing directors' decisions in acquisitions, compelling reasons may persuade

51 Ibid. 705.
52 836 A.2d 531 (Del Ch. 2003).
53 787 A.2d 691 (Del Ch. 2001).

the court to grant shareholder applications in certain circumstances. As indicated in the cases examined, the reasoning of the courts in its decisions to refuse shareholder application includes the failure of shareholders to clearly identify lack of fairness in the deals negotiated by the directors leading to a breach of duty. Others include the need to protect overall shareholder interests. This implies that if any of these can be proved by shareholders, the court would likely grant their application and review directors' decisions that were taken in relation to an acquisition. For example, in *Topps Co.*,[54] dissident shareholders sought to halt a shareholder vote on the company's proposed acquisition by Eisner. They contend that the board of the company (Topps board) breached its fiduciary duty by failing to negotiate towards obtaining a better sale value. The board had entered a standstill agreement with Eisner. In light of the agreement, the board refused to negotiate with a competing bidder, Upper Deck. Eisner had insisted on the standstill agreement to protect its earlier negotiations to acquire Topps. Granting the injunction, the court held that it was likely that plaintiffs would prevail on their claim that the board of the target company breached its duty by refusing to negotiate in good faith with the competing bidder and by not releasing competing bidder from a standstill agreement so that the bidder could communicate with stockholders. The court held that the refusal of the board to waive the standstill agreement prevented the shareholders from the opportunity to accept a potentially more attractive higher priced deal.[55]

Similarly, in *Netsmart Technologies, Inc.*,[56] shareholder plaintiffs allege that the process engaged by the board in selling the company was poorly-motivated and tactically flawed, and that the Netsmart board made no attempt to generate interests from strategic buyers. They also allege that the proxy statement which the board distributed to shareholders in advance of their vote omits important information. Granting the injunction, the court held that there was no reasonable factual basis for the board to conclude that other strategic buyers would not have been interested in acquiring the company at the time. It was further held that the board failed to disclose the projections used to perform the discounted cash flow valuation supporting its fairness opinion. This prevents shareholders from the ability to make informed decisions. A reasonable shareholder that is deciding to accept a one-time payment of cash and forsake any future interest in the firm would be interested in knowing the best estimate of the company's expected future cash flows.

Further, in *Del Monte Foods Co.*,[57] the court observed that the board breached its fiduciary duties in the process leading to negotiations for the acquisition of the company. The board authorised the financial advisor of the company to provide financing services to the bidder. This led the financial advisor to secretly manipulate the sale process and obtain secret monetary value at the expense of the

54 926 2d 58 (Del Ch. 2007).
55 Ibid. 92.
56 924 A.2d 171 (Del Ch. 2007).
57 25 A.3d 813 (Del Ch. 2011).

company. An injunction was granted to restrain the target board from proceeding with the scheduled shareholder vote to enable shareholders the opportunity to receive a topping bid free of financial misconduct. The decision of the courts in *Del Monte Foods Co.*,[58] *Netsmart Technologie, Inc.*[59] *and Topps Co.*[60] clearly indicate that the court is likely to intervene in reviewing the role of directors in relation to acquisitions where there has been a breach of directors' fiduciary duties and where shareholder interests is undermined or threatened. It is a difficult task to successfully persuade the court to decide in favour of shareholder because the shareholder must show that there has been a manifest breach of fiduciary duty, rather than a likely breach of duty. Also, the business judgment rule is mostly applied in favour of directors, since the court is not willing to be drawn into the internal arrangements of corporate entities; neither is the court willing to challenge a director who is usually considered to be best suited to make investment decisions for their companies. This is evident in the long list of shareholder applications that were denied by the court in Table 8.1.

The long list of shareholder litigations in the United States differs sharply from the list of shareholder litigation in the United Kingdom in relation to the same subject matter within the same period of time. This disparity does not indicate the differences between shareholder litigation in the United States and United Kingdom generally, it mainly relates to litigations in relation to acquisitions. The reason for the limited number of shareholder litigation can be attributed to the non-interventionist approach of the court in the UK, particularly in relation to shareholder actions on the conduct of directors when acquisitions are made. As indicated earlier, directors' duties are not owed to shareholders except in special circumstances.[61] Other litigations challenging the propriety of acquisitions are restricted to the jurisdiction of the *Takeover Panel*, subject to limited judicial review.[62] These were not examined: only shareholder actions relating to director conduct was examined. The next section concludes the chapter.

8.5 Conclusion

This chapter examined the scope of judicial intervention in acquisitions in the United Kingdom and the state of Delaware. Specifically, it identifies the extent to which shareholders can successfully challenge director conduct when a takeover is made. Some relevant judicial decisions were examined based on a case search methodology covering a period of 18 years of corporate acquisitions in the United Kingdom and the United States. The case search revealed a larger number of shareholder takeover litigations in Delaware than the United Kingdom.

58 Ibid.
59 924 A.2d 171 (Del Ch. 2007).
60 926 2d 58 (Del Ch. 2007).
61 See 8.3.
62 *Companies Act 2006, Part 28*; *R v Panel on Takeovers and Mergers, Ex parte Datafin Plc* [1987] QB 815.

A negligible number of cases in the United Kingdom were filed to challenge directors' conduct. Out of the six cases that were examined, four cases were decided against shareholders and one of the cases decided in favour of shareholders was partly decided in favour of directors.[63] The decisions of the court indicate that shareholders, especially minority shareholders, have limited scope of protection through judicial intervention. The court would only intervene in circumstances where the interest of shareholders would likely be undermined, especially where the intervention would ensure a fair and equal treatment of all shareholders.[64] However, in the absence of a special factual relationship between directors and shareholders, a claim founded on a breach of fiduciary duty would not likely succeed.[65] This implies that when a takeover is made, directors are not generally bound to act for shareholders. This includes providing relevant information to shareholders that can aid shareholders in making informed decisions. Since directors do not owe fiduciary duties to shareholders, directors are not bound to provide all the relevant information that can aid shareholders in decisions relating to acquisitions.[66] This indicates that judicial intervention has a very limited scope of protection for shareholders in the absence of substantive regulations that specifically protect shareholder interests. It may also indicate that directors are not bound to provide sufficient and 'helpful' advice or information to shareholders. This encourages box-ticking exercises, since directors are required to merely provide information to the shareholder without specifying the nature and usefulness of the information, in the absence of a special relationship between the directors and shareholders. For example, several losses post-acquisition may have been caused by lack of access to relevant and useful information before shareholder votes were held.

Shareholder litigation in Delaware was shown to be significantly higher than those instituted in the United Kingdom within the same period. Out of the 39 cases identified, 25 cases were decided against shareholders. Among the 14 cases that were decided in shareholder favour, some were partly decided in favour of defendant directors. Similarly to the attitude of the courts in the UK, the court in Delaware is not keen on intervening in matters relating to takeovers. The main reason for the non-intervention approach of the court is attributed to recognition of directors as best suited for making investment decisions for companies.[67] The court in Delaware is also concerned with decisions that protect the general interests of shareholders.[68] It also considers whether a takeover defence was reasonable and proportional, since directors are permitted to oppose bids.

63 *Vald Nielsen Holding A/S v Baldorino* [2019] EWHC 1926 (Comm).

64 *Diamix Plc.* [2002] EWHC 770 (Ch).

65 *Vald Nielsen Holding A/S v Baldorino* [2019] EWHC 1926 (Comm).

66 *Sharp v Blank* [2015] EWHC 3220 (Ch).

67 The business judgement rule applies in relation to acquisition. *Pennaco Energy* 787 A.2d 691 (Del Ch. 2001).

68 *Del Monte Foods Co.*, 25 A.3d 813 (Del Ch. 2011); *Netsmart Technologie, Inc.* 924 A.2d 171 (Del Ch. 2007); *Topps Co.*, 926 2d 58 (Del Ch. 2007).

Alternatively, the court would likely intervene when there is lack of fairness in the deals negotiated by the directors leading to a breach of duty. Although there is scope for the court to intervene, shareholders must show that the intervention of the court would remedy a wrong that cannot be remedied without the intervention of the court. For example, the court refused to intervene in *Yucaipa American Alliance Fund II, L.P. v Riggio*[69] because the poison pill would not ultimately prevent the claimant shareholder from the opportunity to obtain control of the company through a fairly contested proxy contest. The poison pill would not absolutely prevent a change of control. Since other options can be explored to avoid the poison pill, the court refused to intervene. Alternatively, in *Topps Co.*,[70] the court intervened because the refusal of the board to waive the standstill agreement would prevent the shareholders from the opportunity to accept a potentially more attractive higher priced deal. These imply that the court would only intervene in an action by shareholders in exceptional circumstances.

This suggests that the ultimate protective measure that can largely enhance shareholder interests is by a regulatory control of the role of the board, since the courts cannot create new rules for shareholders in the UK or in Delaware. They merely interpret the existing regulations that define the role of board when acquisitions are made.

Furthermore, it can be observed from Table 8.1 that the claimants were mainly target shareholders – only two cases were filed by acquiring shareholders and their applications were denied. This further implies that litigation may not be a suitable platform for protecting shareholder interests, especially shareholders of acquiring companies. This appears to have been further confirmed by the insignificant number of shareholder litigations on corporate acquisitions in the UK.

References

Barnett, E. and Amanda Andrews, 'AOL Merger Was "the Biggest Mistake in Corporate History", Believes Time Warner Chief Jeff Bewkes' *The Telegraph* 28 September 2010 www.telegraph.co.uk/finance/newsbysector/mediatechnologyandtelecoms/media/8031227/AOL-merger-was-the-biggest-mistake-in-corporate-history-believes-Time-Warner-chief-Jeff-Bewkes.html accessed 30 June 2019.

CNN Money 4 February 2000 https://money.cnn.com/2000/02/04/europe/vodafone/ accessed 11 July 2018. Edmund L. Andrews and Andrew Ross Sorkin, 'Europe's Megadeal: The Overview; $183 Billion Deal in Europe to Join Two Wireless Giants' *New York Times* 4 February 2000 www.nytimes.com/2000/02/04/business/europe-s-megadeal-overview-183-billion-deal-europe-join-2-wireless-giants.html accessed 11 July 2018.

Georgina, Tsagas, 'A Long-Term Vision for UK Firms? Revisiting the Target Director's Advisory Role Since the Takeover of Cadbury's PLC' (2014) 14 *Journal of Corporate Law Studies* 241.

69 1A.3d 310 (Del Ch. 2010).
70 926 2d 58 (Del Ch. 2007).

Jeanne Dugan, Ianthe and Ariana Eunjung Cha, 'AOL to Acquire Time Warner for 183 Billion Merger' *The Washington Post* 11 January 2000 www.washingtonpost.com/archive/politics/2000/01/11/aol-to-acquire-time-warner-in-record-183-billion-merger/f3bf2f07-c32b-4052-b5a6–8489bb9d7013/?noredirect=on&utm_term=.69ae04545d2d accessed 30 April 2018; 'AOL Buyout of Time Warner: Merger Frenzy Sweeping Corporate America' *World Socialist Web* 14 January 2000 www.wsws.org/en/articles/2000/01/merg-j14.html accessed 2 May 2018; Seth Sutel 'AOL Buys Time Warner for $162 billion' *ABC News* 10 January 2000 http://abcnews.go.com/Business/Decade/aol-buys-time-warner-162-billion/story?id=9279138 accessed 30 June 2019.

Jennifer, Payne, 'Schemes of Arrangement, Takeovers and Minority Shareholder Protection' (2011) 11 *Journal of Corporate Law Studies* 67.

Leon, Ferera and Hannah Mehta, 'Scheming to Get around the Takeover Code: Does It Work?' (2008) 23 *Butterworths Journal of International Banking & Financial Law* 476.

9 A new paradigm for takeover administration

9.1 Introduction

This chapter concludes the book. It begins with a brief analytical reflection of the underlying framework of the book. Next, it highlights the themes that connect the chapters. It identifies the central role of management boards as the determinants of the values of corporate acquisitions to the various corporate actors, including shareholders in acquiring and target companies and employees. Then it concludes.

9.2 The dominant role of managements in takeovers

The book begins by highlighting some challenges to takeovers, especially in relation to shareholder and employee interests. It examined the extent to which the interests of shareholders and employees can be protected in takeovers. Since the role of management boards is central to takeover administration and regulation, the objective extended to analysing the role of the board and the scope of the regulatory functions. In light of the similarity of the nature of corporate acquisitions in different jurisdiction, a comparative approach was adopted in pursuit of the underlying objective of the book. Acquisitions affect similar interests irrespective of the jurisdiction where it occurs: shareholders of target and acquiring companies, employees, creditors, the board, the community and the government and regulatory agents. The extent to which the interest of these constituents is affected is determined by reference to the existing regulatory framework in any particular jurisdictions. Hence a comparative approach was justified to ascertain the scope of differences and similarities of the problems. The regulatory framework in the United Kingdom and the United States (Delaware) were compared because of the significant acquisitions deals that have been concluded by companies in both jurisdictions.

One of the main challenges of regulating corporate entities is its threat to managerial functions. Management boards may be deterred from exhibiting their expertise if their conducts are overly scrutinised. Chapter 2 addressed this concern. It identifies the relevance of the regulatory framework of institutions. It showed that the institutional framework for takeover regulations is not meant to undermine the role of the board; rather, it is aimed at professionalising the role

of the board by promoting the competitive function of the market, especially in relation to acquisitions. It showed that regulations can be used to mitigate transaction costs when a takeover is made, to ultimately promote the role of the board towards the company and to protect the property rights of shareholders. The regulatory role of mitigating transaction costs was also shown to affect employee interests. The chapter ultimately showed that regulating takeovers would be unnecessary if the market functions flawlessly. It emphasised that the aim of takeover regulations is to promote market functions, by encouraging corporate actors and investors to operate in a platform that is devoid of manipulations and individual or group dominance.

To understand the web of interests that is affected by corporate acquisitions, the theoretical framework for takeovers was examined in Chapter 3. The examination showed that the role of management boards is central to synergistic gains, hubris and the disciplinary role of takeovers. The extent to which any of these takeover characteristics can occur was shown to be dependent on the acquisition objectives of management boards, subject to regulatory controls examined in Chapter 2. Further, the effects of takeovers on the interests of corporate constituents, such as shareholders and employees, were also shown to be dependent on the acquisition objectives of the board. Agency conflicts between management board and shareholders were examined in light of the economic analysis of the corporation as a going concern. This demonstrated the extent to which the economic interests of the corporation and particularly shareholders can be undermined by agency conflicts, in the absence of the desirable institutional framework examined in Chapter 2.

To demonstrate the current challenges of corporate acquisitions, the regulatory framework for takeovers in the United Kingdom and the United States (Delaware) were examined in Chapters 4 and 5 respectively. The regulatory frameworks were examined to show that regulations were introduced to address the challenges at the level of the market. The market challenges which were highlighted in Chapter 2 were demonstrated with the analyses of the takeover challenges in the early periods in the United Kingdom and the United States. These challenges which led to the development of the institutional framework for takeover regulations were highlighted by a brief examination of the historical development of takeover regulation in both jurisdictions. Similar problems in both jurisdictions showed that the takeover markets experienced several challenges. These challenges were mainly caused by the dominant role of managements. The market was weak, because property rights were not freely controlled by shareholders and the management board were the determinants of the outcome of takeovers. The development of the regulatory institutions has been shown to have positively enhanced the development of takeovers, however challenges still exist in both jurisdictions. Management boards still wield much influence over takeovers and this is undermining corporate value, shareholder and employee interests.

In further demonstration of the dominant role of management boards, Chapter 6 examined the extent to which the function of the market for corporate control is being undermined by the board. The market for corporate control is expected to serve as an alternative disciplinary mechanism to corporate governance

regulation. Chapter 6 highlighted the extensive scope of management functions. It showed that the limitation of corporate governance regulation over the role of managements has gradually been extended to the market for corporate control which is exhibited through takeovers. The chapter showed that managements are extending their dominance to takeovers to weaken its disciplinary role over managements and this is undermining the role of the market as an alternative disciplinary mechanism. Managements are achieving this by influencing the role of the market, engaging in costly acquisitions and determining the outcome of takeovers. Engaging in costly acquisitions often leads to losses to acquiring shareholders; the need to mitigate further corporate expenditure and to achieve synergy in the combined company becomes necessary, leading to employee dismissal. Hence in Chapter 7, the need to address the threat of takeovers to employee interests was examined. An analysis of the extent to which employee interests complement the interests of shareholders in the acquiring company was linked to costly acquisitions. Costly acquisitions can lead to losses to acquiring shareholders; it can also enhance the need to dismiss employees. The chapter shows that the complementary function of acquiring shareholder interests and employee interests can apply where managements are restrained with limited capacity to dismiss employees as a result of takeovers. This can ensure that costly acquisitions must be clearly justified without the need to dismiss employees. The restriction on employee dismissal can ultimately ensure that costly acquisitions are limited to acquisitions that are most likely to lead to synergistic gains for the combined company, including economic gains to acquiring shareholders.

In light of the dominant role of managements, the extent to which shareholders can seek judicial redress was examined in Chapter 8. From the analysis of judicial intervention in the United Kingdom and the United States, it was shown that the courts provide limited protection to shareholder interests. In light of the fact that the courts merely interpret existing regulations without enacting them, a review of regulations is necessary to ensure that shareholder interests are adequately protected from the dominant role of managements. Negligible cases were filed in the United Kingdom in the period under review, mainly because the board do not owe a duty to the shareholders personally; their duty is owed to the company, except in certain exceptional circumstances. In contrast to the United Kingdom, a significant number of cases were filed in the United States (Delaware). Most of the cases were resolved against shareholders. Although the decisions from Delaware courts showed that shareholders are active litigants, the court is nevertheless bound by the existing rules which are often interpreted in favour of directors as either having the capacity to defend takeover bids or promoting the sale of the company in a reasonable way where sale is inevitable.

9.3 Professionalising managerial decisions and enhancing market functions

The challenges that undermined takeovers in the early period of takeovers in the United Kingdom and the United States were influenced by the dominant role

of management boards. The regulatory framework that has been developed to address this problem; to strengthen market functions are being dominated by managements in recent times to enhance the scope of managerial control over takeover outcomes. While management boards should be encouraged to exhibit their expertise in running corporate entities as going concerns, the scope of the expertise should be limited to managerial and supervisory functions without stifling market functions. The limitation of corporate governance rules in monitoring the board and management functions is evident in the continuous corporate scandals and failures despite the existence of corporate governance rules and codes. Similar challenges apply to takeovers. Takeover codes and rules have limited application to managerial discipline. *The UK Takeover Code* and the *European Union Takeover Directive* provide limited restrictions on the role of the boards of target and acquiring companies. Similar limitations exist in Delaware; directors can defend bids in permitted circumstances. In both jurisdictions, acquiring managements can engage in acquisitions without much external control. This is encouraging costly acquisitions since management boards are determining the outcomes of takeovers. A mechanism for challenging costly acquisitions is desirable. This can ensure that while the board can freely engage in acquisitions, there should be a requirement of ascertaining the implications of the costs of acquisitions on corporate value, shareholder interests, and other relevant stakeholders such as employee.

This can promote the professionalisation of management functions. Justification of the potential for synergistic gains can transform management functions from merely engaging in investment for their companies to identifying avenues for a high propensity of economic value. This can address the issue of costly acquisition by limiting costly acquisitions to only those categories of acquisition where high costs of transacting are inevitable yet synergistic gains are highly likely. This can also ensure that the occurrence of employee dismissal is either unlikely or implemented for strictly synergistic purposes with desirable compensation for loss of employment. The reduction of costly acquisitions would serve both shareholder interests and employee interests. This would also address the needless difference between shareholder and stakeholder value, in takeovers, particularly in relation to shareholders and employees.

Although the role of corporate management is central to takeover administration, other factors can influence the outcomes and effects of takeovers on the economic value of corporate entities. For example, the capital structure of the payments used to complete acquisition deals may include a high percentage of debt capital. This could determine the extent to which synergistic gains can be achieved. Since capital structure is dependent on managerial preference, the choice of capital structure is linked to management functions. Thus, research into the relationship between the role of management boards and capital structure and its impact on corporate value post-takeovers is desirable.

Index

Note: Page numbers in *italics* indicate figures and page numbers in **bold** indicate tables on the corresponding pages.

www.ingramcontent.com/pod-product-compliance
Ingram Content Group UK Ltd.
Pitfield, Milton Keynes, MK11 3LW, UK
UKHW011009180926
475701UK00004B/650
9781032238258